The Normans

TIMOTHY BAKER was Baring Scholar at Hertford College, Oxford, where he read history and later did postgraduate work and teaching, principally dealing with the Middle Ages and the Anglo-Saxon period. He is at present a member of the research team engaged in compiling, through the biographies of individual MP's, the official history of Parliament. Mr. Baker was responsible for the masterly condensation of the text of Sir Winston Churchill's *A History of the English-speaking Peoples*.

JACKET DESIGN/RICHARD SMITH

THE NORMANS

By Timothy Baker

THE MACMILLAN COMPANY, NEW YORK

Library of Congress Catalog Card Number: 66-28738

Second Printing 1967

The Macmillan Company, New York

Printed in the United States of America

Contents

DA
195
B25

List of Illustrations

(Photographs from the Bayeux Tapestry by John R. Freeman [Photographers] Ltd)

Genealogical Tables

Maps

Acknowledgements

*T*HIS book is indebted to so many people's research that it is not possible to do more than refer to the bibliography. I must, however, thank Dr J. J. G. Alexander for his help on manuscript illumination and Miss Hope Muntz, who has read most of the typescript and made invaluable suggestions; neither is responsible for the book's shortcomings, but both have saved it from a number of errors. I am also grateful to the editorial staff at Cassell & Co. for their patience and trouble. To my wife I owe more than I can say.

CHAPTER ONE

The Normans in France

*I*N the summer of 911 tradition says that an expedient and rather discreditable pact was made beside a stream between two steep hills at Saint-Clair-sur-Epte, on the highroad from Paris to Rouen. Charles the Simple, king of the Franks, met Rollo, leader of one of the Viking armies whose intermittent invasions had been racking France for seventy years. The king, heir to the western rump of Charlemagne's divided empire, beset by pirates from without and undermined by mighty subjects from within, was not so much simple as unlucky; a rival had triumphed in his childhood and others were to reign before his death in prison. For the moment he was leagued with his eventual supplanter, Robert of Neustria, and could hope for a breathing space, since the Scandinavian raiders had been defeated before Chartres.

Norman history begins with the meeting of Charles and Rollo. The pagan chief promised to marry Charles's daughter, to receive baptism and do homage to the king in return for an area later known as Upper Normandy; this land was to be held as long as the Viking should keep peace with his lord and help to defend the kingdom against other enemies, although it seems that he was entirely free to attack the Christian Bretons. A similar agreement had been reached in England, between King Alfred and his Danish opponent Guthrum over thirty years before, but attempts to colonize France had so far met with no success. Charles was not making a heavy sacrifice, for the land which he ceded was part of Robert's great duchy or march of Neustria, which stretched from the Loire to beyond the Seine. Robert, with a Viking army in possession, could hardly object, while for the king, with two vassals where there had been one, there was safety in numbers. As with many treaties which have since become landmarks, the prospects of survival seemed dim.

The new order almost foundered in the making. Feudal custom, then emerging, required that when land was given by the king as a fief, to be held on conditions, the recipient should kneel to perform the act of homage, whereby he became the king's man. Details of the ceremony might vary and in practice its significance depended on the strength of the parties, but Rollo certainly in some way became Charles's vassal. Descriptions of the meeting at Saint-Clair-sur-Epte all stem from that of Dudo, dean of Saint-Quentin, who wrote a history in praise of the early Norman dukes one hundred years later. Although Dudo has been convicted of eking out knowledge with invention, one of his stories aptly symbolizes William the Conqueror's ancestors. Rollo, expected to kiss the royal foot, recoiled in anger but finally singled out a reluctant follower to perform the act. The Viking then seized the king's foot and, amid gales of laughter, jerked it up to his mouth, laying Charles flat on his back.

Already the Normans had unseated a king.

*

Europe in Rollo's day owed much to Constantine the Great, the first Roman emperor to be baptized and to give the unwieldy empire a second capital in the east.

During the fifth century the west had succumbed to
Germanic invaders who settled in Britannia, Gaul,
Iberia and Italy, eventually accepting Christianity and, in
the last three provinces, maintaining a debased Latin
culture; here political unity dissolved and for more than
three centuries only the eminence of her bishop recalled
the glory of Rome. Meanwhile imperial rule persisted at
Constantinople and over a fluctuating but normally
much diminished area, the Eastern or Byzantine Empire;
this sophisticated and increasingly hellenized society
soon became estranged from the more backward west,
none the less it survived many perils to act as Europe's
bulwark against Asia for a thousand years.

On Christmas Day 800 Byzantium was challenged
when the Frankish ruler Charlemagne, master of western
Europe save for Britain and Iberia, tried to revive the
ancient unity by being crowned at Rome. The artistic
renaissance which he also sought to promote was far-
reaching and helps to bear out the view that the centuries
which followed the collapse of Rome ought never to have
been named the Dark Ages. The Carolingian Empire,
however, disintegrated within a generation, leaving the
title of Holy Roman Emperor and a Europe which was
once again a prey to local wars and invasions. Islam,
checked in Spain, established itself in Sicily, Sardinia
and Corsica; Slavonic tribes swept across the Balkans,
cutting off the Eastern Empire; oriental Magyars and
yet more Slavs pressed against Germany from the east,
while Vikings descended from Scandinavia. Europe in
the early tenth century may therefore be divided between
Constantinople, isolated at the south-eastern tip; the
unstable Christian kingdoms of the west; the menacing
fringe areas of the south, which now formed highly
civilized Moslem states, and those of the north and east,
which had always been barbarian. Assailed on all sides,
Christians in their prayers singled out a supreme and

common terror: 'From the fury of the Northmen, O Lord, deliver us.'

The Vikings, called after the typical *vik* or creek haunted by their long ships, might be any of the Scandinavian adventurers who swarmed about Europe from the eighth to the eleventh centuries. No one knows what caused this upsurge but it may have been an expanding population, with polygamy producing younger sons who resented the growth of royal power at home and were attracted by the disarray of Europe. In the east, marauders from Sweden gave their name to Russia and encamped before Constantinople, others in the west burned Seville and poured into the Mediterranean to sack Pisa, while yet more reached out to Iceland, Greenland and America.

Sophistication was strangely blended with barbarism in these northerners. Welcomed as traders before they became dreaded as pirates, the Vikings had a weakness for luxury, especially in dress, and were already ingenious in fashioning metal ornaments, as well as in stone-carving. They were skilled in building fortifications and siege-engines and, although daring on occasion, were masters of all the ruses of war. Above all, they excelled in seamanship. The dragon-carved ships, shallow, clinker-built, low in the middle and pointed at either end, could cross oceans or sneak up rivers into the heart of an unsuspecting countryside. Although these vessels were not large enough for a mass migration, some reached seventy-five feet in length and could carry up to a hundred and twenty men with unrivalled speed. While western Europe still basked in the security of Charlemagne's rule, the pirates had briefly hovered off the south of France, at Narbonne; the Emperor, rising from his table to gaze at the sinister fleet, had wept for his descendants.

Viking society, like that in Germany, was divided between the thrall, who tended the land, the churl, a craftsman but often also an adventurer, and the earl or noble, who was essentially a fighting man. This society, under its aristocratic leaders, was bound by laws which were often complex and always strictly enforced, but it was basically free. Self-reliance was encouraged and the Norse gods had only a feeble grip on many rovers, who found little difficulty in blending two faiths, or in having none. Love of fighting was finely expressed in epic poems and stories, whose source of inspiration still makes it hard for them to be appreciated. In the eyes of Christendom, the Vikings' skills were eclipsed by their savagery: the custom of cutting a blood-eagle by splaying out the ribs of a fallen foe, the tossing of children on their spears and the famous berserk fury in the heat of a battle.

Cruel, grasping and sly, the Vikings have generally been regarded with a fascinated horror. Rollo of Normandy, for historical rather than personal reasons, remains an exception, since his homage and the unlooked-for success of his settlement have won him renown as the first Norman duke. His origins are none the less obscure and the name is recorded only in its Latin form. He is thought to have been Rolf 'the Ganger', so called because he had to walk everywhere, no horse being strong enough to bear him. This Rolf, too lawless for ninth-century Norway, fled to Scotland, probably crossed to Ireland, married a Christian woman and perhaps had made his way to France by 905. The Norman Rollo is first definitely mentioned when repulsed before Chartres and then defeated by a relief force on 20 July 911.

If Rollo himself was Norwegian, the bulk of his following came from Denmark. Irish chroniclers drew a clear distinction between the Norwegian or 'white' invaders and the Danish or 'black' ones, but there are no such descriptions of what happened in Normandy. Both types of marauder had appeared in France and their exact relative strength will never be known. Their total number

is also uncertain; an ordered colonization by the rank-and-
file of the Danish army took place in parts of England,
where innumerable place-names are some guide to the
Viking numbers, but in France the newcomers seem to
have been more aristocratic. Some half-dozen endings of
Norman place-names, amongst them *-tot*, *-beuf* and
-fleur, are definitely Scandinavian and others, such as the
very common *-bec*, are probably northern, but there is
nothing so widespread as the Danish *-by* which is so well
known in England. Hybrids, with the Latin *villa* tacked
on to a Viking's personal name, are common in Normandy and rare in the more thoroughly Danish parts of
England; this suggests that the pre-Norman peasantry
survived and that a new lord simply substituted his own
name for that of his Frankish predecessor. It would
explain why fair-haired Normans, although found today,
are relatively rare. The number of settlers, however, was
to increase with time, especially to the west of Rouen.
Rollo's men were the first of many and his fief in 911
merely the kernel of the future duchy.

*

There was nothing very distinctive about the area where
Rollo and his army made their home. Charles's grant is
thought to have comprised that part of the lower Seine
basin which made up the counties of Rouen, Lisieux
and Evreux, with the wooded plateau of the Pays de
Caux to the north-east, between the rivers Bresle and
Epte and the sea. This ill-defined zone was Upper
Normandy, with Rouen at its centre blocking the
approach to Paris up the Seine, already an archbishop's
seat, a magnet for trade and a natural capital for the
future state. Rollo pressed westwards into the districts
of Bayeux and Sées in 924 and his son into those of
Avranches and Coutances nine years later, so adding
Lower Normandy and filling the outlines of the historic

duchy. The result was a fertile province of low hills, forests, orchards and pastures, with a long sea-coast and a damp climate—France's nearest approach to the English countryside (Map I).

The weaknesses in this state presented a decisive challenge to its rulers. The boundaries were political, not geographical: the western uplands continued those of Brittany, the plains in the east merged with Picardy, the valley of the Seine led straight into the Île-de-France and, to the south, Maine and Perche were separated from Normandy only by a hilly watershed. Moreover, the duchy was dwarfed by the lands which its sons were to conquer. On the eve of his invasion of England, William's domains were smaller than Harold's earldom of Wessex; the longest direct journey on Norman soil, from Eu in the north-east to Couesnon in the south-west, was less than a hundred and ninety miles, and nowhere was the duchy more than seventy miles wide. Harold could march two hundred miles from London to Stamford Bridge, but a third of that distance would have brought William from Rouen to the gates of Paris and did bring him from Saint-Valery to Pevensey Bay.

Normandy had enjoyed some kind of organized existence for five hundred years before it acquired its name from the Northmen. Christianity had triumphed early in the fourth century, whose closing years had seen Rouen made the centre of a new province of Roman Gaul, Lugdunensis Secunda. Later the Gallo-Roman population of Celts and Belgae had intermingled with Saxon and Frankish invaders, but in language and physique it remained basically non-Germanic. After political divisions had been wiped out, ecclesiastical boundaries had lived on, as elsewhere, preserving the old limits until new importance was given to them, as *pagi* or administrative units under the Frankish kings. Yet all this time, in peace or anarchy, Normandy's fate had been shared by other provinces, since the triumph of Frankish law had been added to that of Christianity as a tie with the rest of Gaul. Normandy had always been a subdivision; it was left to the Vikings to give it a life of its own.

*

The omens did not favour Rollo. There was no sign that the pact of Saint-Clair would bring more than an interlude of peace to a distracted land and Charles might reasonably hope that the colony's life would be short. In England the area of Viking settlement known as the Danelaw was already being subjected by Alfred's successors; in Ireland, the freest field for development, Viking power was divided and on the wane. The golden age of the northern pirates has been well described as 'a sickly capricious thing, a triumph not for political sense, but merely for audacity, enthusiasm and lust'. Every Scandinavian colony seemed to lack cohesion and, deprived of a strong leader, to fall an easy prey to resurgent native forces. In one sense, Normandy followed the pattern, for French customs were to be adopted, but politically the duchy was to have a destiny of its own.

Rollo's reign was, and remains, a dark time. There is no contemporary Norman chronicle to trace his life nor is there a charter to record his gifts, although many deeds of charity were foisted upon him after death. His acceptance of Christianity, in accordance with his promise at Saint-Clair, was as momentous as the meeting itself, but baptism did not mean true conversion; under his rule it is doubtful if a single one of the former monasteries survived and the duke himself is said to have offered up human sacrifices to the old gods before he died. Rollo is presumed to have granted land orally to his Scandinavian followers, giving them the traditional freehold and hereditary rights, and to have formed some rough legal code as security. Fresh bands continued to arrive from the north. In 925 the colonists clashed with the Franks in the east, at Eu, and there Rollo may have met his end; certainly he was dead before the Breton wars of 933. He can be judged only by results, by the fact of his settlement's survival, in itself remarkable, and by the conquests which he made to the west.

The story of Rollo's successors is one of Vikings changing into Frenchmen but, paradoxically, ensuring an independent existence in the process. Four generations produced five dukes—William I Longsword, Richard I the Fearless, Richard II the Good, the short-lived Richard III and finally Robert I the Magnificent, father of William the Conqueror. Resounding names did not make up for doubtful legitimacy and no succession went unchallenged. At first the Frankish kings could look on these men merely as a new line of counts of Rouen, in theory no more than provincial governors, and the ducal title varied with the sympathies of those who recorded it. Until the end of the century Normandy was 'the land of the Northmen', and a chronicler exulted at the death in 996 of Richard I, 'duke of the pirates'. The pen being no match for the sword, Rollo's line continued to prosper (Table I).

Scandinavian influence remained dominant for at least fifty years after Rollo's death. William Longsword had probably been born before his father reached France and he secured his own heir by a Danish woman, in spite of having a French wife. He is said to have been brought up by a francophile Dane, named Botho, and to have blended the ways of a Viking with those of a Frenchman. William added the Channel Islands, as well as Avranchin and Cotentin, after a war with Brittany in which he failed to seize the Breton capital, and there is some evidence of his attachment to the Church, although this is still second-hand. The story of the second duke, depressingly like

TABLE I

The Norman Ducal Dynasty

ROLLO, duke of Normandy c. 911–25/33

WILLIAM I (Longsword), duke of Normandy 925/33–42

RICHARD I (the Fearless), duke of Normandy 942–96;
m. Gunnor

RICHARD II (the Good), duke of Normandy 996–1026; m. (1) Judith, sister of Geoffrey, count of Brittany, (2) Papia from Evermeu

Emma; m. (1) Æthelred II, king of England, (2) Cnut, king of England, Denmark and Norway
(see Table II)

Hawisa; m. Geoffrey of Rennes, count of Brittany
— Alain III, count of Brittany

Robert, archbishop of Rouen 989–1037
— Counts of Evreux

Godfrey
— Gilbert of Brionne

William
— Counts of Eu

Children of Richard II:

(1) RICHARD III, duke of Normandy 1026–7; m. Adela
— Nicholas, abbot of Saint-Ouen

(1) ROBERT I (the Magnificent), duke of Normandy 1027–35

(1) William, a monk at Fécamp

(1) Alice; m. Renaud, a count of Burgundy
— Gui of Burgundy

(1) Eleanor; m. Baldwin IV, count of Flanders
— Baldwin V, count of Flanders

(1) A 3rd daughter

(2) Mauger, archbishop of Rouen 1037–54

(2) William, count of Arques

Children of Robert I:

Adelaide; m. (1) Enguerrand, count of Ponthieu, (2) Lambert of Lens, (3) Odo, count of Champagne

WILLIAM II (the Conqueror), duke of Normandy 1035–87, King William I of England 1066–87; m. Matilda of Flanders
(see Table V)

Children of Baldwin V:

Baldwin, count of Flanders — Counts of ...

Matilda ...

that of his father, is enlivened by signs of conflicting traditions. He too entrusted his heir to Botho and sent the boy to Bayeux, where he could learn the ancestral tongue which was now forgotten at Rouen. French had already triumphed in the oldest area of occupation, but it was still necessary for the ruler to speak Old Norse. It is possible that French was weaker in the west because of earlier Saxon settlements, or because these lands had only been won with the help of fresh invaders from the north. William himself strayed too far from the ways of his fathers, for his murder by the count of Flanders in 942 set in train a bloody pagan reaction.

The early years of Richard I were ones of confusion and misery. Faced with a Danish invasion, the ten-year-old prince apostatized, while the Christians were divided between rival protectors in King Louis IV and Hugh the Great, the respective sons of Charles the Simple and Robert of Neustria. The king challenged the invaders, seized Richard and might have kept his duchy, if further Scandinavians had not arrived to tip the scales by capturing Louis and transferring him to Hugh. Eventually the northerners withdrew or settled down and Normandy, under its restored and reconverted ruler, emerged with a stronger will than before to resist inroads by the French Crown.

At Gisors in 965 Richard made peace with Louis's son, Lothair, after a meeting second in importance only to that of their grandfathers. Rollo's line had endured half a century of turmoil, in which statesmanship had been eclipsed in the struggle for personal survival. During the next eighty years the area of Viking settlement was to be transformed into the Normandy known to history.

*

One reason for the colony's survival was the strife between Charlemagne's heirs and the upstart house of

Neustria. Norman obligations to the Crown had been recognized, when convenient: Rollo had marched to Charles's help against Robert of Neustria and his son-in-law and successor as rival king, Raoul, but William had acknowledged Raoul in 927 and perhaps was confirmed in his western conquests as the price for his fidelity. Spasmodically, the power of the old royal line was revived under Louis IV and Lothair, so that William did homage to Louis in 936, but as early as 942 several Normans were acknowledging the overlordship of Robert's successor, Hugh the Great. Gisors was decisive, for later charters show that Norman allegiance was then transferred to Hugh's son, Hugh Capet, Richard's brother-in-law and immediate neighbour. Carolingian rule flickered out in 987 and Hugh mounted the throne. Thereafter relations between kings and dukes were generally good and of benefit to both parties; French support was to make possible the accession and achievements of William the Conqueror.

The triumph of Christianity was inevitable if the Normans were to have any dealings with the rest of France. Again the peace secured at Gisors was crucial, for the work of the Church could now be resumed. When the Vikings swept over the diocese of Rouen, a few monks from the house of Fontanelles had escaped to Flanders. There they maintained a tenuous existence until Flanders became the centre of a religious revival in the mid-tenth century. This inspired St Dunstan to re-establish monasticism in England and also impelled Mainard, from the abbey of St Peter at Ghent, to lead a band of exiles back to Normandy. Already under William Longsword a few monks from Aquitaine had ventured back to their gutted home at Jumièges and now, in 960 or 961, Mainard founded the new house of Saint-Wandrille on the site of Fontanelles, which he had obtained from Duke Richard. In the year after Gisors

Richard installed monks in the former sanctuary of le Mont-Saint-Michel, where they were joined by Mainard and ruled by him for the next twenty-five years; soon the duke established another house, Saint-Ouen, in Rouen itself. The old bishoprics had been reconstituted by 990 and secular canons, who differed from monks in not being bound by a common rule, had been brought to another pre-Viking site at Fécamp. None the less it was the monasteries, the sole centres of education, which were to be the mainspring of religious and intellectual activity.

Richard I's reign saw the haphazard beginning of organized religious life. Richard the Good, who succeeded in 996, has been given his nickname too readily, but it was he who brought the Norman Church into touch with Europe's foremost monastic centre at Cluny in Burgundy. The inmates of Cluny and her daughter houses had adopted the sixth-century code of St Benedict of Nursia, who gave his name to the famous rule amplified nearly three hundred years later by Benedict of Aniane. The black-cowled Benedictines formed the only regular order yet known in western Europe, with their lives a cycle of work, private meditation and elaborate services. As pious benefactions multiplied monastic wealth, this routine was inevitably to be modified, more attention being lavished on the beauty and formality of the liturgy than on manual labour or on study. Every musical and decorative device was exploited to embellish the religious services, so that when Cluny was at the height of her fame it was said that a monk could scarcely find half an hour to himself, even on Midsummer Day. Tranquil refuges were at least provided, where there was no time for sin even if there was little time for thought. Every age is an age of violence, just as it is an age of transition, but the tenth century had peculiar need of such havens.

The Piedmontese William of Volpiano, abbot of the

Cluniac house of Saint-Bénigne at Dijon, was invited to Fécamp in 1001 and at once substituted monks for the canons whom he found there; he is said then to have reformed Saint-Ouen, Jumièges and le Mont-Saint-Michel. William of Volpiano was a happy if unlikely choice, for to piety he added diplomacy and a truly Norman efficiency, while he also showed an intellectual curiosity not common among saints: music, medicine, geometry and architecture all engaged his interest. A man of such all-round learning is particularly attractive when compared with the ignorance which surrounded him or with the narrow specialism of later days. His successor Abbot John was another many-sided man, whose devotional work still finds its place in twentieth-century missals. John, like all the towering figures in Norman monasticism, came from south of the Alps; his impact is a tribute to the eager receptiveness which the Normans were to show in every field.

There was still a sense of kinship with Scandinavia. This may indeed explain why the earliest Norman monasteries, save le Mont-Saint-Michel, were all in Upper Normandy, where French influence was stronger than in the west (Map I). Richard II, like his forebears, was the offspring of a Danish woman, although his father had later married her, and he, too, did not scruple to welcome armies from the north. Flemish and Burgundian annalists spied a Viking streak in the atrocities of the good duke's soldiers and in 1014 more northern pirates found a welcome at Rouen, after their sack of Dol. A Viking army was thus greeted in Normandy within twenty years of the Conqueror's birth.

Nowhere did Viking blood show more than in the Normans' relations with England. While Alfred's heirs were slowly mastering the Danelaw, they had extended marriage alliances to France, Germany and the Low Countries, but never to Normandy. In the last quarter of

the tenth century, when the northerners again turned
upon England, their ships found shelter in the duchy. A
papal envoy had to be sent to London and then, with an
English embassy, to Rouen in 991, and another quarrel
was raging nine years later, perhaps because the raiders
were being pursued into Norman harbours. Boastful
chronicles of a later date are a poor guide to what happened, but in 1000 Æthelred II arranged an expedition
to the Cotentin peninsula. It misfired, like most of his
projects, but was followed by a peace treaty and the king's
marriage to Richard's half-Danish sister, Emma. For
England the peace too may be said to have miscarried,
for Æthelred seems to have been denied help against
Sweyn Forkbeard of Denmark seven years later. By his
foreign match, unprecedented since the mid-ninth
century, the luckless king merely gained some half-
Norman children, one of whom was to displace the line
of his eldest son, Edmund Ironside, and to pave the way
for William. The Conqueror's lineal claim to the English
throne, such as it was, also sprang from this marriage, for
he was the great-nephew of Æthelred and Emma
(Table I).

None the less it was sentiment, not similarity, that now
linked Norway and Denmark with their offshoot. Richard
II often served the king as his vassal, and his circle was
French in speech and ways, with all the aristocratic
feelings of feudal France. The duke is said to have
desired that every one of his attendants should be a
gentil hume—perhaps the earliest reference to a 'gentleman'—and a stupendous upheaval of the peasantry on
his accession may have been fired by hatred of the new
order. This revolt indicates that the Norman peasants
were more Scandinavian than the evidence would otherwise suggest and that men hungered after the freedom of
their roving fathers. At any rate, the work of suppression
should have satisfied the most ferocious Viking. Raoul of

Ivry, Richard's uncle, led the hunt for mutinous peasants, and mass mutilations advertised the ducal vengeance.

The duke received his fugitive sister after Sweyn Forkbeard had finally dislodged the West Saxon line and, when Emma regained her throne by the simple expedient of marrying Sweyn's son, Cnut, her children continued to receive shelter at the Norman court. Richard the Good was a cautious ruler, however, and gave no military help to his nephews. He probably settled the succession before his death and was duly followed in 1026 by his eldest son. Richard III reigned for less than a year and was rumoured to have been poisoned by his brother, Robert the Magnificent, once wrongly known as Robert the Devil.

A young man of less than twenty, Robert at first indulged in wild schemes for asserting his cousins' rights in England, but the threat to Cnut never materialized. Albeit the first romantic figure among the Norman dukes, Robert possessed all the forcefulness and much of the cunning of his race. In 1031 he helped Henry I to the throne of France against the jealous queen mother and, in return, he may have been granted the French Vexin, a heavily garrisoned frontier district between Rouen and Paris, over which later disputes were to lead to endless wars. His short reign saw the lay magnates turn to monastic foundations and also the departure of Norman adventurers to southern Italy, an event no doubt unwelcome to the duke but destined to bring glory to his race.

Robert had a high reputation as an energetic ruler and a benefactor of the clergy when he died at Nicaea in Asia Minor, on his way back from Jerusalem, in July 1035. As he was still unmarried, he had guarded against the unlikely event of his death by persuading the chief men of the duchy to accept as his heir a bastard of seven or possibly eight years old. This boy had been born to Herleve, nicknamed Arlette, who was probably the daughter of Fulbert, a tanner of Falaise. One story says that she was dancing in the road, another that she was washing at a stream, when the duke spied her from his castle on the rock. Robert's family had maintained the Viking habit of contracting regular unions which none the less fell short of Christian marriage, so that the sequel to his meeting was blessed by tradition.

It was twelve years before William the Bastard was secure. Richard II and Emma had left another brother, Robert, archbishop of Rouen and count of Evreux, while more remote but still legitimate claims could be advanced by Gui of Burgundy and Alain of Brittany; there was even a son of Richard III who, fortunately for himself, became a monk. Irregular birth had never been a bar, and in that case there were two other eligible adults, the sons of Richard II. In England, where minors might be passed over, veneration for the royal house would have impeded the accession of a bastard save in the direst emergency; Norman conventions were more fluid. In this welter of claims, the child succeeded by default. While England endured Cnut's uncongenial sons before Earl Godwine presented her with Edward the Confessor, the duchy which had sheltered Æthelred's children was given over to rebellion and private vendetta. One by one, the protectors appointed for William by his father met violent ends.

Supported mainly in the more civilized east, the young duke survived many perils until 1047, when rumours of an ambush forced him to escape by night and throw himself into the arms of Henry of France. The king himself had previously taken advantage of Normandy's disarray to ravage Hiesmois but now, doubtless fearing that there might soon be a more formidable duke, he repaid the debt which he owed to Robert the Magnificent. Henry marched with his protégé against Gui of Burgundy and the other rebels, who met them on a gently undulating plateau to the south-east of Caen, known as Val-ès-Dunes.

There followed an incident which shows how even the most turbulent of men set store by outward forms. Ralph Tesson, a leading conspirator who had sworn to smite William at the first opportunity but now scented danger, galloped up to the young duke on his own. He then struck William lightly on the shoulder with his glove, in fulfilment of his vow, was gravely thanked by his lord and rode off, to watch which way the battle would go. A series of cavalry charges followed, unhampered by archery, Ralph's fears were justified, and in the end he intervened on the right side. In the first pitched battle of his life, William conquered.

Val-ès-Dunes marks the end of the second phase of Norman history, when a new, essentially French state was emerging. Only six written acts survive from the reign of Richard I, but fifty are known from that of Richard II, two from Richard III and over thirty from the seven years of Robert I. These reflect a more elaborate government, making it possible to look in some detail at Norman society on the eve of its collision with England.

*

The Normans, above all, are associated with feudalism and its introduction to England. As such, they were among the midwives of the medieval world or of the Middle Ages. In the blaze of the Renaissance, men were to give this name to the second half of the long night which separated the classical age from their own day, but their scorn was unjustified. There is a sharp contrast between the chaos which followed the fall of Rome and the ordered Carolingian world, both of which are included in 'the Dark Ages', and between this period and the new Western Europe, Latin, Christian and feudal, which was approaching.

Today anything which is held to be antiquated can be derided as 'feudal'. No adjective has been more debased.

Feudalism was justified by the need for protection when the Roman Empire broke up, and its origins lay in the rise of cavalry. Military horsemen or knights being expensive to maintain, the simplest way to ensure a proper supply was to reward the knight with land, which he would hold in return for military service. The recipient promised to serve the grantor, the former thereby becoming the vassal and the latter his lord. A distinction between land owned outright and land held on conditions had been recognized by the Romans and by the German tribes who overran the Western Empire. The early Frankish Church often received revocable land, when it was known as a *beneficium*, and the description was later applied to estates granted to knights; such military benefices were the forerunners of the feudal fiefs.

Haphazard growth and lack of definition make the early history of feudalism a confusing subject and even its palmiest days, after the Norman conquest of England, were to be bedevilled by disputes over what was due from a vassal to his lord. It is important to remember that the fully developed feudal society, described below, did not exist in Normandy at the time of Val-ès-Dunes, nor even by 1066. Random practice preceded uniform theory and the Conquest was to allow William to impose on England a feudal pattern more rigid than anything yet experienced by his native duchy. None the less a feudal society was beginning to emerge by the time that William started his effective rule as duke of Normandy.

The essence of feudalism was the tenure of land by military service. For example, the duke granted land to a man in return for the obligation to provide five fully equipped knights; the recipient thereby became the duke's tenant-in-chief and the land, which was his barony, consisted of five knights' fees. The number of knights was normally five, or one of its multiples or fractions, and the customary period of service eventually became forty days a year at the tenant's expense, any extra service being paid for by the lord. In addition, there were obligations to guard the lord's castles and to pay him various sums, which are now known as 'feudal incidents'. These included a 'relief', when the tenant entered on his inheritance, and contributions towards the knighting of the lord's eldest son and the marriage of his eldest daughter. In Normandy, most estates had not been granted for life or at will but were hereditary. Under Richard II it was usual for the right of inheritance to pass to all the sons or, in default, to daughters; if a child succeeded, his wardship, which included the profit of his lands, the custody of his person and the arrangement of his marriage, belonged to the lord.

The barons or tenants-in-chief were important men, who held their land directly of the duke. As such, they were his vassals and held fiefs, but these terms have a wider meaning; any man who did homage for his land was a vassal and any land so held was a fief. The ducal practice of granting land to tenants-in-chief was repeated when the latter made grants, on similar conditions, to under-tenants. This process, called subinfeudation, produced an extremely complex pattern of tenure, with men holding fractions of knights' fees, often of several lords. Its advantages for the barons were obvious: if one owed the duke the service of five knights, he could impose the service of perhaps ten knights on his own tenants, thus ensuring an extra force of five knights for his own disposal.

Norman society was therefore a pyramid, organized for war, with its layers cemented by rights and duties. Outside the Church all men of consequence bore arms, while humbler men tilled the soil. At the bottom of the pyramid were the *villani* or villeins, tied to the land and, in return for their plots, forced to render special services to the lord, including work on the ground reserved for his personal support, the demesne. In Richard II's time there was a slightly superior class of peasants, called *hospites*, who were not bound by regular labour for the lord but rendered occasional services. Above them came the *vavassores* or smaller freeholders, who were bound by military service but only to fight on foot. Then came the knightly class and at the top the duke, who himself owed knight-service to the king of France. This society, with its horizontal layers, was similar to that of the duchy's neighbours, and men felt more in common with their social counterparts there than with those above or below them at home. Far removed from the freebooters from which it had sprung, feudal Normandy shows how regular services and protection are needed when men have settled down, particularly when they are surrounded by enemies. In adopting military tenure, the practical-minded descendants of Rollo's pirates had abandoned Scandinavia for France and had left England far behind.

All the laborious discussions about the nature and extent of military obligations and the responsibility for their introduction spring from two needs: to discover the strength of the duchy, compared with that of her neighbours, and to see if this strength was at the disposal of the dukes. Normandy has been linked with Flanders and Barcelona as one of the most highly developed feudal states of the mid-eleventh century. Richard II, Robert and William therefore presided over an advanced society, but this did not mean that they wielded special authority. Unhappily, while the layers of feudal society were horizontal, the bonds were vertical; the ties which bound men to their lord did not bind them to one another, so that the spectre of private warfare was constantly coming to life.

There is no direct evidence that the Norman dukes could impose fixed quotas of military service on all their tenants before 1066, although they had probably managed to do so upon the great landowning monasteries, which

ranked as baronies, and perhaps upon the bishops.
Certainly these dues were enforced on the Church far
more strictly than on the laity, and baronial obligations
were always lighter than they were to be in the Conqueror's England. If services had lain heavily on the
barons, emigrations to Italy would never have been
possible on a large scale, nor would private warfare have
been so easy in the years before Val-ès-Dunes. Feudalism
was developing not as part of the duke's policy, but
because it suited an aristocracy which had a unique gift
for organization and a keen eye to its own advantage.

*

The dukes none the less had their rights. Every ruler's
main tasks were to act as general and as judge, and in
neither of these were Rollo's descendants backward. The
administration of justice in the early eleventh century,
although it required a knowledge of custom, did not call
for impressive learning or eloquence. Defendants were
commonly made to undergo an ordeal to test their
truthfulness; women held a red-hot iron, which was
supposed to blister the hands of the guilty, while men
were more commonly bound and thrown into consecrated
water. This obvious if primitive way of determining
God's will may sometimes have defeated its own ends, for
in ordeal by water the hallowed element would receive
only an innocent man, who thus had to sink. The martial
Normans often preferred a new form of ordeal, by battle,
but a more lasting claim to fame would be their occasional
use of a jury, if only this could be proved. After many
attempts to trace this famous institution to English or
Norse customs, it was at last generally credited to the
Frankish kings, who would summon groups of dis-
interested neighbours to declare on oath what they knew
concerning rights to land. The Normans were then
believed to have inherited the jury, although there is no

record of its actual employment and it has since been pointed out that they were not, as a race, given to swearing judicial oaths. The whole question of its early use is again in doubt.

While justice has always, in theory, been the end of government, it is not easy to agree on who should govern. Feudalism, which brought landed wealth and military power to a protecting aristocracy, also allowed private persons to enjoy wide judicial powers. A Norman lord exercised justice over his tenants at his feudal court but for certain cases he needed a special grant, since they were otherwise reserved for the duke. In 1091 this monopoly embraced murder, assault on journeys to or from the ducal court, attacks on pilgrims and violations of the currency, while arson, rape and attacks on houses were left to the barons. In fact the monopoly was often infringed by grants and, with every allowance for pious forgeries, it seems that several monasteries were given immunity and exercise of the ruler's rights. At least, in that society of self-reliant warriors, it was recognized that the duke had a unique responsibility for law and order.

Another feature of Normandy, as of other feudal states, was the separate jurisdiction of the Church. Again a haze covers the scene for most of the eleventh century, but the council of Lillebonne in 1080 shows that by then ecclesiastical courts were well established. It is also clear that archdeacons, who were responsible to the bishop for supervising the clergy within a defined area, were known in Normandy under William, and that the priests who served cathedrals were being organized into chapters, separately endowed and with specific duties. The bishop punished offences in churches and churchyards and drew fines from clerks or members of his household, but his jurisdiction over laymen is uncertain. A priest was subject to his lord for his secular holding, while forest offences were also beyond the scope of the Church.

Like all the stronger princes of the age, the dukes of the eleventh century could appoint prelates and sometimes, in an emergency, engineer their deposition. This meant that, in the last resort, there was unlikely to be defiance from a bishop or abbot and Rollo's successors, pious but prudent, never allowed a bishop to exercise the secular powers of a count, even in his own cathedral city; there was always a ducal agent, a *vicomte*, to do that. An attempt to limit private war by threatening spiritual penalties, known as the Truce of God, was introduced from Flanders a few months after Val-ès-Dunes. The need to make violence especially heinous from Wednesday evening to Monday morning and during the seasons beginning at Advent, Lent and Rogationtide may be a shocking comment on the times, but the responsibility for enforcing the Truce brought prestige to the bishops and to the dukes who assisted them. Church courts and the Truce of God were unknown across the Channel, perhaps because there they were not so sorely needed.

*

Revenues, although they make for dull reading, are the sinews of the state. Despite the lack of financial records for Normandy earlier than 1180 it is possible to piece together the dukes' sources of wealth. Extensive domains and forests had never been granted away but stayed in the dukes' hands, scattered throughout the duchy, with sundry mills, saltpans and fishing rights, including a monopoly of whales and other 'great fish'. The dukes enjoyed the sole right to issue coins, which may not have been in widespread circulation but which were being struck at Bayeux and Rouen before the Conquest. Wrecks and treasure-trove were reserved, together with profits from the coinage, and there were also tolls and certain urban properties. Feudal dues, judicial fines and forfeitures made up the rest of the ducal income. Lack of information about the collection of these motley sums, which did not include a national tax like the English Danegeld, does not prove immaturity. Richard II had a special treasury or *camera* for financial windfalls, and his officials clearly knew the difference between ordinary and extraordinary income.

Finance was bound up with administration and in Normandy, as everywhere, military, judicial and fiscal duties might be combined in the same office. The chief local agents of the duke were the *vicomtes*, of whom there were over twenty and whose title was sometimes interchangeable with that of *prévôt*. Their districts, perhaps based on older Frankish divisions, in general were much smaller than the English shires and more like the rapes of Sussex. Under Richard II there were also four or five counties—Mortain, Hiesmois, Evreux, Brionne and Eu—which served as fiefs for his kinsmen, but these were no larger or wealthier than the *vicomtes*, into and from which they might be changed. The only difference was that the duke retained no important estates in the counties and left the local administration to their holders.

Active government needs a reliable income, which can be collected efficiently. Here the use of the *vicomte* as a fiscal unit is startlingly modern. Later records show that by the mid-eleventh century the dukes were granting fixed sums from the revenue of a certain area, a habit which placed them far ahead of their southern neighbours in Anjou, of the French royal domains and probably even of England. In early medieval societies, when the prince wished to grant an income he might well make it in kind or, if it was to be in money, assign it on a specific feudal source. It was precocious to assign so many grants on the cash receipts from a considerable district. Feudalism, the source of military strength, was not allowed to hamper

the development of an administration based, more conveniently, on geography. Norman genius for government
was already at work.

The duke, who presided over every aspect of the state,
could hardly take every decision himself. Counsel was
available from his court or *curia*, a body of parallel growth
to the one which served the French kings but of indeterminate numbers and times of meeting. It represented both birth and office, for membership extended to
the ducal family, the bishops, a few great nobles, some
household officials and the *vicomtes*. These persons, whose
business was more to witness than to assent, might
advise on a wide range of subjects, including the invasion
of England, and mete out justice to barons, in disputes
over jurisdiction or in any case that touched the duke's
rights. The *curia* was also the obvious place for issuing
charters and recording agreements, for trials by ordeal
and battle and perhaps for sworn inquests. There was no
fixed division of function and justices are not mentioned,
although they may have existed. Certainly a few members,
usually one or two bishops and a *vicomte*, tended to give
decisions. Like many Norman institutions whose history
is uncharted, this central council may have been highly
effective; its members were certainly fewer than the
better known English *witan*.

There was little machinery for putting decisions into
effect. Apart from the *vicomtes*, the dukes had a number of
attendants whose titles are the same as those found in the
French royal household, but these personal servants can
hardly be considered officers of state. There seems to have
been no formal chancery where documents were drawn up,
although one chancellor makes a fleeting appearance
under Richard II and the ducal chaplains might act as
household clerks. Charters, expressing the duke's will,
arose as written records of oral gifts; in a world of
illiterate laymen, they needed authentication, which

William the Conqueror sometimes provided with a cross.

The English sealed writs, or short letters from the king to the shire courts, were not known on the Continent. There was a chamberlain in charge of the *camera* or chamber where such extraordinary revenue as reached the duke was lodged, but most sums were raised and spent locally; even the title of chamberlain was accorded to different dignitaries at the same time. In comparison with England, the structure of government was undeveloped.

*

There were two partial exceptions to the general administrative framework of *vicomtes* and the more confused pattern of overlapping public and private justice. These were the forests and the towns, both of which are obscure. The wide ducal forests were already under a special jurisdiction, which dated back to Frankish days and was to become the notorious forest code of the Anglo-Norman kings. Mysterious pleas of the forest probably showed the dukes at their harshest, for certain assaults were unlawful only there and no one was exempt, but nothing definite is known save the names of a handful of foresters. In England the kings also reserved such areas and the old myth of widespread depopulation to suit William the Conqueror's passion for hunting has long since been modified. None the less, the elaboration of a separate code was in keeping with the Norman search for maximum efficiency; with its use of mutilation as a deterrent, it was one more terror for the poor.

Townsmen, by their occupation, always needed to escape from the system which hampered life in the countryside. Feudalism, with its forced labour, complicated payments and restrictions on movement and business, was stifling for industry and commerce, the two activities which brought men together. The early townsmen, however, did not presume to demand freedom from obligations to the lords from whom they had acquired their land; they merely sought recognition of their peculiar interests. In theory, all that was coveted was a collective lordship, owing, for example, communal military service, and even this feeling had not visibly developed by the mid-eleventh century. The dukes remained large urban landowners and every major town had its *vicomte*, while none enjoyed the independence of the medieval municipal body, the commune. Nothing more positive is known of early municipal government, even for Rouen, with its history from Roman times. Yet individual customs were evolving, for many new centres known as *burgi* sprang up in the middle of the century, taking their laws from older ones. Those of Breteuil were to be transplanted by the conquerors to the Welsh borders and Ireland, while the privileged area of one league around a town or castle, found in Norman England, was known much earlier in the duchy.

The main towns were the seats of the seven bishoprics which made up historic Normandy—Rouen, the metropolitan see in the east, Evreux, Lisieux, Sées, Bayeux and, in the west, Coutances and Avranches; to these should be added Caen, a ducal foundation which was flourishing under Richard II, and a number of seaports. The status of such places is even harder to assess because so little is known of the activities carried on there. Rouen was to become famous for its tanneries, one of which was already enjoying the protection of the eastern ramparts by William's time. Men from the city had traded in wine and large fish with the Londoners of Æthelred II and were using their own wharf at Dowgate under Edward the Confessor. The best wine came from farther south but fishing was widespread off the Norman coast; the large fish were called and may sometimes have been whales, or at least lesser cetaceans such as porpoises, whose oil was

highly prized. Charlemagne's successors had sadly
neglected the sea, to their own cost, and it was the
Scandinavians who brought new life to the abandoned
ports of northern France. The forests around Rouen
supplied timber, first for piracy and later for more peaceful voyages, so that the city became a busy port once
again. Other, less sheltered, harbours had been revived
by Richard II's time, especially Honfleur, Harfleur,
Barfleur and Dieppe, where herrings were being salted
in 1030. These activities cannot have freed many men
from their feudal duties but at least urban life had
begun.

*

In the very long run, Europe's development was to be
decided by the towns. For the moment, the men who
worked counted for nothing, while chroniclers exalted
the men who fought and recounted the splendour of
princes. This attitude was reasonable, although it frus-
trates any inquiry about how ordinary people used to live.
Prosperity depended upon the skill of a small martial
class and upon the success of an individual ruler. Amidst
constant warfare, every community needed warriors for
its defence and one warrior more powerful than the rest,
who could keep his fellows from rending one another and
from oppressing their social inferiors. Normandy lacked
strong rule during William's minority and its provision
was to be his lifelong task, but Norman military enterprise,
which he was to channel towards his own ends, was
already advanced. If it had been otherwise, there would
have been no duchy for him to govern.

The need to fight for survival had forced the early
colonists to abandon the traditional Viking habit of
fighting on foot. No longer pirates who crept up rivers in
shallow ships to plunder and depart, but landholders who
had to keep what they had won, the Normans perfected

the mounted warfare already practised by the Franks. For this, knights wore conical iron helmets, with nose-guards, and hauberks or mail shirts, which reached to the knees and had short, wide sleeves (Plates I, II); there might also be tighter pieces of mail for the lower legs and forearms. Various types of padding were necessary under this mail and a further defence lay in the heavy shields of wood, covered with hide and strengthened with metal. Those who could not afford the full armour might use boiled leather, which was also the main protection for foot soldiers. Offensive weapons were the lance, the javelin or throwing spear, the long, broad-bladed sword and often a mace, which was usually a simple cudgel but might have a metal head. This last was a great boon for warlike churchmen: the sword would have shed Christian blood, while the mace merely produced concussion.

The careful breeding and management of heavy war-horses or destriers was one of the secrets of Norman success. Armour gave protection and horses, which lived well on the fat pastures of the duchy, gave mobility. This combination made cavalry the supreme arm, with no need, as had the lighter Roman horsemen, for cover from masses of infantry. The resulting warfare was not an elevated science. When there was fighting in open country, organization and tactics were at a discount and individual prowess was everything; archery might first succeed in weakening the enemy, but knights could be overcome only by other knights after a headlong collision. Rashness, however, was far from dominating every campaign; the Conqueror himself preferred sieges and devastations to the hazards of a pitched battle.

The Normans went further, with the ruthless logic for which they are famous, and extended the possibilities of cavalry action by building castles, again in emulation of those around them, particularly of the nobles of Anjou. Castles are so closely associated with the medieval world

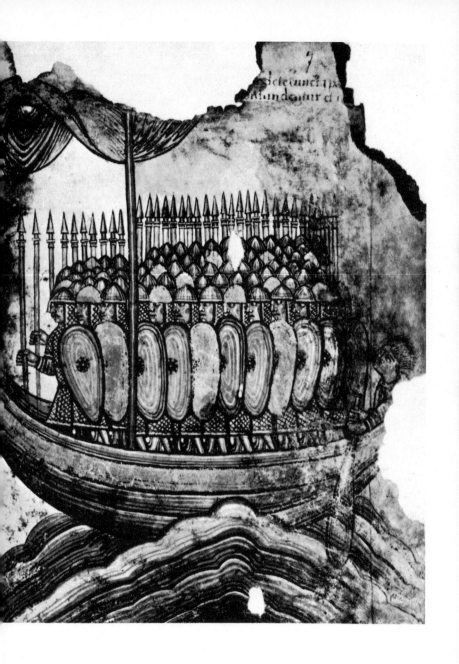

I Norman soldiers on board ship *(Bibliothèque Nationale)*

II Duke William bestows arms on Earl Harold. Both men wear knee-length hauberks and conical helmets with nose-guards. The tabs sticking out from William's head and shoulders indicate his rank. (From the Bayeux Tapestry)

III   The castle at Dol. Although the architectural details are formal and unrealistic, this flimsy structure is clearly a wooden building on a mound, with a drawbridge at the left. Conan of Brittany escapes by sliding down a rope—a mistake, since Conan in fact was besieging Dol and was forced to flee by the Normans' advance. (From the Bayeux Tapestry)

IV Ploughing scenes
(a) Detail from the Bayeux Tapestry
(b) From a manuscript containing the first English
calendar pictures, early eleventh century.
Since this artist often includes classical details copied
from Continental works, his scenes do not always illustrate
Old English manners with complete accuracy.
(Cotton MSS Julius A VI f.3, *British Museum*)

V   (a) Seal of Edward the Confessor
(b) Silver penny of Harold II
(c) Silver penny of William I
(All *British Museum*)

HIC HAROLD MARE NAVIGAVIT

VI Earl Harold feasts at Bosham. The earl is drinking from a bowl while attendants tell him that it is time to leave. Englishmen and Normans are both shown with short garments and long

VII   The site of the battle of Hastings, Battle, Sussex. The top
of the ridge on which the English took their stand was probably
open country; part of the lower slopes may have been tilled.
Fishponds now mark what was once a swampy meadow,
the source of the Asten. *(Aerofilms)*

VIII   A portion of the *Domesday* survey for Surrey—'Gilbert son of Richer de Aigle holds Whitley.' His lands are followed by those of Geoffrey de Mandeville in the hundreds of Brixton, Wallington and Woking. The names of places and of tenants struck out are meant to be underlined. *(Public Records Office)*

that it is hard to realize that they were once a novelty.
In the Byzantine Empire they had been used for centuries;
in western Europe, from Roman until Viking days,
defences were normally reserved for towns. Purely
military strongholds had then been introduced by the
Frankish kings in their efforts to check the northerners,
but it was turbulent subjects who were mainly responsible
for the spread of castles. These were built by the Normans
in very simple forms, consisting of a *motte* or moated
mound, with a bailey or base-court attached, fortified
with wood. Several are shown in the Bayeux Tapestry
(Plate III), although these do not include a bailey, and
one of many which still exist is at Domfront, built around
1030 by the elder Guillaume de Talvas, first of the rapa-
cious lords of Bellême. Like military tenure, castles were
a source of potential strength to the state, so long as their
building could be controlled by the duke. William's
success in this made him a formidable threat to lands
where such strongholds were unknown.

*

The blood of the Vikings, who had revelled in war,
undoubtedly contributed to Norman triumphs in the
field. These and other achievements, however, were the
work of a few. When posterity thinks of the Normans, it
naturally thinks of the knightly class. The decision to
invade England was a political one, taken by the duke
and his barons, who regarded him as essentially one of
themselves, albeit with special privileges and duties.
The bishops, scions of the great houses if not ducal
bastards, in background and usually in habits were a
part of this proud aristocracy.

Pride was justified by deeds more than by lineage.
None of the men who dominate William's minority or
reign boast a long family history, which is scarcely
surprising, considering the irregularity of the ducal line

itself. Richard I's Danish mistress Gunnor, whom he afterwards married, had relatives whose advancement accounts for some of the oldest families. The rise of the nobility which fought at Hastings is only traceable to Richard II's reign and territorial surnames were still rare; in the eleventh century, as in the nineteenth, they were the choice of parvenus.

The dukes seem to have resembled their leading subjects, although there were doubtless many men of less vigour, who failed to make their mark. Guileful, mercenary and hard-living, torn between the chase and the battlefield, the Norman noble could unite bravery with unspeakable cruelty. Some of the leading figures of William's minority were bywords for treachery, like nearly every member of the house of Bellême, into which women married at their peril; the Christian devotion of one wife so infuriated her husband that he had her strangled on the way back from church, although another, the ill-famed Mabel of Montgomery, survived for longer, thanks to an encyclopedic knowledge of poisons. Others were noted for more straightforward cruelty, like Ralph of Tosny, who was reported to beguile the dinner hours while a Crusader in Spain by being served with the boiled heads of infidels.

There was a more attractive side to many of Ralph's fellows. Close-cropped, clean-shaven and comparatively clean of body, they dressed richly and could behave with impressive formality. The survival of swords with a gentleman's civilian attire until the eighteenth century conjures up pictures of earlier and progressively fiercer ages, when hot-tempered barons stalked about, bristling with weapons. In reality, nothing warlike was carried by Norman nobles during their leisure and it was some two hundred years before even the dagger was worn at court. William of Malmesbury records that the Normans are so inured to war that they can scarcely live without it, that they weigh treason by its chance of success and will change their opinions for money; he also admits the discrimination in food and clothing of these men, who live with economy and are 'the most polite of peoples'. Part of this description by the foremost Anglo-Norman historian fits in well with the bloodstained history and rugged achievements of Rollo's heirs, part is an early and startling tribute to the civilizing influence of France. The Normans, with Viking impulses under Latin manners, were a complex race.

A ruling class may despise learning, as did most of the Norman nobility, without being entirely boorish. The rigid medieval separation of society into workers, warriors and churchmen meant that there was no need for a baron to be literate. If he sent or received a letter, there were clerks to serve him, if he wanted peaceful entertainment, there were poets and harpers; no one yet read to him aloud, since his speech was French and books, mainly on theology, history and law, were still in Latin, but there are other ways of influencing people for the good. Spectacle was a source of delight for all classes in medieval Europe, even for the practical Normans, whose strong point was not their imagination. Today especially, when the printed word is again being challenged by sounds and pictures, this outlook deserves understanding.

Another aspect of the Norman character appeared only in the second quarter of the eleventh century. There was an upsurge of piety, or at least of religious generosity, from which it is barely distinguishable. So far, in contrast to England, the ruling family alone had inspired the monastic revival. Its patronage had been vital for Normandy's development; William of Volpiano, in whose native country education was more highly esteemed, had taken care to found schools for future monks, which ordinary clerical aspirants and even the interested laity could attend. Now the barons suddenly followed suit, the fearsome lord of Bellême in the van, so that the war-torn years of the Conqueror's youth were ones of unprece-dented benevolence by the men whose 'adulterine' or unlicensed castles riddled the land. The patrons' motives were naturally mixed; they expected to benefit in the next world, ordaining prayers for themselves and their kin, they also liked the social competition of lavish good works, and some arranged that their grants of lands should be rewarded by annual payments in cash. The result was none the less a stimulus to worship and learning and a help to those who preferred a quiet life. It does not in the least detract from the importance of these founda-tions that they were largely the work of ruthless and successful men, faced with the prospect of dying in bed.

Occasionally altruism is more obvious, as in Herluin, a knight of one of William's hapless guardians Count Gilbert of Brionne, whose disgust with the world led him to make a retreat for himself at Le Bec. Herluin had his disciples, whose revulsion against the violence of their time shows at least that the Normans could produce men who reacted against the excesses of their own race. Moreover, about 1042 a renowned teacher of law and letters sought solitude at Le Bec and founded a school there. His name was Lanfranc; he was to be one of the greatest archbishops of Canterbury and his school was to be a beacon for the north.

*

It is vital to look back to the foundation of the duchy, since the early dangers helped to cast the Normans into their historic mould. If there had been more colonists, swords could readily have been beaten into ploughshares and the settled communities would have fallen easy victims, as in England, to revived native power; paradoxically, the colonists might then have remained close to the Vikings, except in religion, again like their counterparts in the Danelaw. In the island Danes had remained Danes but become farmers, while in the duchy they had become Frenchmen but remained fighters. Scandinavians and Anglo-Saxons had more in common with one another, in customs and language, than either had with the Latin races, so that any influence on English life was bound to be more momentous if it came from across the Channel rather than over the North Sea.

Europe had a foretaste of Norman prowess and ambition while William was still young, when resourceful members of the Hauteville family entrenched themselves in Apulia, at the south-eastern tip of Italy. Their penetration of the rest of southern Italy was a triumph of private enterprise, achieved in close alliance with the papacy and displayed in their recognition as dukes of Apulia and Calabria seven years before the conquest of England. In the course of the 1070s and 1080s Sicily was to be wrested from the Arabs to form the centre of a rich and exotic kingdom, which the Normans were to rule for a century; from there they were briefly to acquire lands in northern Africa and the Balkans, to dominate Rome and to menace Constantinople itself. William's work had its parallel by the Mediterranean and during his lifetime the Normans came to straddle the western world.

Explanations of this achievement are naturally distorted by the pride of conquerors or tainted with the rancour of subject races. The Italian Geoffrey of Malaterra says that the Normans were cunning and greedy but eloquent, hard-working and apt at warfare, and he ascribes their success above all to imitation. This is only a half-truth, for in all spheres they were more than imitators, they were developers, but Geoffrey rightly pinpoints their distinguishing quality of *effrenatissima*, a combination of ceaseless enterprise with lawlessness. William of Malmesbury would have agreed, although he does not attempt a specific explanation; writing at the other end of

Europe, he remarks that the Normans envied their equals and wished to vie with their superiors.

The restive Norman nobility was therefore a tremendous force, for good or evil. Military skill made it a constant internal threat, even to Rollo's masterful descendants; a negative answer to this problem was to allow emigration, which in the end dissipated the dukes' own strength, a positive one would be to direct this energy against a chosen target. William, seeing Italy reel under the blows of Norman adventurers, could not fail to covet a prize nearer home.

CHAPTER TWO

England at the Accession of Edward the Confessor

*T*HE Normans' early development is relatively obscure and their historical fame rests on their expansion in the eleventh century. If carving out Mediterranean principalities was a spectacular feat, the almost equally heroic conquest of England has proved more fateful for the world. The value of William's work is constantly disputed by those who see the Old English kingdom as a sick body, in need of a blood transfusion, and those who mourn a vigorous individual growth, cut off in its prime. It is therefore essential to survey the land which Edward the Confessor was called to rule, so as to find out whether England actively contributed to 'Norman' achievements or whether she simply provided a freer field for Norman enterprise.

*

England's history, from the earliest times, has been shaped by the country's rough division into a highland and a lowland zone. Wherever the line is drawn, from the Trent to Southampton Water or from the Humber to the Exe, there remains a contrast between the backward

lands of the north and west and the more favoured region
to the south-east; not until the industrial revolution did
the balance of population and wealth shift towards the
north. The southern lowlands have their counterpart in
those of northern France, to which they were once joined,
and these areas lay open to the same influences. England
was only later to find safety as an island fortress; in the
Dark Ages, the seas were less of a barrier than were
mountains, forests and swamps.

Geography determined that men on both sides of the
Channel should meet the same forces and, more often
than not, that on both sides they should succumb. The
Celtic population of each land had submitted to the
Belgae and then to the Romans, who found that they
could best defend Gaul by conquering most of the island
to the north, which became the province of Britannia. The
defences erected by Rome in their turn gave way early
in the fifth century before the onslaughts of Germanic
invaders, themselves under pressure from new tribes
pouring out of Asia. When the Franks overran Gaul,
Britannia was left to the Angles, Saxons and Jutes. These
kindred peoples had already intermingled before they
left the north-west coastlands of Germany, so it is not
surprising that their tribal identities gradually dissolved
in their new home: King Alfred spoke of 'Englishmen',
although Continental writers preferred the term 'Anglo-
Saxons' to distinguish the islanders from the Saxons of
Germany.

Finally, in the ninth century, both Franks and English
were faced with the Vikings. In England it seemed that
every native kingdom would be submerged during the
860s, when Danish raids were changed into attempts at
permanent conquest. At the battle of Ashdown in 871,
Alfred of Wessex miraculously checked the invaders and
won a respite, followed by a further victory at Edington
in 878 which led to the baptism of Guthrum, the Danish

leader. Guthrum's warriors were now forced either to settle in the area assigned to them, the Danelaw, or to seek their fortune elsewhere. Whenever resistance stiffened on one side of the Channel the Vikings turned to the other. The successful stand of Alfred and, after his death in 899, of his son Edward the Elder, was indirectly responsible for Rollo's settlement in Normandy.

The inhabitants of England, as of Normandy, were therefore of mixed stock. The extent to which the English invaders had displaced their various British predecessors is not known. Some Britons had been exterminated and probably many more had been enslaved, while those who remained independent had been driven into the fastnesses of Cornwall, Wales and Cumberland. Certainly there was less Roman blood north of the Channel than there was in Gaul: in Britannia little more than a hundred thousand immigrants had been added to a population of about one million, and Latin had failed to survive, whereas in Gaul, Italy and Spain the Germanic invaders had adopted the speech which they found, so ensuring a future for the Romance languages.

The Scandinavian influx is equally hard to measure. Place and personal names suggest that a warrior class was superimposed on the English of the Danelaw, although its numbers must have been swollen by later immigrants either from over the North Sea or, in the north-west, from the Norwegian colonies in Ireland. Viking settlers were most sparse in the southern Danelaw, between the Thames and the Welland, more plentiful in East Anglia and more still in the north, between the Welland and the Tees; beyond this, an English enclave held its ground (Map II). William the Conqueror's *Domesday* survey was to show that some forty per cent of the peasantry bore Danish names in East Anglia and sixty per cent in Lincolnshire.

*

The Anglo-Saxon colonists transformed England's landscape. The towns and villas of Roman Britain, with their high material civilization, had adorned a countryside where farming had barely changed since the Iron Age. Very little new land, save in the Fens, had been brought under cultivation and villages had been most plentiful on the chalk and limestone uplands of the south, where the light soil could easily be turned. The German tribes were more hardy, settling first on the eastern seaboard and then, under constant pressure to win new homes, stealing into the heart of the country up the great river systems of the Thames, the Humber and the Wash. They started a gigantic attack on the thick forests and heavy, untouched clays of the Midlands. The work, agonizingly slow, was being stubbornly pursued when the Vikings descended and had still to be finished when the Normans came. The Scandinavians played their part, by populating the neglected northern dales, but the main credit for reducing the wilderness belongs to the Anglo-Saxon peasant. His achievement is the unhonoured glory of Old English history.

The cultivated land was divided into strips, which formed part of an open field extending perhaps to several hundred acres. The size of a peasant's individual strip was determined not by some primitive ideal of fair shares but by what could be cultivated in one day with a mould-board plough, which turned the furrow as well as cutting the sod. The most economic method was to plough in a straight line, turn once and plough back, so that the average strip consisted of two parallel furrows; its length would be a furrow long or furlong of two hundred and twenty yards and its total width would be twenty-two yards, giving rise to the modern acre. Since different soils and contours caused strips to vary in size it was many centuries before the acre, a term for a day's ploughing, became a standard measurement (Plates IVa, b).

Open fields were necessary because of the shortage of plough-teams: the *Domesday* survey was to estimate that there was one team to every two and a half rural households in Oxfordshire and one to every five housholds in Norfolk. Two fields were also necessary for each community, one being left to lie fallow while the other was sown with spring and winter corn. Each man sowed and ploughed in succession, so that his total holding was scattered, the cropped strip lying with others in one field, the fallow strip with his neighbours' fallow in the other field. The direction of the strips altered with the drainage and so arose the apparently confused agricultural pattern of the two-field system, each field a cartographer's nightmare of individual holdings.

Open fields formed only one part of the rural scene. Every village had its common meadow lands for pasture and usually some wasteland, which provided brushwood and could be used for rough grazing. In the west the emphasis lay more on livestock than on arable and many hills unsuitable for cultivation were turned over to sheep. Some free tenants did not live in villages at all but secured a lord's permission to clear part of his forest, reclaim some marshland or encroach on the fringe of an inhospitable moor; these peasants in their isolated farmsteads might be joined by their kin, so that new hamlets sprang up with smaller, individual fields. Monasteries were active in extending cultivation, especially in the wooded Severn valley and the fenlands around Ely, but the main burden was shouldered by individuals. The whole process of exploiting woodlands, marshes and heath was so slow that in the eleventh century half of the kingdom was still technically 'waste'. England's pre-Conquest population of one to one and a half million was too small for her resources.

It is possible to picture the face of rural England around the year 1000. The land was fertile, as in Normandy, but unevenly settled: a quarter of the population inhabited the four coastal counties between the Thames and the Humber, being particularly dense on the Norfolk coast, and many of the rest lived in the south Midlands, in Oxfordshire, Berkshire and Wiltshire. Royal forests, not necessarily waste but as restricted to ordinary men as the hunting preserves of the Norman dukes, seem to have extended to every county save Norfolk, Suffolk and Kent. The wilderness had retreated in some areas before villages of wattle-and-daub houses, either in one street or around a square, beyond which stretched vast, unfenced fields, with pasture land at the fringe; elsewhere, it pressed closely on isolated farmsteads. Villages were most common in the south and east, individual homes in the north and west, but so varied was the scene that nearly every county possessed both. Famine, flood, pestilence and war repeatedly destroyed thousands of these homes; in those that survived life went on in the same way from one century to the next. Neither Guthrum the Dane nor William the Norman could alter the form which the English countryside was taking.

*

The unity towards which England had been groping painfully for generations was forged in the Vikings' fire. In the course of the tenth century the energetic West Saxon kings beat off new invasions, wore down the Scandinavian conquests and even completed the subjection of the Britons in Cornwall. The strongest of the old tribal kingdoms—Mercia in the Midlands, Kent and East Anglia—whose rulers had all been paramount in their day, finally submitted to Alfred's line. The neighbouring Welsh and Scottish princes acknowledged the overlordship of Edgar (959–975), the first king to receive the special sanction of the Church by being crowned and anointed in a ceremony adapted from the consecration of a bishop. Edgar ceded Lothian to Scotland and reigned in peace from the Channel to the Tweed, albeit over Norwegians and Danes, who still enjoyed their own laws, and over Britons, as well as over Englishmen.

England's fate was the opposite to that of northern France, where the Viking colony prospered only to lose its Scandinavian character. Then suddenly the West Saxon dominion was overthrown by a new wave of attacks during the reign of Æthelred II (978–1016). This king, immortalized as 'the Unready' or more accurately as 'the Redeless', lacking in counsel, vainly tried every expedient: massive bribes supplied by an ever more crippling tax known as the Danegeld, threats and overtures to the Normans, a massacre of Danish subjects on St Brice's Day 1000 and a series of fatally uncoordinated campaigns. At the end of 1013 Sweyn of Denmark forced Æthelred to flee to Normandy, from where he returned on his supplanter's death in the following spring only to die himself two years later. Edmund Ironside, Æthelred's heir by his first and English wife, continued in the field against Cnut, Sweyn's younger son who had won the allegiance of the invading army. The new rivals fought each other to a standstill and then divided the kingdom, as Alfred and Guthrum had done, after which Edmund suddenly died on 30 November 1016. In times of crisis the throne did not pass to a child but to the most suitable royal prince or ætheling. The West Saxon line, which traced its descent back to the fifth-century Cerdic, could put forward no national leader. England, exhausted, submitted at once to Cnut.

In the person of Æthelred II, the royal house for the first time had failed to meet its responsibilities; now, with Edmund dead, for the first time it forfeited its rights. The persistence of the old line posed no challenge to the Dane. Edmund Ironside left a younger brother, whose flight did not save him from Cnut's murderous agents,

TABLE II

The Old English Royal Dynasty

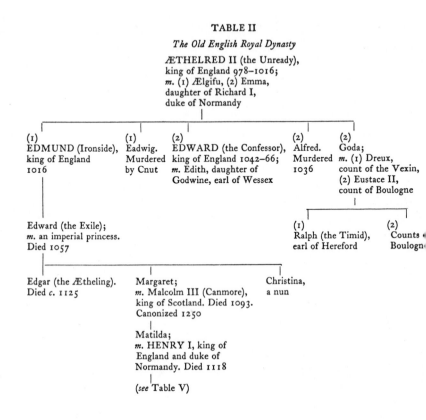

ÆTHELRED II (the Unready),
king of England 978–1016;
m. (1) Ælgifu, (2) Emma,
daughter of Richard I,
duke of Normandy

(1)
EDMUND (Ironside),
king of England
1016

(1)
Eadwig.
Murdered
by Cnut

(2)
EDWARD (the Confessor),
king of England 1042–66;
m. Edith, daughter of
Godwine, earl of Wessex

(2)
Alfred.
Murdered
1036

(2)
Goda;
m. (1) Dreux,
count of the Vexin,
(2) Eustace II,
count of Boulogne

Edward (the Exile);
m. an imperial princess.
Died 1057

(1)
Ralph (the Timid),
earl of Hereford

(2)
Counts
Boulogn

Edgar (the Ætheling).
Died *c.* 1125

Margaret;
m. Malcolm III (Canmore),
king of Scotland. Died 1093.
Canonized 1250

Christina,
a nun

Matilda;
m. HENRY I, king of
England and duke of
Normandy. Died 1118

(*see* Table V)

and an heir, who found a far-off refuge in Hungary.
There remained Æthelred's two sons by his second wife,
Emma of Normandy; these were Edward, the future
King Edward the Confessor, and Alfred, who were
brought up at the court of their uncle, Richard the Good.
Any chance that the Norman duke might intervene on
behalf of his sister's children vanished with Cnut's own
marriage to Emma in 1017 (Table II).

A Scandinavian at last ruled the whole of England.
Cnut soon succeeded his elder brother as king of Denmark
and for a time he subdued Norway, presiding over a
maritime empire which made him a commanding figure

in Europe. The work of Alfred and his heirs was not destroyed, for the situation resembled that of a century earlier, save that the ruler's nationality had been reversed: then the English kings had extended their sway over Danish colonists whose separate identity was recognized, now a Danish king respected the customs of his English subjects. Cnut looked on England as the jewel of his empire. After some initial months of repression he confirmed the laws of Edgar and felt strong enough to disband most of the fleet. Sweyn had been a tardy convert to Christianity and his son proved a lavish benefactor of English houses, although capable of the deepest treachery towards his enemies; he even visited Rome, as no other English monarch was to do before George V. While William the Conqueror grew to manhood, English society remained intact. Indeed it was only under Cnut that the simple territorial title *Rex Angliae*, king of England, came into use.

Cnut's wide interests forced him to delegate power, which in England became monopolized by three dominant figures. Each of them enjoyed the Danish title of *jarl* or earl and each governed a block of shires which in size recalled the chief kingdoms of pre-Viking days; when lesser earldoms were created out of the larger units, it was usually to satisfy the kinsmen of these great regional governors. The vulnerable north was ruled by Siward of Northumbria, a warlike Dane who married an English-woman, the Midlands by the noble and native-born Leofric of Mercia, the south by Godwine of Wessex. Godwine, an Englishman of obscure background, owed much to his marriage to Gytha, sister of the Danish Earl Ulf, who had married Cnut's sister, Estrith. As earl of Wessex he controlled the traditional preserve of the Old English kings and so became, in Cnut's absence, the first power in the land. All three earls and their English sons were to play a decisive part in the Norman Conquest.

Cnut's rule in England may later have been an object lesson for William, since it showed that Englishmen's first requirements were respect for their customs and the maintenance of order. These being guaranteed, the country had quietly endured a Danish king. Why, on the same terms, should it not accept a Norman? When Cnut died at Shaftesbury in November 1035, however, there was no question of William's succession. The bastard duke was a boy some seven years old and many lives stood between him and home.

*

Cnut, like many Norman dukes, was a father before the Church made him a husband. Harold Harefoot, supposedly his son by the Englishwoman Ælfgifu of Northampton, coveted England in the absence of Harthacnut, the late king's heir by Emma of Normandy, for whom had been destined the thrones of both England and Denmark (Table III). Earl Godwine, with Harthacnut detained across the North Sea, eventually acquiesced in Harold's election and sought favour by an act of treachery that was to have dire consequences. Alfred, the younger of Æthelred's sons by Emma, left the safety of Normandy to visit his mother in 1036, whereupon Godwine arrested him and allowed him to be blinded so savagely that the ætheling died. In the following year Emma herself sought refuge in Flanders. Godwine's support had allowed King Harold to triumph over her sons, whether by Æthelred or Cnut.

The colourless Harold died childless in March 1040 while his half-brother, having settled the affairs of Denmark, was preparing an invasion. Harthacnut was at once accepted in England. The new ruler arrived with a mighty fleet and soon provoked violence by levying the money needed to pay off its crews. Harold Harefoot was ignominiously exhumed, Queen Emma was restored and

TABLE III

The Scandinavian Kings of England

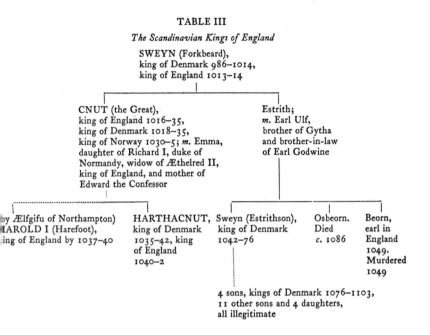

SWEYN (Forkbeard),
king of Denmark 986–1014,
king of England 1013–14

CNUT (the Great),
king of England 1016–35,
king of Denmark 1018–35,
king of Norway 1030–5; *m.* Emma,
daughter of Richard I, duke of
Normandy, widow of Æthelred II,
king of England, and mother of
Edward the Confessor

Estrith;
m. Earl Ulf,
brother of Gytha
and brother-in-law
of Earl Godwine

by Ælfgifu of Northampton)
HAROLD I (Harefoot),
king of England by 1037–40

HARTHACNUT,
king of Denmark
1035–42, king
of England
1040–2

Sweyn (Estrithson),
king of Denmark
1042–76

Osbeorn.
Died
c. 1086

Beorn,
earl in
England
1049.
Murdered
1049

4 sons, kings of Denmark 1076–1103,
11 other sons and 4 daughters,
all illegitimate

Godwine called to account, not apparently as a supporter of the late king but for having procured Alfred's death. The earl made his peace by offering a magnificent ship, complete with eighty fighting men, and swearing that Harold alone had been responsible for the atrocity. Harthacnut was the last of the male line of the Danish royal family; being also childless and in poor health he turned to his legitimate half-brother, the sole surviving son of Æthelred and Emma, who had the courage to leave Normandy in 1041 after a quarter of a century in exile. Nothing good is written of Cnut's fleeting sons, who are always dismissed as worthless youths; possibly they were so, although in the eyes of history most youths who did not live to prove themselves are worthless. Harthacnut, out of kindness or policy, at any rate brought

forward an obvious successor before collapsing at a
wedding feast on 8 June 1042.

Popular enthusiasm in London probably at once
ensured the ætheling's accession. If the role of Godwine
has been exaggerated by apologists, his acquiescence as
earl of Wessex was certainly essential. Godwine was not
the man to jeopardize his unique authority by taking up
arms against the only available candidate, and he joined
the other earls in acclaiming the brother of the man whom
he had murdered. In the person of King Edward, the
West Saxon house was restored.

*

The fate of kingdoms was finally decided by their
military resources and by the rulers' capacity to use them.
It is easy, with hindsight, to say that in the mid-eleventh
century the future lay with the feudal prince, whose
vassals were trained in warfare and depended for their
position upon fulfilling military obligations. This knowledge leads students of Old English history, armed with
varying and complex definitions, to detect dubious
symptoms of feudalism in the darkest ages. The presence
of these symptoms inevitably has become the most
popular criterion—all too often the sole criterion—by
which the progress of King Edward's England is judged.

English society, like that of Normandy, was a pyramid.
The foundation, almost hidden from modern eyes, was
made up of numberless *theows* or slaves, who had no
existence in law; some were descendants of the Britons,
others of Englishmen who had fallen on evil days. Then
came the churls, the Anglo-Saxon *ceorls*, the typical
English peasants, from whom the early Victorians traced
all the rugged independence which they most admired.
Degrees of freedom varied widely and a treatise on estate
management called the *Rectitudines Singularum Person-
arum* divides the Anglo-Saxon peasantry into three main

groups: the *geneatas*, who were the radknights of *Domesday*, the *kotsetlan* or cottagers and the *geburas*. Above all these churls were the thegns, formerly called *gesiths*, an aristocracy whose origins lay in services performed for the king. The question is whether or not these classes were bound together by ties similar to those in Normandy. Was there a private contract for one man to serve another, sanctified by an oath of homage? Was this contract based on land? Were the services to be performed essentially military?

The great Whig writers would have been distressed to know the extent to which Old English history saw the depression of the churls and, towards the end, of many lesser thegns. Lordship, the superiority of one man over another, had been acknowledged in the earliest times, even by the primitive Germanic tribesmen among whom the strongest bonds had been those of kindred. In England the churl or thegn could 'commend' himself to the protection of a superior, by taking an oath and promising annual payments; this practice gathered strength over the centuries between the Anglo-Saxon invasions and the Norman Conquest. Kings rewarded followers with grants of land, in practice subjecting many to the authority of a few. They later strove to weaken the ties which bound a man first and foremost to help or revenge his own relatives and, as kinship declined, protection was sought elsewhere. Commendation was also stimulated, in England as in France, by Scandinavian attacks and by natural disasters which in a subsistence economy could speedily reduce the sturdiest of peasant families to starvation.

The process by which the churls lost their independence is obscure, and its results were uneven. The English did not speak of a 'manor', although this already existed as the estate of an individual lord, worked and administered as an economic unit; such a manor very rarely coincided with a village. Persons or lands could be commended, sometimes to different lords, so that the pattern of tenure in many villages became one of extreme confusion. Peasants who retained full control of their lands and performed only light services for their lord were common in the Danelaw, where they were known as sokemen, and the *Domesday* survey was to show that in Lincolnshire, the centre of Scandinavian settlement, they made up half the population. None the less, the peasants as a whole were becoming villeins, in varying degrees of servitude, whose lot differed little from those of Normandy.

Personal contracts between the humble and the great were therefore common. There were also contracts based on land, affecting the tenure of thegns and prelates as well as of peasants and implied in the distinction between folkland, bookland and loanland. The first was owned outright, by custom; the second was also owned fully, by those who had acquired the security of a charter, a document originally developed to safeguard the Church; the third type of land, as its name implies, was held on conditions. Dependent tenures feature as early as the laws of Ine of Wessex (688–726) but are best known from some seventy leases granted by the tenth-century bishop, Oswald of Worcester. The services which he imposed varied considerably, from carrying his messages to offering him hospitality, and loanland was normally granted only for three lives. It therefore differed from a feudal tenement, a fief, which was held in return for military service and was fully hereditary. Dependent tenants were not yet military tenants.

There were of course military obligations. Theoretically every free man was bound to join the royal fyrd or army in an emergency, and not the least of Alfred's achievements had been to summon only a fraction of this force at a time, thereby extending the period of service. Unhappily these peasant soldiers could not for long be kept from their land. A readier defence lay in the king's thegns, whose numbers were swollen under Cnut by his chosen companions in arms or housecarles, Anglo-Danish courtiers who were lavishly endowed with lands. At first sight England appears to have known a military caste similar to the Norman nobility; land, however, was given to these warriors merely to increase their status, and their duty to fight for the king was a personal one. The house-carles, superb fighters and great landowners, were not feudal tenants.

The Old English rulers did not take their military duties lightly. England's best defence was to meet invaders at sea; Alfred had built a fleet of Viking-style ships so large that his subjects could barely handle them, and later kings maintained their right to impress any vessel in a crisis. The cost was so heavy that even the mighty Cnut, who reached England with forty ships, lost no time in reducing his standing fleet to sixteen, and Harthacnut's efforts to pay the crews of sixty-two ships provoked the murder of two of his housecarles. This preoccupation with sea-borne enemies made it inevitable that mounted warfare would be perfected else-where.

*

The difference between Latin and Teuton is particularly obvious in their notions of justice. The Romans had regarded laws as enactments by the supreme power of the state, the emperor, while for a German tribe they were antique, unchangeable customs binding on everyone, including the king himself. The law-codes or dooms of the Anglo-Saxon rulers, and indeed every judgement in an Old English court, were therefore in theory mere defini-tions of custom. The limitation was only theoretical, since changing circumstances demanded fresh decisions. The spirit behind the theory, cautious and conservative, remained very different from that of the bold, innovating Romans and their heirs.

If every allowance is made for the dimness and brevity of Norman history it is still clear that there was more legal activity in England. A unique collection of dooms has survived, beginning with those issued by Æthelberht of Kent around the year 600, which form the earliest body of law expressed in any Germanic tongue. The dooms of his Kentish successors and of neighbouring kings shed further light on society and the progress of Christianity; they attach great importance to each man's wergild, the price at which his life was assessed and which would have to be paid by his killer. These codes became more than simple tariffs of offences as kinship weakened and the authority of superiors was emphasized, until Alfred limited the blood-feud, by exempting a culprit's kin from vengeance and stressing the duty of a man to his lord. The later Old English kings continued as law-givers, their interest contrasting sharply with the barren reigns of William and his Norman sons. In the duchy itself, no written statement of custom survives from before the Conquest.

The mere fact of legislation by a king in Alfred's time was crucial, since monarchs were everywhere allowing this power to slip away from them. A feature of feudalism as central as the linking of land tenure with military service was its association of lordship with judicial power. Private justice had been known under Alfred and to some extent its growth was in the interests of the king, since kinship could be weakened and order enforced by making lords responsible for the misdemeanours of their retainers and eventually for the causes of all their tenants. Fiscal rights were certainly granted away and the king may then have lost interest in cases from which he drew no profit; hence certain lords assumed the right to hold courts, with the result that England, like Normandy, appeared to be familiar with complete feudal immunities.

By the mid-eleventh century it was normal for a wealthy thegn to hold his lands 'with sake and with soke, with toll and with team, and with infangenetheof'. The first phrase, 'cause and suit', had become a vague formula, but *toll* and *team* represented the lord's right to levy a sum on the sale of goods or livestock on his estate and his right to hold a court to settle disputes over ownership; *infangenetheof* was the right to exercise summary justice over a thief caught red-handed. Graver offences, as in Normandy, could be dealt with only by the ruler; Cnut reserved for himself all cases of harbouring outlaws, forcible entry, ambushes, neglect of fyrd-service and breach of the king's special peace, save when this higher jurisdiction was conferred on anyone as a signal favour. By 1066 several great lords, bishops and monasteries were exercising these traditional royal rights of justice, but they could not have done so without a specific grant. The feudal belief that a landlord had the right to hold a private court was not recognized, and justice in theory remained royal justice.

It is simple, by selecting the similarities between England and Normandy, to show that English society before the Conquest was to all intents and purposes feudal; by stressing the differences, it is equally simple to show that it was not. Any verdict must be qualified.

The social gulf between the English peasant and the thegn was as wide as that between the Norman peasant and the knight, for processes had long been at work pressing society into its feudal mould, when every man would have his lord and every piece of land was to be charged with duties. On the other hand, when Edward was crowned no overall pattern of tenure existed and hereditary tenure by knight-service was unknown; the military side of feudalism remained undeveloped. This was a weakness, with the Normans for neighbours. Private jurisdictions, by-products of feudalism, were also undeveloped in that they were common but did not yet exist as of right. This tardiness, and the imposing structure of royal administration, was a source of strength.

*

The king's justice was administered, in a unique and orderly fashion, through the courts of the shire and the hundred. The shire has many origins. It began as an administrative district created by the West Saxon kings around one of their towns, Dorchester becoming the centre of Dorset, Wilton that of Wiltshire. Other shires corresponded to former tribal kingdoms, Kent, Essex or Sussex, while yet others might be subdivisions of an old kingdom, such as that of East Anglia, which split into Norfolk and Suffolk. In what was once Mercia artificial groupings such as Shropshire and Warwickshire resulted from the copying in the tenth century of West Saxon institutions, while to the east yet more shires appeared as Alfred's heirs reduced the Danelaw, the boundaries being drawn neatly around existing towns or encampments. By the mid-eleventh century the whole of England south of the Tees was divided into shires and only Rutland, arising from the dower lands of Edward's queen, had yet to establish itself. Away from the disorganized northern frontier, the shires of the Confessor's England are those of the England of today.

The shire court is first mentioned long after the earliest shires had come into being; none the less it was probably descended from a tribal gathering, the folk-moot, and so was of ancient, popular origin. In Alfred's Wessex every shire had its own chief man, the ealdorman, appointed by the king. Over the next hundred years the ealdormen dwindled in number, taking control of several shires and so growing in stature; under Cnut this trend was carried so far that the earl, as the ealdorman was henceforth called, was virtually a viceroy, remote from local business. The foremost figure in the shire therefore became the king's shire-reeve or sheriff, who normally presided over the court, although the earl and the bishop might still do so if their affairs permitted. The shire court met twice a year to judge all manner of suits between free men and its decisions were final.

The interests of the ordinary peasant did not extend beyond his own hundred. This was a unit of obscure origin and in Wessex may once have consisted of a hundred hides, the hide being a variable piece of land which would support a churl and his family. The hundred, a German military term mentioned by the first-century Roman historian Tacitus, appears as an administrative area in England only under Edgar and may not have existed much earlier; in the northern Danelaw its equivalent was known as a wapentake. Intermediate units add confusion to the pattern of shires and hundreds; at the time of *Domesday* the size of Yorkshire had already led to its division into three parts, the Anglo-Danish *thrithings*, while Sussex boasted six rapes and Kent at least six lathes. None the less it was at the hundred courts, which met every four weeks in the open air under the king's reeve or his bailiff, that most day-to-day business was done.

The hundred, if it contained roughly a hundred churls' families, embraced several villages. In each village still smaller meetings were held, perhaps originally to discuss common farming projects but later also to assign police duties among the inhabitants; it was there that every man not of high social standing had to be enrolled in a tithing or group of ten, which was responsible for producing for trial any member accused of wrongdoing. Thus the king of England's laws could be administered through his officers of the shire and the hundred, and good behaviour enforced at the very lowest level. No comparable hierarchy of courts is known elsewhere. In Normandy the duke's command was far less certain to be obeyed and at the same time the peasant there never knew the responsibility for regulating his own life that was borne by the English churl.

*

Shires and hundreds were administrative as well as judicial units. As such, they allowed the Old English kings to develop a fiscal machinery unmatched across the Channel. The royal income came mainly from those estates which had not been granted away, as did that of other rulers, and from an old-established *feorm* or food-rent, which had arisen from the custom of entertaining the king when he stopped on a journey. Before Alfred's time kings and churchmen or nobles who received royal lands were extending their modest right to receive provisions for twenty-four hours into a formidable rent. The rest of the king's ordinary revenue came from the profits of justice, a monopoly of the coinage, tolls and windfalls similar to those enjoyed by the duke in Normandy.

These resources, of motley character and often paid in kind, did not include feudal incidents. England's superiority lay in the ease with which money could be raised in an emergency by a royal order to the sheriffs, who would divide the sums demanded of them among the hundred, at which level the tax was assessed on groups of hides. Æthelred II raised many such extraordinary levies under the name of Danegeld and the dismal repetition of his orders no doubt improved the system while it impoverished the country. Largely as a result of Æthelred's expedients, Scandinavian museums today boast more Anglo-Saxon coins than do those of England; these are the fruit of the first taxes to be levied in Europe on a national scale.

*

The peculiar strength of England lay in its local institutions, which responded to orders from a royal government whose own methods were relatively advanced. A writing office had developed out of the king's chapel and charters were being issued in the seventh century, long before the country had been brought under one ruler. The chief clerk evidently did not enjoy the dignified style of 'chancellor' before the Conquest, but his department was already highly specialized. Royal orders were being dispatched throughout the kingdom in the form of summary letters, authenticated with a double-sided seal, in which the use of English rather than Latin must have acquainted an unusually large body of laymen with the workings of government. These sealed writs were a novelty, later adopted throughout Europe (Plate Va).

The treasury, like the chancery, was evolving its own traditions. It was inevitable that public revenues should still be identified with the king's personal income, so long as most of them were paid in kind as a food-rent. Cash, however, was also collected and kept in a treasure-chest, which originally was placed with the king's other belongings in the wardrobe adjoining his chamber. Kings continued to move while their revenues swelled and commitments increased, so that by Cnut's time the treasury normally stayed in one place. The site was Winchester, in the heart of Wessex, an obvious choice for Alfred's successors, who rarely strayed far from the bounds of their ancestral kingdom except on campaign. It was also under Cnut that the office, if not the title, of treasurer became known. The rule of the Dane saw not the frustration but the logical development of earlier trends; these trends stretch back long before the foundation of Normandy.

Towering above all these bodies was the monarchy itself, linked with that most famous of all pre-Conquest institutions, the *witenagemot*. Under modern analysis this council has all but dissolved. The *wita* (plural *witan*) was a man consulted by the king; the *witenagemot* strictly speaking was not a distinct body at all, it was any occasion on which the *witan* gave their advice. These counsellors included members of the royal house, the earls and prelates, a few thegns who held court offices or were influential in the locality where the *witan* happened to meet, and the occasional minor cleric. Twenty-six gatherings of varying size have so far been traced to the twenty-four years of the Confessor's reign, so the king evidently heard these mixed advisors at least once a year, when there was an average attendance of thirty to forty people. A wide range of political, diplomatic and judicial business was discussed; dooms were never issued without full consultation and grants of land, if made at other times, were also attested by the *witan*.

The king summoned his own *witan* and consulted them as a matter of practical politics, not because there was a constitution which forced him to do so. Any general advisory body, however remote in time, however vague its composition, can be hailed as an embryo parliament, and the *witan* were once viewed through a romantic haze. Now they can be seen only as a parallel to the narrower circle of ducal advisers in Normandy, not as the forbears of democracy. Even their power to choose a king is doubtful, for the fact that the throne was not necessarily hereditary does not mean that the issue hung upon an election; the succession was usually settled during the previous reign and in an emergency the obvious candidate easily asserted himself before seeking formal recognition. The *witan* were not chosen to represent any class, race or region, nor were they like modern legislators who are supposed to check the executive government. There was no idea of an inherent conflict of interest, so that king and *witan* had the identical task of giving decisions which were lawful. It was this respect for the law, often lacking in individuals but normally assumed to be present, that was the safeguard against tyranny.

*

It is now generally admitted that the administration of England was superior to that of Normandy, although the duchy was better organized for war. Another weakness in Old English society, of which sometimes too much has been made, was the condition of the Church. Here it is important to separate moral judgements from practical ones; many failings which may help to justify the Conquest did not make the Norman victory more likely.

The Church in England boasted a glorious past: in the Venerable Bede she had produced the West's most famous historian of the Dark Ages and during the eighth century her intrepid missionaries had led the conversion of the German peoples on the Continent. Then, in England as in northern France, the Vikings had burned the monasteries and organized religion had been almost extinguished. Alfred's introduction of foreigners to a house at Athelney did not prove fruitful and new foundations received their impetus only from St Dunstan, whom the pious Edgar made archbishop of Canterbury in 960. Dunstan and his fellow bishops, Oswald of Worcester and Æthelwold of Winchester, reintroduced the Benedictine rule and set in train a movement which was barely affected by the wars which brought Cnut to the throne, so that England contained some thirty-five monasteries by the reign of Edward the Confessor. Royal support was essential in the early stages, as was that of the dukes in Normandy, but the nobility in the south of England began to follow suit fifty years before the Norman barons turned to pious foundations. Moreover, England's leading figures in the monastic revival, while they looked to Europe and especially to the Cluniac foundation of Fleury, were all of native birth.

This achievement, with the literary and artistic renaissance which it inspired, is undeniable. It has been belittled on the grounds that the pace of reform soon slackened, that many monks and priests were negligent or sinful, that their superiors were subservient to the State and that the clergy as a whole were too insular. The first three charges are true but inadequate. The momentum of the late tenth century had been lost by the time that Normandy underwent its own reformation, but this natural decline was lessened by two new foundations under Cnut. The sins of the clergy and people are known either from the attempts to stamp them out or from Norman and Anglo-Norman writers; the stern homilies of English churchmen have no echo in the duchy, where silence may testify to indifference as much as to purity. Rulers controlled the appointment of prelates on both sides of the Channel and they continued to do so without dispute so long as the papacy remained unreformed.

The most serious charge against the pre-Conquest Church is that it was cut off from foreign influences and therefore backward. In fact the tenth-century monastic revival could never have taken place if Dunstan, Oswald and many other English churchmen had not been personally acquainted with Continental developments. Æthelwold, the most forceful of the reformers, ensured a measure of uniformity in the new monasteries by drawing up a code, the *Regularis Concordia*, which was based on the current observances of a wide range of houses in the Loire valley, the Low Countries and Lorraine. Furthermore, England continued to send royal alms, later known as Peter's Pence, to Rome from Alfred's reign until 1066; pilgrims were numerous, archbishops of Canterbury normally journeyed to receive their *pallium* or stole from the Pope himself, and English bishops attended the great Church councils of the mid-eleventh century, while foreigners were often appointed to English sees. If the Church in England was peculiar, it was in its veneration of the papacy.

The internal organization of the English Church was certainly open to improvement. Pleas of the clergy were not heard in special courts but in those of the shire, where the bishop was entitled to sit with the earl and the sheriff, or of the hundred. This overlapping jurisdiction proved offensive to the tidy-minded Normans, yet hardly anything is known of their own early ecclesiastical courts and, once again, the main impetus to reform was to come from Rome after the papacy itself had been reformed. In other respects the English Church had less excuse for lagging behind. Some of the cathedrals were monastic and others were served by loosely organized priests who bore little resemblance to the canons of a Norman cathedral chapter; bishoprics were unequal in size and there were few territorial archdeacons. At the lowest level, however, parishes were growing up around the churches founded by kings and nobles, with priests enjoying an assured if humble living from payments in kind known as tithes, which were stringently enforced by King Edgar.

Few of these ecclesiastical weaknesses impaired the strength of the kingdom. The absence of separate courts naturally hindered the advance of the Church as a force in her own right; it was less certain that their introduction would be a blessing for the State. England was in danger because her military resources were not being exploited as were those of Normandy. In this respect the Church, holding vast estates unburdened with knight-service, bore the same responsibility as the laity.

*

The tenure of land without military duties was one danger to the Old English state. Another weakness, less susceptible to reform, was the gulf between Anglo-Saxon and Scandinavian. Half the country had been colonized by Vikings, admittedly in unknown numbers, and it had taken the West Saxon kings over fifty years to subject all these settlers. Conquest was wisely followed by conciliation and no attempt was made to displace Danish landholders, whose separate customs were recognized in Æthelred II's Wantage Code. This was issued at a time when strife between the races was being rekindled by a new wave of attacks, which Æthelred's Danish subjects did little to resist. The English finally submitted to Cnut and in 1042 the Danelaw accepted Edward the Confessor; on neither occasion had there been any choice. The Danes were Christian and had given Canterbury an eminent archbishop in Dunstan's predecessor, Oda, but their leaders were rarely devout and until Cnut the monastic revival passed them by. The hundred and fifty years since Alfred's death had proved that both races could live together; it was equally clear that they did not view each other with enthusiasm.

The legal differences were fundamental. Although trial in the Danelaw was still by ordeal there was an upper bench of learned thegns or lawmen who could interpret the customary rules; the Wantage Code contains the first assertion of the later axiom that when opinions differ the majority view should prevail. The code also mentions twelve leading thegns who could initiate prosecutions and so formed what later became known as a jury of presentment; this was not the same as the Frankish jury, which held an inquisition. The Frankish institution, used widely by the Normans after they came to England, is now generally preferred as the ancestor of the traditional English jury, but that of the Danelaw was equally foreign to the Anglo-Saxons.

A separate legal code reflected different social conditions. The large number of free men and the relatively light services even of the poorer peasants have already been noted; moreover, the compensation due to a lord for slaying his man varied with the rank of the victim and not, as in Wessex or English Mercia, with that of the lord. This greater degree of personal freedom was based on the individual's greater economic prosperity. In the Danelaw men reckoned by twelves instead of by tens and if the variable Anglo-Saxon hide had once in theory contained about a hundred acres its Anglo-Danish equivalent, the ploughland, sometimes known by the Latin name of *carucata* or carucate, was of some hundred and twenty acres. The typical peasant holding in the Danelaw was an oxgang, the Latin *bovata*, of some fifteen acres, or one-eighth of a ploughland. It represented the holding of a man who could contribute one ox to an eight-ox team and it excelled the fraction of a hide which eventually became the normal holding of the depressed English churl.

The contrast between a thegn-ridden English society and the democracy of the Danelaw can be overstressed. Conditions were not uniform inside either area: the laws of English Mercia were technically different from those of Wessex, the Mercian churl's holding was larger than that of his West Saxon counterpart and Kent had a unique class of prosperous peasants. Danish customs varied between Northumbria and the area of the 'five boroughs'—Lincoln, Nottingham, Derby, Leicester and Stamford—and again between East Anglia and the south-east Midlands. The Wantage Code was issued for the Five Boroughs and may not accurately reflect conditions in the sparser areas of Danish settlement; the system of ploughlands and oxgangs was not uniform in East Anglia and hides remained in the more anglicized south-eastern Midlands. England, united only in the tenth century, was a kingdom of some legal and great economic and social diversity, and the contrast between English and Danish conditions is only one of many that can be made; it is the one most easily made because of the

different terms used and no doubt it was the most important, but non-racial variations are often forgotten.

In the last resort, Danes and Englishmen had more in
common with one another than with any race south of the
Channel. Most Anglo-Danish differences were those of
nomenclature and degree rather than of kind. An imposing administrative network extended over the whole
kingdom and the absence of military tenure meant that
nowhere could society be termed feudal, whatever the
local variations. Above all, Danes could understand
English, even when they did not speak it. The crucial
question in the middle of the eleventh century was
whether these ties were strong enough to bind the races
together against a new threat, from the south.

*

England, like Normandy, boasted towns of diverse
origin, many with a long if savagely interrupted history.
Germanic tribesmen had naturally encamped within old
Roman walls, so bringing new life to London, Canterbury,
York and to the dozens of places which now end in
'-chester'. More towns had grown up around monasteries,
some of them also amid Roman ruins and others, like Dun-
wich or Whitby, on new sites, while yet others became
commercial or even industrial centres, again often connected with a monastery. The Danish invasions had
forced Alfred to strengthen the existing towns and to
establish fortified posts or *burhs*, of which Oxford is an
example; his successors created boroughs as a military
device in their reduction of the Danelaw and, if that was
not necessary, set up administrative centres for the new
shires. By the eleventh century the traditional distinction
between a port or market town and a *burh* or defensible
position had long been blurred.

The average town under the Confessor was a royal
foundation, consisting of a market, a mint and fenced

tenements or holdings; these were surrounded by walls
or earthen ramparts and then by open fields and meadows,
shared out among the chief inhabitants. In a royal town
the burgesses would be hereditary tenants of the king,
paying a money rent for their land and tolls on their
transactions, as well as rendering any special services or
payments that had been laid on them. Sometimes the
Church or a lay magnate would acquire urban plots as an
investment, after which the burgesses normally paid a
customary rent to the king and an agreed one to their
lord; by King Edward's time, however, it was normal for
a third of the royal revenues from a borough to be enjoyed
by the local earl. The few borough courts which are
mentioned can easily be confused with shire or hundred
courts which happened to meet in the town; where they
became separate it was a matter of expediency and not of
right. Unique in its elaborate internal government was
London, divided into wards, each with an alderman to
preside over its own court, the Anglo-Norman wardmoot;
for graver matters there were the husting court, which
met weekly, and a great folkmoot, which assembled
three times a year.

The pre-eminence of London is hard to exaggerate.
King Edward's city stretched along the north bank of the
Thames for a mile, to the east of the river Fleet, and
inland for half a mile. This rough rectangle was still
sheltered by its much repaired Roman walls, although
there were already settlements around it, as well as a
wooden bridge to the suburb of Southwark and a string
of large houses along the road to Westminster. The site
covered the valley of the Walbrook and the low hills to
east and west, now crowned by Leadenhall Market and
St Paul's, and its importance arose from the possibility
of bridging a river where it was still tidal. Although
government still centred on a mobile court, London was
England's commercial capital and the only borough

where men of thegnly rank formed a distinct urban aristocracy. London alone of the pre-Conquest towns would be recognized as one today, with a population of perhaps twenty thousand. *Domesday Book*, which does not include London or Winchester, shows that York was the next largest town, with over eight thousand, that Norwich had over six thousand six hundred and Lincoln slightly less.

Every community, from the meanest hamlet to the grandest monastic household, could have been self-sufficient. The more prosperous did not choose to be so. The Romans' most lasting legacy had been their roads, which helped Anglo-Saxon penetration before they fell into decay. In the turbulence which followed the long, straight roads were neglected and men travelled the safest rather than the quickest way from market to market. None the less, they travelled, on horseback if they could afford it, and with their heavier baggage following in long carts. Free men were bound to attend their shire and hundred courts and, although the number that did so dwindled, the country dwellers of eleventh-century England were probably more mobile than their descendants from the thirteenth century until late Stuart times. While it was often quicker to journey by water, rivers were as much of an overall hindrance as a help, since they had to be bridged. This was such a major task that *brycg bot* and *burh bot*, bridge building and fortress building, were included with service in the host as essential public burdens, from which very few were exempt.

The possibility of travel everywhere stimulated the desire for novelties, whether they were fish from the east coast at a country market or spices from the orient at the king's court. London was fed by trade, which developed rapidly in later Anglo-Saxon times. Prosperity may already have been founded on wool, for there were probably more sheep in England during the eleventh century, before arable farming had expanded over pastures, than there were two hundred years later; English cloth, which had featured in a commercial treaty made with Charlemagne in 796, enjoyed a wider demand as Europe recovered from the Viking devastations. Much early trade was in the hands of Frisians but Englishmen were travelling as far as Italy by Cnut's reign and the status of thegn was given to any merchant who crossed the Channel three times. Slaves, horses, hunting-dogs, furs, silver and weapons were all exported, while wine, silk and spices found their way to London. As in Normandy, the volume of trade cannot have been large enough to support more than a fraction of the people divorced from the soil, perhaps one in ten. This was less important than the fact that commerce, the great civilizer, was at work.

*

There are no chronicles to extol a beaten race. William of Malmesbury contrasts the Normans, living frugally in splendid surroundings, with the English, who indulge themselves amidst squalor. He tells of ignorant clergy and indifferent laity and of how the rich used to prey upon the poor by seizing their property or making maidservants pregnant and selling them into slavery abroad:

> The English at this time wore short garments, reaching to the mid-knee; they had their hair cropped, their beards shaven, their arms laden with golden bracelets, their skin adorned with punctured designs; they were wont to eat until they became surfeited and to drink until they were sick. These latter qualities they imparted to their conquerors; as to the rest, they adopted their manners (Plate VI).

This last passage is particularly interesting, since excesses at table have often been ascribed to the islanders.

None the less, William went on to point out that not all the English were included in his strictures. It is a pity that his most famous remarks have led such trenchant writers as Carlyle and Macaulay into seeing pre-Conquest life as a drunken orgy, for their picture is quite incompatible with the Old English heritage in literature and art. His opinion that the people put dissipation before the accumulation of wealth was expressed in a work which was finished in 1125, long after the native aristocracy had been dispossessed, and it is plain that he was generalizing from isolated tales of vice.

William of Malmesbury also ignores political achievements. England in the mid-eleventh century was in many ways ahead of her neighbours. Larger than the northwestern maritime states of the Continent—Flanders, Boulogne, Normandy and Brittany—she was also more compact than the sprawling kingdoms of Norway and Denmark. The counts and dukes of the Continental seaboard were not sovereign, for they owed allegiance to an emperor or to a king of France, and the lords of Scandinavia were still Viking chiefs, whose dominions splintered and coalesced with the fortunes of war. The West Saxon line was the oldest in Europe, its kings were free from the irksome if theoretical duty to serve another prince and at the same time they enjoyed a prestige founded not on mere personal prowess but on religious veneration. They wielded the ruler's traditional authority as lawgiver, policeman and tax collector with unique effectiveness. It is small wonder that Cnut cherished their throne above all his other spoils.

England, a rich prize, was not simply there for the taking. It had been Cnut's particular fortune to find a people already almost battered into submission and to have his one native rival cut off by death. He had also, as a Dane, been welcomed by men who might not so readily accept an invader from the south. The kingdom was endangered by its cumbersome system of defence and by the gulf between Englishmen and Danes; the first weakness had been fully exploited for Cnut by the campaigns of his father, the second had worked in his own favour. It was unlikely that a Norman in the following generation would triumph with such ease.

CHAPTER THREE

Edward the Confessor, William and the Godwines

THE reign of Edward the Confessor forms the long, dark prologue to the Conquest. A few of her fellow countrymen had accompanied Emma from Normandy in 1002 but it is only under her half-Norman son that English society becomes sharply aware of the new power across the Channel. Edward's lack of children and his Norman leanings leave the succession in the balance. The resulting drama stems from personal ambitions and the main contenders, being for the most part related, are themselves of mixed stock. None the less, behind the rivals it can be seen that national issues are at stake. England is reaching the cross-roads, for she is ceasing to be an outpost of the northern world and is not yet irrevocably tied to Latin Europe.

*

The new king himself was insecure. According to modern doctrine he was not even the West Saxon heir so long as the son of Edmund Ironside still lived at the court of Hungary. Primogeniture, however, was not yet established and Edward the Exile presented no problem in 1042; his claim lay dormant, to be revived later. William of Normandy also failed to challenge King Edward, with whom he could boast no common ancestor more recent than Richard the Fearless. In 1042 the duke was aged about fourteen and beset with enemies, whereas the king was in his thirties; time and Edward's own favour offered the best chance of a Norman succession. A nearer lineal claim was that of Sweyn, son of Cnut's sister Estrith by a Danish nobleman, Earl Ulf; no doubt his ancestry would have made Sweyn Estrithson particularly welcome in the Danelaw and he had the further advantage of being a nephew of Earl Godwine, who had married Ulf's sister Gytha. Fortunately Sweyn had succeeded Harthacnut in Denmark and the defence of his kingdom against Magnus of Norway forced him to seek English help.

King Magnus was the common enemy, the paramount threat to Edward as well as to Sweyn. The Norwegian's claims were based only on a treaty made with Harthacnut as king of Denmark in 1038 or 1039, which had provided that if either should die without heirs the other would inherit his kingdom. This pact had left Harthacnut free to succeed Harold Harefoot in England and now it was invoked by Magnus against both of Harthacnut's successors. England lay under constant fear of invasion, which became acute after Sweyn was driven out of Denmark early in 1047. The danger passed with Magnus's sudden death in the autumn but was revived by his successor Harald Hardrada, clouding the last years of Edward's reign and reaching a grim climax in 1066.

*

England, thus perilously placed, needed a statesman and a warrior king. She received a devout but enigmatic figure, possessed of many traits not normally found together, a man of flawed holiness. Ascetic, artistic, intent on the collection of relics, Edward combined piety with a lifelong passion for hunting; he wore the trappings of royalty with reluctance but never forgot his dignity, and he would jest with his courtiers until he was crossed, when his benevolence might be shaken by childish outbursts of rage. The king was married to Godwine's daughter Edith in 1045 but, for spiritual or physical reasons that remain a mystery, he probably never consummated the marriage. This enhanced the reputation of a man whose mere appearance encouraged veneration. A long beard distinguishes Edward from the other persons in the Bayeux Tapestry and a protégé of Queen Edith has left a vivid picture of the king as a man of medium build and regal bearing, with striking milk-white hair, full rosy cheeks, thin, snowy hands and tapering fingers that were almost transparent. This has led to suggestions that Edward was an albino; it also helps to explain his future title, 'the Confessor', since it is the portrait of a medieval saint.

It is uncertain how far Edward's obsession with the next world distracted him from his earthly kingdom. Although to all appearances only fitfully interested in politics, he may have withdrawn from affairs in dislike of Godwine and it is probable that throughout the first nine years of his reign the king was biding his time, until he could be rid of his brother's betrayer. Edward was to score one notable victory, which saves him from being dismissed as a man incapable of decision. None the less, latent energy in the ruler is small comfort to his people and Æthelred II had shown that such spasms were no substitute for constant attention to the internal fissures and external pressures which menaced the Old English state. Æthelred had failed as a leader and his son, moved by loftier visions, proved no better. No more could have been expected: Edward was a monk at heart, half Norman by birth and wholly Norman by upbringing.

The mystery of Edward's interest in politics veils the

true balance of power within England, between the king and the earls. The emergence of three pre-eminent families under Cnut may be seen as a mortal threat to the monarchy and so to the strength of the State; in this case Edward was inevitably the puppet of magnates more powerful than himself. On the other hand it is worth pointing out that the new, larger earldoms were still erected or split up at the king's behest and that in 1051, on the single occasion when Edward acted decisively against the Godwines, their hold was broken. There will therefore always be disputes as to whether the monarchy had started permanently to decline or whether the entrenchment of viceroys sprang from Edward's apathy. Was the centralized fabric constructed by Alfred's heirs still sound or was it now crumbling behind an imposing façade? On the answer to this question hangs one of the main arguments for or against the Norman Conquest.

Edward's role is also crucial to any assessment of the Norman challenge. The king certainly preferred the speech and company of Frenchmen to those of his own subjects, who were offended at the number of foreigners in his household and in the royal chapel. His sister Goda had married first Dreux or Drogo, count of the Vexin, and then Eustace, count of Boulogne; Ralph the Timid, her son by Dreux, accompanied his uncle to England and by 1050 was enjoying the earldom of Hereford. None the less, Edward's leanings can be exaggerated. The majority of his courtiers remained Anglo-Danish and only two foreigners ranked as leading landowners, both of them probably not Normans but Bretons. Even in the Church, the king's favourite sphere, only three Normans were given bishoprics in the course of a reign lasting twenty-four years; it is not clear if three other foreign bishops from Lorraine owed their appointments to Edward or to the house of Godwine. Perhaps Edward systematically imported Normans, placing as many as he

TABLE IV

The Family of Godwine, Earl of Wessex

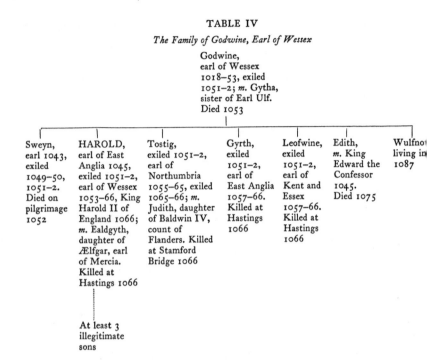

Godwine,
earl of Wessex
1018–53, exiled
1051–2; *m.* Gytha,
sister of Earl Ulf.
Died 1053

| Sweyn, earl 1043, exiled 1049–50, 1051–2. Died on pilgrimage 1052 | HAROLD, earl of East Anglia 1045, exiled 1051–2, earl of Wessex 1053–66, King Harold II of England 1066; *m.* Ealdgyth, daughter of Ælfgar, earl of Mercia. Killed at Hastings 1066 | Tostig, exiled 1051–2, earl of Northumbria 1055–65, exiled 1065–66; *m.* Judith, daughter of Baldwin IV, count of Flanders. Killed at Stamford Bridge 1066 | Gyrth, exiled 1051–2, earl of East Anglia 1057–66. Killed at Hastings 1066 | Leofwine, exiled 1051–2, earl of Kent and Essex 1057–66. Killed at Hastings 1066 | Edith, *m.* King Edward the Confessor 1045. Died 1075 | Wulfno living in 1087 |

At least 3
illegitimate
sons

dared in key positions to frustrate the Godwines, but he did not proceed far along this road and it is more likely that he simply wanted congenial company. The only certainty is that he hoped for a Norman successor and that, if his wishes had prevailed, untold misery would have been avoided.

The responsibility for the Conquest rests on the house of Godwine. Although the man who wrote the *Vita Ædwardi* for Queen Edith was a foreigner, perhaps a Flemish monk, and was ostensibly a royal hagiographer, it is the Godwines who are the true heroes. The mighty earl himself, hailed by the people as 'the father and tutor of the kingdom', bears no resemblance here to the monster of Norman chroniclers. So many contradictions mean that he can only be judged from his career. His unprecedented rise under Cnut and his survival in the following reigns show that Godwine was able, perhaps more in council than on the battlefield, and that he was adroit. He was probably eloquent, as his apologist says, and certainly careful to cultivate supporters, while doing everything possible to extend the power of his house. Alone among the magnates of his time, he is unconnected with religious benefactions. He was a wordly politician with nothing, save perhaps some outward graces, to commend him to King Edward, and he was the father of a turbulent brood.

It is fanciful to see the earl of Wessex as a doughty champion of Old English liberty, although his second son and eventual successor, Harold, came nearer to being a national figure. Their family dominated the south where the king kept his court, and was distrusted by its rivals in Mercia and Northumbria. Earldoms were eventually secured for five of Godwine's six sons—Sweyn, Harold, Tostig, Gyrth and Leofwine—but Northumbria was held only for ten uneasy years, after the death of Earl Siward, and Mercia was never wrested from Leofric's line. The Godwines commanded little support in the Midlands and the north, where obedience had to be required in the name of the king and then not always with success. Moreover, their attachment to the old West Saxon dynasty was shallow; the earl was a protégé of Cnut, he had sacrificed the ætheling Alfred in favour of Harold Harefoot and then ingratiated himself with Harthacnut before turning to Cerdic's line. His children were half Danish and, if they disliked Normans, it was partly because this was an Anglo-Danish, not an exclusively English, sentiment, and more because they feared for their own position.

No one in these early years could have foretold the events of 1066. There were the dwindling possibility that King Edward might have children, the overriding threat from Norway until 1047 and the uncertainty of Duke William's survival, while no Godwine could yet aspire to the throne itself. Only gradually does there emerge the prospect of a Norman succession and even then it is not at first clear that there will be a Norman conquest. The personal manœuvres around Edward the Confessor were to have historic consequences, for it was these which led Harold and William to the field of Hastings.

*

The reign opened dramatically with the disgrace of Queen Emma. The first Norman in England, wife of two monarchs and mother of two more, Emma holds a unique place in the kingdom's history. This merely focuses attention on her coldness towards the children of her first marriage, whom she had deserted for the bed of their supplanter and whose rights she had never upheld. Now she was accused of intriguing with Magnus of Norway and accordingly, in the autumn of 1043, the king and his earls arrested her at Winchester. This unnatural mother, her property confiscated, lingered on in retirement until 6 March 1052.

Emma's eclipse did not remove the menace of invasion. In 1045 the unwarlike Edward himself took command of a fleet off Sandwich and in the following year more ships were gathered after a false alarm. England owed much to the stubborn defiance of Magnus by Sweyn Estrithson, whose brothers Beorn and Osbeorn were welcomed by Edward and who, in the extremity of 1047, requested the help of fifty ships, which was refused. When Magnus was succeeded by Harald Hardrada a few months later, the latter made peace with England in order to deal with the newly restored Sweyn, who once more fruitlessly asked for help. Godwine's historic reputation as a patriotic Englishman is laid bare:

the earl of Wessex, the husband of Sweyn's aunt, would gladly have sent a fleet, but he was overruled. It was Earl Leofric who spoke for a substantial body of English opinion that evidently wanted nothing to do with the turmoil of the Scandinavian world.

A consistent national policy needed the co-operation of all three great earls and on this Godwine could never rely. None the less, his hold over the king, to which the influence of Queen Edith was soon added, allowed him to advance his house. Sweyn Godwineson received an earldom in the Severn valley in 1043, Harold was made earl of East Anglia two years later and a Danish nephew, Beorn Estrithson, became an earl in the eastern Midlands in 1049. In this way the whole of south-eastern, southern and south-western England fell to the earl of Wessex and his kin.

Fortunately for their enemies, the Godwines were too insatiable to make a united family. Sweyn in particular had all the rapacity of the Vikings. He committed an extraordinary outrage by seducing the abbess of Leominster in 1046 and then abandoned his earldom, which was divided between Harold and Beorn. Sweyn briefly sought refuge in Denmark until another crime ensured his expulsion, whereupon he reappeared before the English king whose forces had mustered against a new Viking threat at Sandwich in 1049. Finding Edward unfriendly, Sweyn won the trust of Earl Beorn, lured him on board ship at Bosham and there vengefully murdered him. The earl of Wessex himself did not dare to dispute the sentence of outlawry which was immediately passed at an assembly of the whole royal army; Sweyn, deserted by most of his own sailors, escaped to Flanders. Not for the last time, an unruly Godwine had shaken the prestige of the whole family.

Edward's kingdom never seemed so secure as in the months following Sweyn's banishment, while Earl

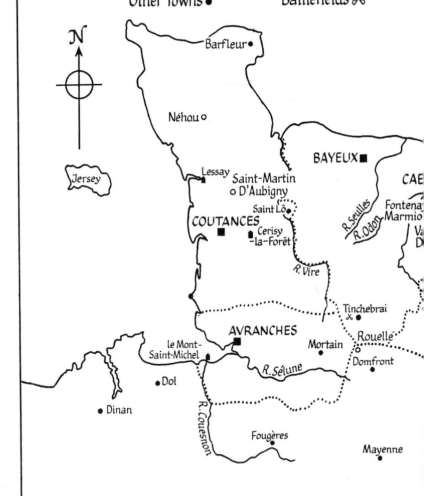

THE DUCHY OF NORMANDY IN 1066

Bishoprics ■   Established centres of Baronies ○   Major Abbeys ▮

Other Towns ●   Battlefields ✕

N

Barfleur ●

Néhou ○

Jersey

BAYEUX ■

Lessay ▮

CAE...

Saint-Martin ○ D'Aubigny

Saint Lô ●

R. Seulles

R. Odon

Fontena... Marmio...

Va... D...

COUTANCES ■

Cerisy ▮ -la-Forêt

R. Vire

Tinchebrai ✕ ●

Rouellé ○

AVRANCHES ■

le Mont-Saint-Michel

Mortain ●

Domfront ●

R. Sélune

Dol ●

Dinan ●

R. Couesnon

Fougères ●

Mayenne ●

Rennes ●

Laval ●

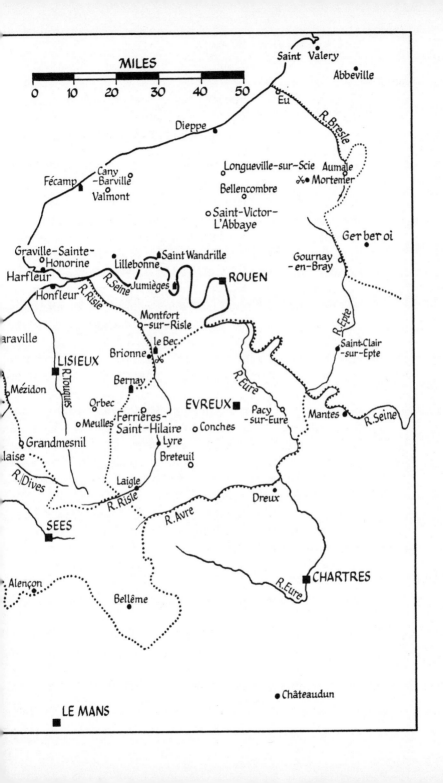

Godwine held his peace. Since the end of Æthelred's reign there had been a permanent fleet, numbering fourteen ships in 1049, which could be expanded by general requisitions in an emergency. The king now dispersed even the nucleus of this force, making a bargain with the strategic coastal towns of Kent and Sussex, who would provide ships and men in return for the local profits of justice. Sandwich, Dover, Fordwich, Romney and perhaps Hythe and Hastings were thereby joined in a confederation which was to expand and become famous as the Cinque Ports. Meanwhile England was stripped of a regular naval defence which she soon badly needed. In 1050 Godwine secured the recall of his eldest son, who was given another earldom embracing Herefordshire, Gloucestershire, Oxfordshire, Somerset and Berkshire. The first three were Mercian shires and Sweyn's reinstatement only inflamed the jealousy of rivals.

Disaster, coming in the following year, sprang from deeper causes than the misconduct of Sweyn. Edward had appointed a worldly Norman abbot, Robert of Jumièges, to the see of London in 1044 and five years later the duchy had furnished another dubious prelate in Ulf, bishop of Dorchester. It is ironical that the pious king, yearning for the company of Normans, should have imported men with such flimsy spiritual qualifications. It was disastrous that he made Robert his confidant and, on the death of Archbishop Eadsige in October 1050, that Edward brushed aside Godwine's candidate and appointed Robert to the see of Canterbury. The king and his new metropolitan then proceeded to prevent the consecration of the bishop-elect of London, another adherent of Godwine, and secured the see for a third Norman, William. The threat was clear. All men were by now probably aware that the king would have no children and Godwine may have suspected that the path was being cleared for Duke William. Robert of Jumièges was rumoured to have resurrected the murder of Alfred in his attempts to poison the king's mind against the earl. Poison was probably not needed; what Edward had lacked, and what he now unexpectedly showed, was resolution.

In the summer of 1051 the people of Dover came to blows with the retinue of the king's brother-in-law, Count Eustace of Boulogne, who was returning from a visit to the English court. The count turned back to Edward who, with distasteful alacrity, ordered Godwine to sack the town. Godwine, sensing injustice or perhaps merely unwilling to harry a part of his own earldom, refused. It was an invitation to civil war. He joined his sons Sweyn and Harold in rapidly assembling an army which arrived on 1 September to overawe the king, who was at Tetbury near Gloucester. The earl proclaimed that the people had been humiliated and confirmed his patriotism in later eyes by demanding that a castle built by a Norman in Sweyn's earldom of Herefordshire—the first castle known in England—should be surrendered. In response Leofric and Siward, with the Frenchman Ralph the Timid, rallied to Edward. Grievances on all sides had come to a head and two armies faced each other.

It may have been the unique prestige of the English Crown which averted bloodshed at the eleventh hour. Both sides agreed that the *witan* should meet in London on 24 September, where the Godwines arrived in arms to answer the charges against them. Edward meanwhile had strengthened himself by summoning the militia through-out the kingdom and now appeared with a still greater force, whereupon his opponents' dispirited following melted away. The king struck ruthlessly. Sweyn was again outlawed while Godwine and Harold, lacking assurances for their safety, refused to attend the *witan*. At last the man who had stood behind Edward's throne was told that he had five days in which to leave the country. The earl of Wessex and his wife, with Sweyn, Tostig and Gyrth, embarked at Bosham for Flanders; Harold and Leofwine sailed from Bristol to Ireland; Queen Edith was dispatched to a nunnery. The king, in a bloodless revolution, had broken his fetters.

*

The way was now open for a peaceful Norman succession. Leofric and Siward were essentially local magnates, who left the king free to build up his coterie of foreign advisers. The vast estates forfeited by the Godwines placed in Edward's hands a largesse which he distributed, admittedly in unknown quantities, among Normans. It became clear that he wanted William to succeed him and Norman chroniclers assert that late in 1051 or early in 1052 the duke crossed to England, where Edward recognized him as his heir. This story enjoyed general acceptance until the most recent biographer of William, believing that he was still too insecure to leave the duchy, suggested that Edward's promise had been conveyed to him before the fall of the Godwines, probably by Robert of Jumièges on his journey to Rome for the archbishop's *pallium*. William, as will be seen, was heavily if successfully engaged in Maine during 1051 and unlikely to take what at any time would have been the unusual step of sailing to another land. Norman hopes, moreover, depended not on the duke's movements but on the king's wishes.

It was now that the Confessor's political and military failings sealed the fate of his people. Many Englishmen, alienated by the promotion of foreigners, looked to Godwine, whose native followers had hesitated to attack the king but who was now hiring seamen in Flanders. Count Baldwin V, whose half-sister Judith had married Tostig, leant his support to the exiles. Edward's dispersal of the fleet proved disastrous, for Godwine slipped past the king's hastily collected ships and landed at Dungeness soon after midsummer, to receive widespread promises of support from the south-eastern counties. Storms protected him from the royal vessels, which retreated up the Thames while the earl withdrew to Flanders, there to prepare his final blow. The king's crews deserted in London and Godwine again set sail, proceeding westward to harry the Isle of Wight and Portland before joining a fleet from Ireland under Harold and Leofwine. This adroit co-ordination encouraged Godwine's friends from the south-eastern ports to join him, so that on 14 September an overwhelming naval force anchored near the king's fleet off Southwark. Slowly Edward was joined by soldiers from the north, while London sought terms from Godwine and his pirates yearned for plunder. The king was forced to assemble his *witan*, who accepted the earl's defence of his actions.

The counter-revolution was thorough. Archbishop Robert fled, with his fellow Norman Bishop Ulf of Dorchester, and their property was seized by the triumphant Godwines. All but a handful of Frenchmen were expelled, Earl Ralf and Bishop William of London being among the few who were exempted, as a harmless solace for the king. Queen Edith returned to court and Stigand, bishop of Winchester and a partisan of Godwine, was promoted to the see of Canterbury. This ambitious schemer, the archetype of the worldly medieval prelate, was no worthier than Robert of Jumièges. The Norman carried his grievance to Rome, where his supplanter was condemned by every pope save the uncanonical Benedict X, whose bestowal of the *pallium* conferred a brief legitimacy on Godwine's creature from 1058 to 1059. Stigand's elevation can be defended on the grounds that Robert's flight had created an unprecedented situation, but it cost the Godwines the support of the growing number of reformers in the Church. This party was zealously cultivated by Duke William, who was to reap his reward in papal support against Harold.

Godwine's triumph marks the turning point of Edward's reign. It did not mean that a Godwine would mount the throne, nor did it affect the chances of a Scandinavian claimant, but it weakened the hopes and changed the plans of William. Now, if England was to have a Norman king, there would have to be a Norman Conquest.

*

Edward the Confessor made no more attempts to oust the Godwines and the Norman cause languished, while the king resigned himself to religion and the chase. A series of deaths now cleared the way for the man whom Freeman, the great nineteenth-century historian of the Conquest, hailed as 'the noblest of living Englishmen', Harold Godwineson. His elder brother had never returned to England; like Robert of Normandy and many other men of scandalous life, Sweyn sought atonement by a pilgrimage to Jerusalem, and died on the journey home. Godwine himself suffered a stroke while dining with the king at Easter 1053 and lingered only until 15 April in a distressing condition which was not lost upon moralists.

Harold was now some thirty years old, a tall, strong man who must have benefited from his commanding presence. He was eager for power, like all his family, but ruthlessness never degenerated into treachery, as it had done with his father and Sweyn and as it was to do with Tostig. Harold repeatedly proved his courage and his generalship, while in affairs of state he was sometimes surprisingly moderate. Judgement on his conduct depends on how far he was swayed by personal ambition and how far his interests coincided with those of England; it is not clear when he first coveted the Crown but all his activities under Edward can be presented as those of a loyal and patriotic subject. A mistress named Edith Swan-neck and a number of bastards have allowed Norman writers to blacken him, but Harold was more sensitive to religion than was his father. For what it was worth, Edward must have preferred the younger man. The position of Harold's supporter Stigand clearly disturbed him and a journey to Rome in 1058 no doubt secured the primate's brief recognition there; the earl returned laden with relics, for which he lavishly endowed a collegiate church at Waltham, consecrated before the king and queen in 1060.

When Harold became earl of Wessex he surrendered East Anglia to Ælfgar, the son of Leofric of Mercia, but received Somerset and Berkshire from Sweyn's earldom, while Oxfordshire and Herefordshire passed to Ralph the Timid. For two years only Wessex was ruled by a Godwine until Earl Siward died early in 1055, four months after his eldest son had been slain in battle by Macbeth, the usurping king of Scots. Siward's second son, Waltheof, being too young to rule the exposed and turbulent earldom of Northumbria, Edward bestowed it on Harold's brother, Tostig. Earl Leofric and Earl Ralph both died two years later and Harold, while unable to withhold Mercia from Ælfgar, seized his chance to reorganize the south-east into two new earldoms for his remaining brothers: a truncated East Anglia went to Gyrth and the south-eastern Midlands, with Surrey and Kent, to Leofwine Godwineson. Ælfgar, isolated, sought safety in a Welsh marriage alliance, while Earl Harold bestrode the land.

Plans were laid to thwart a Norman succession. They led to a mysterious episode which might have had historic consequences. After forty years someone recalled that the son of Edmund Ironside was still living at the court of Hungary, where he had married a German princess who bore him three children. It is uncertain whether the name of Edward the Exile was brought up by the king, by Harold or by one of the Godwines' rivals, but it was decided to invite the ætheling to England. Harold himself prepared the reception and even crossed to Flanders in 1056 while Edward, slowly and perhaps with reluctance, journeyed westwards with his family. The man who would now be regarded as *de jure* king of England landed in 1057, only to be seized with a fatal illness before he reached the Confessor's court. No one knows whether this unhappy parallel with 1036 was a coincidence, but after the Conquest suspicion inevitably fastened on Harold. If the earl of Wessex wanted the throne for himself, the ætheling's removal was essential; if his main concern was to exclude William he must have known that a scion of the West Saxon line would command far wider support than a member of the upstart house of Godwine. The ætheling left a son, Edgar, who was too young to defend a disputed succession. The king's early death would leave only one man in England who could offer the hope of effective rule.

The immediate challenge to Harold came not from across the Channel but from Norway, where Harald Hardrada was seated more firmly on the throne, and from the west, where Gruffydd ap Llywelyn was mastering the other independent princes of Wales. Gruffydd's ascendancy provided a buttress for the Godwines' natural rivals, the house of Mercia. As early as 1055 Leofric's heir had been outlawed and had secured help from Gruffydd, forcing Harold to mount an expedition which resulted in an uncertain agreement involving Ælfgar's restoration to East Anglia. Then in 1056 the bishop of Hereford, once a chaplain to Harold, was slain on a military sortie, necessitating a second expedition, whereupon Gruffydd accepted King Edward's overlordship in return for the confirmation of his conquests. In 1058 Ælfgar, now earl of Mercia, was involved in a further rebellion, made doubly dangerous by the appearance of a Viking fleet under Magnus, the son of Harald Hardrada. The events of this year are unchronicled; somehow the danger passed and Ælfgar again was restored. If Harold was supreme at court, the crisis had shown that England was hemmed in by enemies.

The skies cleared with the death of Ælfgar in 1062. His earldom passed to a youthful son, Edwin, and Harold seized the chance for a lightning march into Wales which drove Gruffydd from his capital at Rhuddlan. The onslaught was resumed in May 1063, Harold plundering Wales from the sea while his brother Tostig invaded the north. Three months later Gruffydd's head was presented to the king, while the lesser Welsh princes resumed their sway. The earl of Mercia, a boy deprived of his father's allies, no longer stood between the earl of Wessex and the Crown. Harold Godwineson had reached his apogee.

*

Meanwhile William of Normandy too had been strengthening his position. The battle of Val-ès-Dunes, if it marked the beginning of the duke's effective rule, did not free him from fear. William's weakness was at once shown by his leniency to those rebels who submitted and by the prolonged defiance of Gui of Burgundy, besieged by the duke for three years in the castle of Brionne. Victory itself excited envy and alarm, turning allies into enemies, so that no sooner was one crisis overcome than another began to take shape. Security depended on a series of triumphs and for William the years from 1047 to 1060 were ones of constant danger.

Normandy in the middle of the eleventh century was menaced from the south by the rise of Anjou. A line of counts, as ruthless as their Norman rivals, had extended their power from Angers eastwards along the Loire valley until, under Geoffrey Martel, Anjou became the foremost power in northern France. Geoffrey began to penetrate the county of Maine, which separated him from Normandy, and the death of its native count, Hugh IV, on 26 March 1051 brought the submission of the capital, Le Mans. William reacted by marching south into the territory of the Bellême family, which held Domfront from Maine and Alençon from Normandy and whose terrible heiress Mabel at about this time married the duke's close ally Roger of Montgomery. This was the start of an epic struggle between the Norman and Angevin houses, which ended only when the descendants of Geoffrey succeeded those of William on the throne of England.

Boldness was for the moment successful, for Geoffrey withdrew while William laid siege to Domfront. Nearby the people of Alençon had mocked the duke's birth by hanging hides from their walls and William by a lightning stroke seized their town, where he marked his triumph by lopping off scores of hands and feet. The mutilations are ignored by the duke's contemporary apologist William of Poitiers, who simply boasts that the stronghold 'fell into his hand like a ripe fruit, so that he could glorify himself with the words, "I came, I saw, I conquered"'. These calculated atrocities speedily terrorized the defenders of Domfront into submission and were not lost upon the other towns of northern France, so that the massacre may in the long run have saved lives; unhappily the grisly warning did not penetrate to England.

The immediate result of William's triumph was to reunite the rebellious count of Anjou with the king of France. It is a tribute to the reputation which William had so quickly established that King Henry, alarmed at the prospect of a strong Normandy, now abandoned his role of protector for that of an enemy. The change nearly destroyed William, for the king and Count Geoffrey began to foment rebellion in the duchy and to concert an invasion from the south. William of Arques, the duke's uncle, had retired from the siege of Domfront to his castle in Upper Normandy, from where he defied the nephew whose birth he unjustly despised. The king sent help to Arques but on 25 October 1053 a Norman army, not led by the duke himself, routed these reinforcements near Saint-Aubin, after which the castle was starved out and William of Arques fled to Boulogne. A double attack was mounted early in 1054, the king and Geoffrey marching on Evreux from the south while Henry's brother Odo advanced from the east. The duke took the risk of dividing his forces and awaited the royal onslaught. He never had to meet his king in battle, for news came that Odo's pillaging force had been surprised and over-whelmed at Mortemer. Henry and Geoffrey retreated, so ending the worst military threat of the reign.

The Mortemer campaign was the most crucial of all for Duke William, since the attack came from two directions. It was not the last trial of strength, for in 1057 the royal and Angevin forces again struck from the south. After devastating Hiemois they were caught by the tide while fording the Dives at Varaville and routed with heavy slaughter. The king did not invade Normandy again. War flared up over the Vexin in 1058 and con-tinued until Henry died on 4 August 1060, to be followed by Geoffrey Martel on 14 November. The duke of Normandy, like the earl of Wessex, found that death had removed his foremost enemies.

William had also advanced himself by diplomacy. As early as 1049 a marriage had been projected between him and Matilda, daughter of Count Baldwin V of Flanders and niece of Judith, who had married Tostig Godwineson. The union was forbidden by Leo IX at the council of Reims, perhaps because of a previous contract by Matilda or because the descent of both parties from Rollo placed them within the extremely large circle of relations between whom marriage was prohibited. The pope's motive is clearer than his explanation: Leo favoured the Emperor, who would be weakened by any alliance of Baldwin with a protégé of the king of France. William's estrangement from the king reflected an increase in Norman power which still made the duke a useful ally for Baldwin, while Normandy gained still more from the friendship of wealthy, maritime Flanders. The marriage was therefore celebrated by 1052 and finally recognized by Pope Nicholas II in 1059, on condition that the couple should endow two magnificent abbeys. Saint-Etienne and La Trinité at Caen are lasting reminders that the man who invaded England with papal blessing had for years lived in the shadow of Rome's displeasure.

After 1060 the duke of Normandy had little to fear from his French neighbours. Anjou was rent by civil war between Geoffrey's young nephews, while William's father-in-law ruled France as regent for the boy king, Philip I. The rise of the Norman nobility and the revival of the Church, which have already been noted, continued during these years. Here lay the source of the duchy's strength and William could now turn to harnessing these forces to himself. Lands forfeited by successive rebels were granted to nobles who could otherwise have been rewarded only at the expense of the Church or of the duke's own estates, and William proceeded empirically to build up a network of individual loyalties. Many great families owed their origins to a *vicomte*, in which case William continued to employ them as ducal agents, so keeping them bound to himself. At the same time he extended tenure by knight-service wherever he could, although duties remained vague and were not everywhere accepted. The censures of Rome did not weaken the duke's hold on the Church, nor his interest in its affairs.

He enforced the Truce of God and attended the main ecclesiastical councils, laying the foundations of his reputation as a champion of the faith. William, like his ancestors, was apparently never crowned or anointed as duke of Normandy but his name was included in the litany sung at Rouen, so that he could claim a special ecclesiastical sanction for his rule. This distinction, in France as in England, was otherwise reserved for a king.

William is remembered as the conqueror of England and there are few details of his character or person in youth. He was a well-built man who would one day grow corpulent, always robust in health and temperate in his habits, clever, callous and of inflexible determination. Many hard years had proved him to be a valiant fighter and a capable general, rapid in movement and ruthless in execution. These military gifts, developed by the duke as a mounted warrior, were precisely those shown at sea and among the Welsh mountains by Harold Godwineson.

*

In William the earl of Wessex had a dangerous rival, but one whose chances in 1063 were less than they were to be three years later. Harold was weakened by a sudden misadventure which placed him for a while in William's power and he then received another blow when Northumbria rebelled against Earl Tostig.

The earlier of these episodes probably took place in 1064, constituting the first scenes in the most famous of all sources for the Norman Conquest, the Bayeux Tapestry. King Edward speaks with his attendants, one of them probably Harold, and the earl then rides with his 'knights' to Bosham, where he prays and feasts before taking ship (Plate VI). He reaches the land of Count Gui of Ponthieu, who seizes him and holds him in prison at Beaurain, where they confer together until messengers arrive from Duke William. Another messenger, perhaps an Englishman seeking help, is received by the duke and Gui then takes Harold to him. William leads Harold to his palace, where a mysterious lady with the English name Ælfgifu gestures towards a clerk, no doubt her accomplice in some scandal. The next few scenes show William, accompanied by Harold, marching against Conan of Brittany; they reach le Mont-Saint-Michel and cross the river Couesnon to Dol, where the power-fully built earl drags two Norman soldiers out of the quicksands. Conan flees (Plate III) and his castle of Dinan is besieged until he offers its keys on the point of a lance. Harold receives arms from William (Plate II) and they both leave for Bayeux, where the earl, laying his hands on sacred relics, takes an oath before the duke. The story ends when Harold sails back to England and, in extreme dejection, approaches King Edward.

The Tapestry's version of events leaves several gaps and many of its details might anyway be incorrect. Harold's capture by Gui, attributed in the chronicles to storm or shipwreck, is unexplained, and it is odd to find the Breton campaign of 1064 placed before the earl's promise to William. In spite of the many and often conflicting details which can be gleaned about Harold's journey, no one knows its purpose, nor the circumstances and nature of his oath. He was probably sent by the king to confirm Edward's grant of the succession and William may have seized the chance to extort an extra personal guarantee of assistance from his potential rival.

The results of this adventure at least are clear. Harold, by accompanying the duke on campaign and receiving knighthood, had demonstrated his vassalage in Norman eyes if not in his own. He had sworn a solemn oath and there is probably no truth in a later defence that he was deceived as to the presence or holy nature of the relics, for it was in William's interest to make the occasion as public and solemn as possible. If a man broke his word to his lord he struck at the very roots of society, and the more sacred his vow the more heinous was his offence to the Church. Harold might argue that he acted under duress but so long as he was not released from his promise the victory lay with William. When the earl claimed the throne, the duke was to submit his case to Rome, branding the new king before Europe as a perjurer and a usurper.

The second blow which befell Harold was more material, when in October 1065 the Northumbrians threw off the rule of his brother. Old Siward had been a proven warrior whose Danish birth appealed to the Scandinavians of the northern Danelaw and who had wisely married a descendant of the former English earl. Tostig, the nominee of a West Saxon house, a Dane only on his mother's side and with a Flemish wife, had no local standing nor did he show the tact to conciliate the northern thegns. High-handed, greedy and treacherous, he stained his name with many deeds that foreshadow the historic betrayal of Harold. None the less, this unstable man gave some hope that he would succeed in his daunting task; he kept the peace with extreme severity and wisely supported Malcolm of Scotland against Macbeth, who was defeated in 1057. Tostig must also have been capable of the graces of a courtier, for he was closest to Queen Edith of all her brothers and even the king was fond of him. Edward was so poor a judge of men that his favour does little credit to the earl; by keeping him at court, it did nothing but harm to Northumbria.

Ten years of harsh and fitful rule ended when Tostig, hunting in Wiltshire with the king, learned that his retainers had been slaughtered at York and Lincoln and that Morcar, brother of Edwin of Mercia, had been offered the earldom. This news roused the listless king to one of his outbursts of fury. Morcar accepted the insurgents' offer and marched south to Northampton, where Edwin of Mercia joined him with a force that included some Welshmen. Edward and Tostig urged resistance only to be overruled by Harold, who opened negotiations which led to the confirmation of Morcar and the banishment of Tostig. On 1 November 1065 the distracted king lost one of his few remaining earthly consolations when Tostig and his wife embarked for Flanders.

Harold's failure to support his brother is mysterious. Long-standing feuds often provide convenient explanations of unforeseen events and many later stories testify to the hatred between Harold and Tostig. They are said to have fought together as youths before the king, but Edward's prophecy of disaster in itself discredits this story, for legends about the Confessor are notorious. Nothing in the brothers' careers before 1065 betrays enmity and it would have been surprising if Tostig, with so many potential rivals, had dared to offend Harold. It is more likely that the earl of Wessex decided to make the most of a bad situation by accepting the Northumbrian revolt rather than plunge the kingdom into civil war. Perhaps he was already planning to put away Edith Swan-neck and marry Ealdgyth, sister of Edwin and Morcar, although the marriage probably took place after his accession. At least he must now have been resolved to heal the breach between the Godwines and the house of Leofric.

Once again results are clearer than motives. Harold had taken the only sensible course, yet his power had been weakened. A member of the rival house now held Northumbria, as the result of a popular revolt which had been welcomed and aided in Mercia. The chief consolation was that the north, with its strong tradition of independence, had demanded only a new earl, who placated local separatism by choosing a representative of the former native earls of Northumbria as his deputy. As in 1051-2 men shrank from a struggle which, in the significant words of one chronicler, would have amounted to civil war. The kingdom of England was still intact.

Time did not favour Harold, although he was still the foremost figure in the land. He had been forced into an oath which could be interpreted as making him the duke of Normandy's man. A vengeful brother was plotting in exile, while his earldom passed to the one family which could by itself challenge the Godwines, and whose alliance with Harold could never be easy. Even the Welsh were again raising their heads, for in the autumn of 1065 a force under Gruffydd's son Caradoc swept into Monmouthshire to burn a hunting lodge which the earl had built for King Edward. Edwin and Morcar were young men and Edgar the Ætheling was still a boy, but in the normal course of events every year that passed would increase the stature of Leofric's heirs and make Edgar more eligible for the throne. With the ground slipping beneath him, it was as well for Harold that the king's health began to fail.

Edward never recovered from Tostig's fall. For many years the king had been absorbed in founding an abbey on the island of Thorney in the Thames, beyond the west gate of London. At Christmas 1065 he came to his palace nearby but he was too ill to attend the consecration of the new church, Westminster Abbey, three days later. Many of his chief subjects hurried to the city, where they must have debated the succession.

The Normans, ignoring Harold's usurpation, were to recognize as legitimate only the conditions which prevailed at the close of Edward's reign. For many Englishmen, threatened with new laws and forced to prove their titles, this was to impart a terrible significance to 5 January 1066, 'the day that King Edward was alive and dead'. The final scene is encrusted with legends but even for the bystanders, with so many perils hanging over them, it must have been chilling. The Bayeux Tapestry shows the dying king on a bed of boards and sacking; he is stretching out his right hand in a historic gesture towards a man who is probably Harold, perhaps thereby committing to him the kingdom. The protégé of Queen Edith, who supplies most details of the death bed, says that Edward had lost his speech on 3 January, only to recover it at the last. While the queen warmed his feet in her bosom, the king prophesied woe to the land, appalling everyone around him save Archbishop Stigand, who whispered to Harold that the old man had lost his wits. This account and the *Anglo-Saxon Chronicle* both assert that the Crown was left to Harold and, although the writers are biased, their story rings true. In his last moments, pressed by those around him and alarmed at the dangers which beset England, the king may well have renounced the prejudices of a lifetime.

Edward the Confessor was buried in his new abbey on 6 January. The body was to be translated to Canterbury by Thomas à Becket only to be restored by Henry III to a still grander abbey at Westminster, where it now lies in the Confessor's Shrine behind the high altar. The last monarch of Alfred's line, Edward was the one figure whom Englishmen and Normans could combine to revere. Myths gathered around him, including one that he transmitted to his successors the power of touching to heal scrofula or 'the king's evil', and they did not cease with his canonization in 1161. The miracles veiled an indifferent king, who is more harshly judged today, yet if he was not the saint descried by the Middle Ages, neither was he the fool which his political inaction might suggest. Those who believe that England gained more than she lost from the coming of the Normans must for ever regret that Edward did not have his way.

CHAPTER FOUR

The Struggle for England: the Reign of Harold

O N the morrow of the Confessor's death and on the day of his burial, Harold Godwineson was crowned king of England. The last Old English sovereign was the first to be hallowed at Westminster, where the Bayeux Tapestry shows him enthroned with Stigand standing before him, although it is more likely that the coronation was performed by Archbishop Ealdred of York, whose legitimacy was unquestioned. Harold had moved with typical speed, which the designer of the Tapestry may have meant to condemn by depicting Edward's funeral before his deathbed. The earl had virtually staged a revolution, for he could not boast one drop of West Saxon royal blood. His qualifications were those of the man who was most likely to cope with the threats from abroad. England would have been happier if the coup had failed and William had been acclaimed, but if men desired to resist the Normans they could not have chosen a better leader.

The nature and extent of Harold's support are not clear. He had received the blessing of his dying brother-in-law, the recognition of those notables who were at hand

and the sanction of a coronation, so that he was certainly a legitimate king. No one in the south opposed him and there were many precedents for setting aside a child. Unfortunately it is not known whether the *witan* who had assembled in London represented more than local feeling, nor whether their choice was free. A king from an upstart family, of regional power, had displaced the old royal line, which alone could command national loyalties.

The north, which had already ejected one Godwine, at once showed its discontent. Early in the spring Harold was forced to visit York, where the backing of the archbishop and of Wulfstan, bishop of Worcester, secured his recognition. It was probably at this time that the king married Ealdgyth, sister of Edwin and Morcar, in the hope of ensuring the doubtful allegiance of the two young earls. The number of coins struck all over the country, from dies made in London, suggests that the machinery of government worked as smoothly as ever, but Harold's brief reign was essentially a time of preparation for war. After he had asserted himself in Northumbria he made ready to face invasion, whether by Tostig from Flanders, by Harald Hardrada from Norway or by William from Normandy. The only question was which enemy would be the first to strike.

The earliest reaction came from William, who sent messengers to protest at Harold's seizure of the throne. The duke had seen so much treachery that he may not have expected the earl to keep his oath, but the swiftness of events in England might have taken him by surprise. Inevitably his protest was ignored and William decided to assert his claim by force. An invasion was discussed in the ducal council, where many voiced misgivings before William convinced the barons that his alluring plan was worth the risk. He was well placed to launch an attack. The victories in Brittany had removed the last threat to Normandy's frontiers, confirming the security which the duchy had known since 1060. In the course of time new rulers would emerge to challenge William's primacy in northern France; for the present, the hour of England's greatest peril was the hour of Normandy's greatest safety.

The first task was one of propaganda, to exalt the duke's prowess and emphasize the justice of his cause. Norman envoys were sent to Rome, where no record of their suit survives but where Harold presumably was accused of perjury. Pope Alexander II already favoured William as a true servant of the Church and was biased against Harold for his association with Archbishop Stigand. The breaking of an oath now provided an excuse for a decision based on policy and William's projection of himself as a Christian prince brought tangible gain. Alexander, urged on by Archdeacon Hildebrand, upheld the Norman's claim and dispatched a papal banner to inspire his host, while the advisers of the young Emperor also announced their support. William had become what would later be termed a 'crusader', whose prestige was such that men from neighbouring states, and even from southern France and Italy, were ready to serve him.

Provisions were made for carrying on the government in William's absence. Clerical support was made still more secure by the confirmation of many grants, and the abbey of Fécamp was told that victory would restore to it the manor of Steyning in Sussex, a gift of Edward the Confessor which had been seized by Harold. William and his wife attended the dedication of La Trinité, Caen, in June and at about this time Matilda was given the charge of their eldest son Robert, a boy of about fourteen whom the duke now proclaimed as his heir. The barons swore loyalty and several were directed to stay behind to assist in the government, including Roger of Montgomery and Hugh of Avranches, the future earls of Shrewsbury and Chester. William was sternly testing the strength of the bonds which he had created between himself and his leading subjects; his earlier work proved its value, for the land remained tranquil.

Politics and diplomacy ran parallel with the practical business of preparing the expedition. A standing fleet is not known to have been kept by William's father and whatever navy was at the duke's disposal must have been vastly increased. It was logical that those who had promised military help should also supply transport, and naval quotas apparently were now imposed on individual nobles, the duchess herself setting a fine example with the gift of the *Mora*, which was to bear William across the Channel. Throughout that spring the Norman ports were given over to ship-building. The Bayeux Tapestry shows men felling trees, shaping planks and constructing ships, which are then dragged to the water; a cart follows, laden with armour and a wine cask, while more men bring the knights' hauberks, which are so heavy that each requires two bearers. Horses must have taken up more space than either men, military equipment or victuals; they are shown in nearly every vessel as the fleet crosses the Channel, the largest number in one craft being ten.

Wace, a Channel Islander who was commissioned to write an epic on the Norman dukes a century later, learned from his father that William assembled 696 ships, as well as many small boats. This is a modest figure, for other writers quote round and resounding numbers from 1000 to 3000. The size of the fleet therefore can hardly be estimated, although by contemporary standards it was very large. These vessels began to gather at the mouth of the Dives before Midsummer and by 12 August all were ready.

William's own fervour was the driving force, both in winning support for his plan and in the physical preparations. Few rulers could have gathered such an army, still less could they have held it together for so long and supplied enough provisions to keep it from pillaging the neighbourhood. The fears of the barons, who still spoke of Harold's great resources, were met with brazen confidence. Pride and exaggeration are pardonable in William of Poitiers, writing some five years later, but his story of the treatment of an English spy may well be true. The duke, disdaining to punish his captive, sent him back to Harold of England with these words: 'Tell him that if he does not see me within one year in the place which he now strives to make safe against my coming, he may rest quiet for the rest of his days and need fear no harm from me.'

*

Harold's spies could not tell him when or where the first blow would fall. The south coast was the one most likely to be attacked, from Flanders or from Normandy, and it was in the south that his strength lay. It was therefore natural for the king to return to London after his recognition at York, committing the north to Edwin and Morcar. The vigil which he now started to keep was made more oppressive during the last week of April by Halley's Comet, a portent which blazed every evening in the north-western sky.

The fighting of 1066 was opened by Harold's brother. Tostig, whose cause was compatible with that of William or that of Harald Hardrada, characteristically seems to have been in touch with both princes. It was in the duke's interest to give help to a man whose forays would serve at least to weaken Harold Godwineson, while the king of Norway sent seventeen ships from the Orkneys. Early in May, Tostig ravaged the Isle of Wight and then sailed eastwards to Sandwich, where he landed to gather recruits just as Earl Godwine had done fourteen years earlier. Re-embarking before his brother arrived from London, he plundered along the eastern seaboard with some sixty vessels, only to be routed by Edwin in Lindsey.

Tostig, with his fleet reduced by four-fifths, sought safety with his old ally Malcolm, king of Scots, to await a mightier invader from Norway.

Harold now stationed the militia of the kingdom along the coast and took command of a fleet off the Isle of Wight, confident that Tostig would be followed by William. There followed a lull of three months, which tested the Old English defences as severely as the fiercest war. The levies of Mercia had seen action under Edwin, those of Wessex were kept in suspense while the hammers rang in the ports of Normandy. William, perhaps by disbursing a carefully accumulated treasure, was somehow providing for his swelling host, while the economic life of the duchy continued undisturbed. The duke apparently did all he could to hasten work, no doubt in the hope that he would forestall his Norwegian rival and perhaps unaware that time did not favour the English king. If Harold and his trained housecarles were prepared to wait, the peasants who formed the bulk of the army longed to return to their fields. It proved impossible to support the English levies without plundering the land which they were supposed to defend and as harvest-time drew near their restlessness could not be contained. On 8 September the king was forced to disband the host; he then withdrew to London with his retainers, part of the fleet following him and the rest dispersing on the way.

This decision, if inevitable, was momentous. It exposed the south coast to William, assisting and perhaps ensuring his triumph. It also reveals a weakness in the Old English defence system and so can be used to justify the Conquest. In theory Harold's resources of manpower far surpassed those of the duke of Normandy. Events in the summer of 1066 proved that security rested not solely on numbers, but on organization.

*

ENGLAND AND
NORMANDY IN 1066

MILES

0 20 40 60 80 100

N

NORTH

SEA

Newcastle
Durham
Richmond
Ripon
Tadcaster   York
Pontefract
Chester   Lincoln
Nottingham   Belvoir
Shrewsbury
Lichfield   Stamford   Peterborough   Norwich
Coventry   Ely
Worcester   Warwick   Bury St Edmunds
Hereford   Cambridge
WALES   Gloucester   Colchester
Oxford   Berkhampstead
Bristol
Wells   Bath   London
Rochester   Canterbury
Glastonbury   Winchester   Tonbridge   Dover
Salisbury   Arundel
Exeter   Dorchester   Hastings
Totnes   Pevensey

FLANDERS

ENGLISH CHANNEL

PONTHIEU

Fécamp   Amiens

Channel   Jumièges   Rouen   Beauvais
Islands   Bayeux   Lisieux
Coutances   Caen   Evreux   Paris
le Mont-Saint-Michel   NORMANDY   ÎLE DE
Avranches   FRANCE
Dol   Mortain
Pontorson   BLOIS
Fougères   Orléans
Rennes   MAINE
Le Mans   la Flèche   Tours
BRITTANY
Angers   ANJOU   TOURAINE

POITOU

William responded on 12 September by transferring his invasion force, with some difficulty, to Saint-Valery at the mouth of the Somme. This brought the Normans within closer striking distance and they would certainly have embarked, if a steady north wind had not held them back. For two weeks the wind persisted, while holy relics were borne in procession and the duke fretted and prayed. There was excellent reason for his impatience, for Harold had not only dropped his guard but had been forced to march to the farther end of his kingdom.

It was an extraordinary coincidence that the Norwegian threat, which had hung over England for twenty-four years, should have come to a head within a few weeks of William's bid for the Crown. Harald Hardrada, whose gory epic belongs to European history, was at last free to assert his claim and may have been impelled to haste by the challenge from Normandy and the prospect of an alliance with Tostig. A Viking fleet of three hundred ships arrived off the Tyne, where it was joined by Tostig, who became Hardrada's man. The two allies entered the Humber and on 18 September they landed at Riccall on the Ouse. Two days later Edwin and Morcar faced them at Gate Fulford, two miles south of York, and Hardrada triumphed in the first battle of the autumn. The earls retreated while York cheerfully acknowledged the Norwegian king.

The battle of Fulford made it possible that England would again be absorbed into the northern world. Harold Godwineson, caught between two fires, was probably wise to deal with the invader who had already landed. He did not wait to hear of the Norwegian victory, perhaps doubting the capacity of Edwin and Morcar as well as the loyalty of the people of York, and events proved him right. The Channel wind might change while he was confronting Hardrada, but the risk had to be taken. With a speed that places him among the foremost of warrior kings, Harold made his decision, recalled his levies and marched north.

Hardrada had left York undefended after securing offers of military help and promises of hostages from the citizens. He retired ten miles to Riccall and then moved another twelve miles to await the arrival of the hostages at Stamford Bridge, on the Derwent, which he cannot have reached before the evening of 24 September. This was the night when Harold Godwineson encamped nine miles south of York, at Tadcaster. The rapidity of the English march was the Norwegians' undoing. York offered no resistance on the morning of Monday, 25 September, as the king of England swept through and on to Stamford Bridge.

The battle of Stamford Bridge is rightly legendary, since few victories have been so overwhelming. The invaders were taken by surprise as they lay encamped, mainly on the far side of the river and without adequate guards at the bridge; they had even abandoned their byrnies, leather jerkins sewn with studs or rings of metal, for the day was warm. The story that Harold offered to reinstate his brother but promised Hardrada only burial in seven feet of English earth comes from a thirteenth-century saga, as do most details of the action. The saga's assertions that the English used cavalry and archers are disputable, but the Norwegians certainly defended themselves in the Viking fashion on foot, with axes, swords and spears; the bridge was forced against spirited resistance and then, perhaps after an interval, the main assault was launched against Hardrada's shield-wall, drawn up on a gentle slope about three hundred yards above the river, now known as Battle Flats. Harold's enemies fell, their banner passing from Hardrada to Tostig and finally to the leader of the reinforcements which had arrived, exhausted and too late, from the camp at Riccall. A bloody pursuit followed and the last great Viking action on English soil ended in the last triumph of an Old English army.

Hardrada's son Olaf was permitted to return home with the twenty-four ships which sufficed for the remnants of his father's host. The extent of Harold Godwineson's achievement can be measured by the stature of his victim. Hardrada had campaigned as far afield as Sicily, the Levant and Persia, he had made a fortune while serving in the Varangian guard at Constantinople, he had married a Russian princess and had gouged out the eyes of a Byzantine emperor, before returning to challenge and eventually to succeed his nephew in Norway. There were no more Vikings in this heroic mould.

The king of England probably retired to York after dictating terms on 26 September. He had freed the land from a menace which had been present since Harthacnut died, his authority in the north could no longer be resisted, he had won more glory than the duke of Normandy. Above all he had shown that England's military power, although cumbrous to assemble, was still redoubtable. The price had been heavy, for the northern levies of Edwin and Morcar had been beaten and may well have been decimated, while his own followers must have suffered from exhaustion. Fortunately the wind which had helped Hardrada to England still kept William in the mouth of the Somme, and the campaigning season was drawing to a close.

*

On Wednesday, 27 September, the wind changed. William, who could not have known which Harold was now king of England, embarked that evening. Alone save for one other invading ship, depicted in the Bayeux Tapestry, that of the duke is unburdened with horses; no doubt the *Mora* was exceptionally swift, designed to

assuage an eagerness which invited disaster. In the middle
of the night and in the open sea the ducal galley became
separated from its companions, despite a lantern at the
mast-head. William might have perished ignominiously
if his enemies had been patrolling the Channel, but
England's permanent fleet had proved too costly for
Edward the Confessor and the naval force summoned by
Harold had dispersed or sailed to London. The duke
kept his nerve, eating an ostentatiously merry dinner, and
in due course the ships came together again. Early on
28 September the Norman force landed without difficulty
on the shore of a now dried-up basin, Pevensey Bay.

The construction of fortified strongholds, which was
to be so vital in the subjection of England, started at
once when an inner rampart was dug inside the Roman
fort. Pevensey, none the less, was too exposed and the
invaders, not daring to stray far from their ships, moved
eastward to capture the port of Hastings. William's
caution in clinging for over a fortnight to the sea-shore
shows that he did not belittle the power of his opponent.
At Hastings, on what used to be a peninsula formed by
the swampy estuaries of the Brede and the Asten, William
could erect a castle and lay waste the hinterland. The
Tapestry shows him feasting there with his half-brothers
Odo, bishop of Bayeux, and Robert of Mortain, while a
woman and child escape from their burning home. The
duke had witnessed his rival's impetuous bravery and it
was unlikely to be long before Harold rushed to defend
his own earldom.

The king was probably at York when he learned of the
Normans' landing. The news could not have arrived
there before the evening of 1 October and even if Harold
had already started for the south his prompt response
would have been amazing. The speed which had brought
victory in Wales and in Yorkshire was now intended to
catch William unawares. Harold appears to have covered

the hundred and ninety miles from York to London by
6 October and to have stayed in the capital for five days,
awaiting the arrival of the reinforcements which had been
summoned. On or about 11 October he set out along a
track through the thick forest of the Weald and during
the night of 13–14 October he reached the Sussex
Downs. His men emerged from the trees at Caldbec
Hill, to find themselves on high ground, which was
joined by a lower neck of land to a cross-ridge facing
south-east. In the small hours of Saturday, 14 October,
William, warned by his scouts, marched north-west
from his encampment along the line of the present road
from Hastings to Battle. When he reached the summit of
Telham Hill, three-quarters of a mile to the west of the
highest point along his route, he found that the English
were assembling on the next ridge (Plate VII).

According to the *Anglo-Saxon Chronicle*, it was Harold
who was taken by surprise. The king and his housecarles
had horses but most of the army was on foot; when the
English were sighted by the enemy, some of them were
not yet drawn up and all must have been weary. The
Normans were rested and William had been hoping that
battle would be offered while he could still sustain and
discipline his following in a strange land. The advantage
of numbers probably lay with Harold, who may have had
some seven thousand men to the duke's six thousand, but
the ratio ought to have been higher. The king had led
much of his power to Yorkshire, where it had suffered
heavy losses, more men had fallen behind in the dash
back to London and a twelfth-century writer says that
Harold left the city before half his army had mustered.
Earls Gyrth and Leofwine marched with their brother,
accompanied by such contingents from the Home
Counties as had been able to respond to the summons in
time; Edwin and Morcar, the victims of Fulford, were
absent. William, himself the commander of a motley

host, was faced not by the power of England but by that of the south-east, gathered around the house of Godwine.

Harold's tactics were better than his strategy. He remained on his cross-ridge, setting up his standards by a lone apple tree on its top-most point, a site later marked by the high altar of Battle Abbey. It was a strong defensive position, facing south with the forest behind and the ground falling steeply away some three hundred yards on either side of him; in front, the slope was more gradual. A watercourse or sandstream at the foot of the slope, known in Old English as Sandlacu and in French as Senlac, has given its name to the battle; it denotes the site more accurately than does Hastings but was a term used by only one chronicler, in the following century.

The English were drawn up on foot in the traditional shield-wall, as Hardrada's forces had been at Stamford Bridge. The shire levies formed a tight phalanx, perhaps ten or twelve ranks deep, protected by a front line of experienced housecarles; more housecarles were ranged around the king. These men were the backbone of Harold's force, armed with javelins for hurling at the enemy, with swords and with battle-axes: there were few archers and many of the peasants relied on sticks and stones. If Harold had used cavalry and archers at Stamford Bridge, their absence at Hastings might be explained by the king's haste and the necessity of fighting a defensive battle. Archers, being footmen, would have been left behind in the hasty return south, and the housecarles may have dismounted because cavalry here was more useful for attack than defence. This array might still have held together until its attackers were exhausted and had it done so the English forces would not have been condemned as antiquated. One link with the dawning medieval world was provided by the standards displayed on both sides. William flaunted the papal banner, while

Harold is said to have fought under the dragon of Wessex and his own banner of a Fighting Man. Heraldry, the adoption of personal and hereditary devices, did not appear for another hundred years, but the custom of rallying men to an emblem can be traced to the Vikings and was normal before Hastings.

The fullest contemporary accounts of the battle come from William of Poitiers and the Bayeux Tapestry. William sighted the English at about nine in the morning and his army immediately deployed to the left, down Telham Hill, in order to advance across the intervening valley. The attackers formed three main groups, Bretons on the left, Robert of Beaumont with a mixed body of supporters on the right, the duke in the centre. First came the archers, next perhaps the light footmen, with slings and spears, behind them heavier infantry and in the rear the knights on horseback. The battle started with an exchange of various missiles, during which the English stood firm; William's archers were probably then used until ammunition ran short, when his heavy infantry similarly failed to break the shield-wall; finally the knights charged uphill. Harold's brothers may both have perished in the ensuing struggle but still his ranks held together. The attackers, demoralized, fell back.

Harold was on the verge of triumph. An orderly advance might have routed the retreating horsemen, a refusal to move from his hill would certainly have discouraged any further assault. Bishop Odo, in full armour and wielding a mace, strove to put heart into the Normans, who had heard tales of William's death. Then discipline broke among the exhausted English, some of whom scented victory and rushed down the slope. The knights turned and mowed them down. It appears that this first Norman retreat had been genuine but its success in provoking uncoordinated pursuit probably led to at least two more feigned flights, ending in similar carnage.

IX The late tenth-century tower of Earls Barton Church,
Northants; the battlements are of later date. *(B. T. Batsford Ltd.)*

X   The north transept of St. Albans Abbey,
late eleventh century. (*A. F. Kersting*)

XI The eastern apse of Norwich Cathedral,
late eleventh century. *(B. T. Batsford Ltd.)*

XII   The exterior of Durham Cathedral from the north, the first third of the twelfth century; the central tower was rebuilt in the late fifteenth century. (*A. F. Kersting*)

XIII   Detail of the nave of Durham Cathedral
(National Monuments Record)

XIV The Holy Rood at Romsey, Hants, early eleventh century
(National Monuments Record)

XV (a) Durham Castle Chapel, capital, *c.* 1070
(National Monuments Record)
(b) Canterbury Cathedral Crypt, capital; animals playing
musical instruments, *c.* 1120 *(National Monuments Record)*

XVI (a) The font at Shernborne Church, Norfolk, *c.* 1170
(National Monuments Record)
(b) The font at Great Kimble Church, Bucks, *c.* 1180
(National Monuments Record)

William, uncovering himself, encouraged his host, and Harold's manpower was drained away.

While his men lost their heads, the king himself remained in position. William found that a further cavalry offensive was necessary and this time he reinforced it by his famous order that the archers should aim into the air. After the Norman arrows showered on the heads of the English, the knights charged again. This time they swept over the hill. The Tapestry first shows Harold with three arrows in his shield, plucking another arrow from his eye; in the next scene, dropping his battle-axe, he falls beneath the sword of a mounted Norman. At all events he died at sunset on the spot which he had defended since early morning.

A few housecarles escaped, to effect a temporary rally in the rear which could not dilute William's victory. The survivors of Harold's army were chased until night-fall, when the Normans encamped on the field of what was to prove the most celebrated battle in English history. A search was made for the body of Harold Godwineson, which tradition asserts could not be identified until Edith Swan-neck recognized a mark known only to her. Gytha, the dead king's mother, is said to have offered William the corpse's weight in gold but the Conqueror insisted that Harold should be buried on the shore which he had defended. Later the king permitted the body to be removed to consecrated ground at the collegiate church of Waltham, where it lay until the dissolution of the monasteries.

The result of Hastings has made William's enterprise seem less risky than it was. The victory, albeit one of cavalry over infantry, was not simply one of new techniques over old. There is no sign of the classic feudal cavalry charge, which smashed through foot soldiers unless they firmly presented a line of pikes to make the horses 'refuse'. The English had no pikes and the Normans no lances, each side preferring to rain missiles on the other; by riding in to throw spears and retreat, the knights merely contributed to a barrage which for long failed to dislodge the shield-wall. William was saved from disaster because his cavalry rallied after Harold's men had broken ranks, and the discipline of the victors themselves is so disputed that many experts discount the feasibility of a feigned retreat, which could only have been practised by warriors accustomed to co-operate closely in action. The Normans had carried out such a manœuvre in Italy but it does not follow that they could have done so in the middle of a discouraging battle. If they did not retreat as a ruse, their triumph was one of freshness over fatigue more than one of cunning and experience over simplicity and inexperience. William's barons were professional but so were the king and his housecarles, whose march from the north must have made them even more tired than the peasant levies by the time that they reached the field. It is likely that if the English had been fully rested they would have been proof against the strain.

Until the moment that Harold fell there was always a chance that the battle would go the other way. There would have been a still greater likelihood of English victory if the King had not covered the sixty-odd miles from London so quickly and a still greater one if he had waited there until more men had arrived and all had been properly equipped. A chain of coincidences had worked in William's favour, stretching from these mistakes in Harold's last campaign back to events which were beyond the control of either man: the veering of the wind while Harold was in the north, the invasion of Hardrada and Tostig, the Normans' unreadiness earlier in the summer when the king was waiting for them, the diplomatic calm which had allowed William to contemplate an expedition in the first place, the dispersal sixteen years before of the standing fleet which might have intercepted the duke as he wandered off course. The hypotheses are endless and also important, for they show that the Godwines' stand against William was not a forlorn hope.

Since Harold Godwineson lost at Hastings, it would clearly have been better for his people had he never reigned. If he had won, his earlier achievements suggest that he would have made an oustanding king. A man of his martial enthusiasm, who had fought in Brittany, might even have seen the effectiveness of Norman mounted warfare and have tried to extend its use in England; if the political obstacles could have been overcome it would then have been possible to guard against future Continental invasions. Harold's Danish blood has been unjustly held against him, for it was in the Danelaw that his power was weakest; in his lifetime his cause was certainly dynastic and regional, rather than national, but his fortunes decided the future of England. William of Poitiers reviles Harold as 'a cruel murderer, purse-proud and puffed up with the profits of pillage, an enemy of justice and of all good'. On the other hand St Wulfstan, bishop of Worcester, a man uniquely respected by victors and vanquished, thought highly of the last native king, and both Norse and English legends relate that Harold escaped to live as a hermit. While unhappy peoples have often nursed the hope of a dead hero's survival and adversity has caused many strange figures to be enshrined, it is obvious that William of Poitiers's epithets might more justly be applied to Tostig. If Harold's stature grew with the rigours of the Conquest, the stories of his burial suggest that the greatest of all Normans knew the quality of his opponent.

CHAPTER FIVE

The Subjection of England: the Reign of William

CAESAR was repeatedly attacked by the Britons; William, in a single battle, so crushed the English that they never dared to fight him again.' William of Poitiers, with his flattering classical allusions, is once more misleading. One triumph did not make William king of England, even in name, and in practice it left him master only of the immediate neighbourhood. The Normans had regarded their duke as king from the day of Edward's death, the English had still to accept and to crown him. The resistance of Harold's countrymen meant that years of warfare lay ahead.

The battle of Hastings none the less ends the first stage of the Norman Conquest, by destroying the only army and leader ready to oppose the invaders. On the morning of 14 October 1066 Harold had been the most powerful man in England; by nightfall William had taken his place. Before Hastings the issue had been in doubt; now the brief titanic contest of rivals is over and the struggle degenerates into a long drawn-out process of revolts, devastations, sorties, ambushes, sieges and isolated killings. The victory therefore marks the opening

of William's effective reign, much of which is taken up
with the military subjection of England.

*

William might now have advanced along the road to
London. Instead he retreated for a few days to Hastings
and, receiving no offers of submission, continued north-
eastwards along the coast. A sally by the men of Romney
was punished with a ferocity which proved as effective in
England as it had in France, for Dover quickly surrendered. The invaders then turned inland towards
Canterbury, where they arrived by the end of October
only to be delayed by dysentery for nearly a month. The
Confessor's widow now surrendered Winchester, but still
no recognition came from the largest city in the land.

The mood of London was defiant. Earls Edwin and
Morcar had arrived there, perhaps after Harold had
already set out for Hastings, and the two brothers now
joined Archbishop Stigand and other *witan* in giving their
allegiance to Edgar the Ætheling. This phantom prince,
destined always to be the plaything of stronger men, was
the only one of his family known to have been elected to
the English throne. William accordingly advanced to
repulse the Ætheling's troops at the southern end of
London Bridge; finding that he had insufficient forces
to take the capital by storm, he then razed Southwark to
the ground and proceeded westwards, cleaving a furrow
of destruction through Surrey, the north of Hampshire
and Berkshire. Since his intention was to isolate London
he turned north to cross the Thames at Wallingford.

This encirclement brought quick results. Stigand stole
out to offer his submission at Wallingford, his defection
providing a foretaste of that disunity which was to
undermine all native opposition to the Conqueror. At
Berkhampstead the archbishop's example was followed
by the Ætheling himself, in the company of Edwin,

Morcar, Archbishop Ealdred of York and the chief citizens, to whom William undertook to be a gracious lord. Thus fortified he marched directly on the capital, still prudently harrying, and was probably admitted without resistance.

On Christmas Day 1066 a second coronation took place in the year-old Westminster Abbey, when the anointing was performed as in Harold's case by the archbishop of York. As a conqueror, William was presented to the people for their acclamation, in an addition to the ceremony which survives today; after the question had been put in English and in French, the responses were misinterpreted by the guards outside. Fearing that William had been attacked, they fired the neighbouring houses, so that the ceremony reached its climax against a gruesome background which none the less did not alter its value. King William could now command the obedience of every official who had served King Edward and could claim a sanction for his acts which he had never known as duke of Normandy.

A primitive castle was at once erected by the river, at the south-eastern corner of the city; later in the reign this was to be replaced by a ninety-foot-high stone structure, the White Tower, which still forms the centre of the Tower of London. William of Poitiers admits that it was necessary to overawe the citizens and it may have been at this time that Baynard's Castle, named after the Norman family of Baignard, was set up to watch over them from the south-west. Meanwhile the Conqueror moved to the eastern environs, which had not yet felt his presence. More English nobles were summoned to Barking to give their allegiance, and William levied his first taxes and ordered the first confiscations of property, from the victims of Hastings. By March 1067 he felt strong enough to return to Normandy, leaving the government of his new kingdom to William fitz Osbern and

Odo, bishop of Bayeux. The first of these became earl of Hereford and the second earl of Kent, while Northumbria was taken from Morcar and given to an English associate of Tostig, named Copsi. Edwin and Morcar, with the Ætheling, Stigand and Waltheof, the young son of Siward who had become earl of Huntingdon at the end of Edward's reign, were all kept at court. When William crossed the Channel these leading Englishmen went with him, lest any of them should be a rallying point for rebellion.

*

These early steps show that, while the Conqueror distrusted the English magnates, he did not mean to dispense with them. The political events which follow emphasize a fact which will emerge again in connexion with the administration and the redistribution of land, namely that continued resistance forced William to behave much more harshly towards the English than he had intended. He had rewarded many of his followers and had set some in positions of authority by March 1067. The heirs of Leofric and Siward remained as magnates, Edwin was still earl of Mercia and Copsi, who had displaced Morcar in Northumbria, was also an Englishman or an Anglo-Dane; even the schismatic Stigand was still primate, although it is doubtful if William could for long have tolerated him. Cnut, after a show of force, had governed the kingdom through men of two races and had encouraged intermarriage; the Danish Siward had chosen an English bride and the West Saxon Godwine had taken one from Denmark. William too had cares which would detain him overseas and his own task of defending a state which straddled the Channel would be far easier if Normans could co-operate with and be assimilated into the native aristocracy.

Ruthless examples, followed by offers of conciliation,

formed a favourite stratagem of the Conqueror. It may therefore have been a mistake to leave England after impressing his power only on the south-east, although it seems that even there the lesson of his harshness had not been learned. In Herefordshire a thegn named Edric the Wild helped the sons of King Gruffydd to plunder the county and then retreated to the Welsh mountains, while in Kent a revolt broke out when Bishop Odo was north of the Thames. Count Eustace of Boulogne, an ally of William at Hastings, had quarrelled with the Conqueror and in the autumn of 1067 he occupied the town of Dover at the rebels' invitation, before being routed by the castle garrison. When William returned on 6 December the country was again quiet, but hopes of racial co-operation were dimmed and more serious dangers threatened.

The south-west now offered defiance and William was compelled to march on Exeter, whose men had refused fealty. The thegns of Devonshire submitted more readily than the rebel burgesses, with whom the king made terms after an eighteen days' siege; the city's privileges were confirmed and no plundering took place, although a castle was built there as in other towns. William then marched briefly into Cornwall before returning to Winchester by Easter 1068. His campaign had induced the other south-western cities to offer their submission, so that when three of Harold Godwineson's bastards led a raid from Ireland later in the year they were repulsed by the men of Bristol. William's position in the south was relatively secure by Whitsun, when Matilda of Flanders was crowned at Westminster.

It was now that English defections from William altered the whole course of his reign. Edgar the Ætheling and his family sought refuge with King Malcolm of Scotland, while Edwin and Morcar retired in dudgeon to the north. William undertook what was so far his longest journey in England, reducing the earls to obedience by a march on Warwick and afterwards receiving the submission of York. He travelled back by a more easterly route, through Lincoln, Huntingdon and Cambridge, again marking his progress by erecting castles (Map III). Northumbria lay behind him, seething with discontent.

The earldom which had cast off Tostig and beset Harold did not welcome Copsi, who was at once challenged by Oswulf, a scion of the Old English earls of Northumbria into whose house Siward had married. Both contenders perished in the course of 1067, whereupon Oswulf's cousin Cospatric bought the earldom from William. Morcar, a patron of Oswulf, may well have prompted the new earl to desert to the Ætheling in 1068, so forcing the king to send one of his own countrymen to the north. In January 1069 Robert de Commines marched on Durham, taking no heed of warnings that the English were in arms; the city was encircled by rebels and the first Norman earl of Northumbria was assaulted in the streets, before being burned to death in the house of the English Bishop Æthelwine.

At this news the people of York rose, expelling the Norman garrison, while the Ætheling prepared to descend from Scotland. William, like Harold, gave his enemies no time to exploit their advantage; marching rapidly north, he took York by surprise and commemorated his second visit by a series of executions. Northumbria was again confided to Cospatric and by Easter the king was back at Winchester. The summer of 1069 was a quiet interlude, broken only by another raid by Harold's sons in the west, and it is possible that William found time for a brief visit to Normandy.

So far Wales, Ireland and Scotland had all served as bases for rebels and the count of Boulogne had aided one revolt, but the main challenges had all come from within the kingdom and all had been spasmodic. In the late summer of 1069 a far graver threat was posed when

Sweyn Estrithson, who still reigned in Denmark, at last made a bid for the English throne. His sons and his brother Osbeorn, whose two hundred and forty ships recalled the size of Hardrada's force, raided from Kent along the east coast before anchoring off the Humber. Yorkshire rose once again and the Ætheling arrived to join forces with Cospatric and a new deserter, Waltheof, all of whom in turn linked up with the Danes. York surrendered on 20 September and William was faced with a northern combination as deadly as that which had confronted Harold exactly three years earlier. His plight was worse, for revolts flared up in the south-west from Cornwall to Dorset, while Edric the Wild struck eastwards from Wales as far as Staffordshire and northwards up to Cheshire. The rebellion was almost on a national scale.

If the rebels had followed up their capture of York, it might have been beyond William's power to contain them. Instead the Danes withdrew to the Isle of Axholme in Lindsey and, when William advanced with his customary speed, they fell back on their ships with the booty. Leaving them to be shadowed by the counts of Mortain and Eu, he marched west to subdue Staffordshire, while the insurgents of Devon and Cornwall wasted their strength against Exeter; meanwhile the bishop of Coutances, denuding the south-east of troops, managed to reduce Dorset and Somerset. The king then began to return east until news that the Danes were again moving on York diverted him to the north. As in the Home Counties after Hastings, he began to plunder around his goal in a semicircle until the enemy's morale crumbled. Finally the Danes went back to their ships and were bribed to depart, while William entered York to keep Christmas amidst scenes of indescribable carnage. Waltheof and Cospatric submitted to him during further devastations by the Tees in the New Year and the king completed his triumph by an awe-inspiring winter march across the Pennines to Chester, where the embers of the Mercian revolt were extinguished.

William was again at Winchester by Easter 1070, having survived the upheaval which came nearest of all to throwing off the Norman yoke. His forces had been dangerously scattered and success was owed partly to his own energy, which was never tested so sternly, and still more to the cupidity of the Danes, whose main concern had been booty. None the less, William had secured acceptance only as a conqueror, and disappointment at his failure to win over the English may explain the exemplary vengeance which he wreaked on his third visit to the north.

No king of England scourged his subjects as William did in the winter of 1069–70. Every man and boy was slaughtered on his march to York, and in the New Year the royal army was split up into smaller bands, which laid waste the surrounding countryside so as to make the humblest mode of human life impossible. Fugitives were hunted down and their homes, crops, livestock and even agricultural implements were burned in this sweeping military execution. The implacable Conqueror ensured that Cheshire, Staffordshire and Derbyshire would never revolt again, but the worst calamity befell the land between York and Durham. A whole generation was wiped out in what amounted to genocide, so that Yorkshire was still largely a desert when the *Domesday* survey was carried out in 1086 and the scars were to outlive William's sons. Simeon, a monk of Durham writing some fifty years later, tells of cannibalism and of highways strewn with putrefying corpses, for starvation and pestilence followed in the wake of butchery. Even Norman chroniclers could not excuse such unheard-of barbarity, and William was branded for 'an act which levelled both the bad and the good in one common ruin'.

Native resistance after 1069 was less dangerous, but persistent enough to destroy the last hopes of racial harmony. Early in 1070 Sweyn Estrithson in person took command of the Danish fleet, which again hovered at the mouth of the Humber. During the summer his men sailed to East Anglia, where they landed to assist a new revolt led by a thegn from Lincolnshire called Hereward. Together they seized Peterborough, where the abbey was looted on 2 June, and William once more offered bribes to the Danish king. Sweyn accepted and left for home, while Hereward retreated to fortify his fenland base on the Isle of Ely.

No English magnate could be trusted. The Ætheling's sister, Margaret, had been forced to marry the king of Scots, perhaps at the close of 1069, and Edgar himself was biding his time at Malcolm's court. Hereward gained a number of influential recruits early in 1071, when the submission of Cospatric and Waltheof was counterbalanced by the renewed defection of Leofric's sons, who had remained quiet during the great northern rebellion. Edwin fled towards Scotland, while his brother took refuge in the Fens. The king accordingly turned his power against a centre of resistance which he could no longer afford to ignore.

Spasmodic betrayals and uncoordinated hostilities merely completed the destruction of the English nobility. Edwin was slain by his own men before he reached Scotland, and meanwhile the Isle of Ely was invested by land and water. The stronghold fell, as it was bound to do in the absence of Danish help, and Morcar disappeared into captivity. Hereward himself narrowly escaped, to perform deeds which became folklore, and most of his followers were left to the mercy of William, who 'did as he pleased with them'. Cospatric, restored to Northumbria in 1070, was deposed a second time in 1072, in favour of his former ally Waltheof. The new earl, who had by then been married to William's niece Judith, proved to be the last Anglo-Danish magnate in whom the Conqueror placed any trust.

The error was clear by 1075, when Waltheof was involved in a new kind of conspiracy, hatched in William's absence with two others of very different background, Ralf de Gael, a Breton who was earl of Norfolk and whose father Ralf 'the Staller' had been a friend of King Edward, and Roger, earl of Hereford, the son of William's old associate William fitz Osbern. The revolt seems to have stemmed from feudal grievances; it had little popular support and was crushed before the promised arrival of Danish help. Ralf fled to carry on the struggle from Brittany, Roger was doomed to perpetual imprisonment and on 31 May 1076 Siward's son was beheaded outside Winchester. William was not a merciful man, and the execution of only one leading Englishman after nine years of betrayals shows that his conciliatory approach had not failed for want of trying. It had none the less failed, and the powers of the earls of Northumbria passed to Walcher, the Norman bishop of Durham.

*

English co-operation had been coveted by William because it would have weakened his external enemies; they would not have found allies within his kingdom and he would have been free to combat them on the frontiers. The Conquest had only been possible because Normandy's natural rivals were temporarily neutralized, and its very success was bound to redouble their enmity. The Welsh princes and the king of Scotland were added to the rulers whose dominions touched those of William, to the king of France, the counts of Flanders, Anjou and Brittany, and their border vassals. All these neighbours ruled relatively compact domains, while the Conqueror had constantly to cross the Channel and to contend now with Normandy's traditional ally, the sea power of Scandinavia.

The chief external menace to William's hold on England had always come from Denmark. It is a testimony to the Normans' unpopularity that within three years of Stamford Bridge the Ætheling and Sweyn Estrithson, both of whom claimed the English throne, were acting in concert. It is not certain what agreements they made nor whether the ageing Sweyn expected more than plunder, but the handsome profits which he reaped would not have been gathered so easily if the rebellious English had not helped him. King Malcolm of Scotland was also able to fish in troubled waters by making the Ætheling's cause his own. The northern frontiers of Northumbria had always been vague; the heart of Malcolm's kingdom lay in Perthshire, while southwards the two debatable provinces of Cumbria and Lothian stretched from the Clyde and the Forth respectively. When William was engaged with Hereward in 1070 the Scots began to devastate Lothian, whereupon Earl Cospatric retaliated in the west. The precarious peace of northern France was broken in the same year and thenceforth English disaffection was part of more serious military problems.

The first challenge was sounded in Maine, the former battle-ground of Norman and Angevin interests. William had for a time assured the future by betrothing his heir Robert to Margaret, sister of the young Count Herbert of Maine, the son of Hugh IV. Herbert had died in 1062 and Margaret in 1063, leaving the title to Robert and the administration to his advisers, but a revolt in favour of Hugh IV's sister and her son had succeeded in shaking off Norman rule in 1069. Meanwhile, Fulk le Rechin was establishing himself in Anjou and it was only a matter of time before he took advantage of the confusion in Maine to reassert Angevin authority there. Another peril lay in Flanders, where Baldwin VI died in 1070, leaving a widow, Richildis, who was forced to defend the inheritance of her children against the late count's uncle, Robert le Frison. Richildis in desperation sought Norman help by offering to marry William fitz Osbern, earl of Hereford, who crossed to her aid and was killed at Cassel on 22 February 1071. King William had lost an old friend and Flanders passed to his enemy. The scene was further darkened by the ending of the minority of Philip I of France. The young king was friendly with Fulk of Anjou by 1069 and his early hostility to Robert le Frison so changed after the battle of Cassel that by 1072 Philip had married the new count's half-sister. In the 1070s, as in the 1050s, Normandy was ringed by hostile powers.

These dangers forced William to ignore Malcolm's attack and return to the duchy in the winter of 1071–2. He was back by Easter, preparing yet another northern expedition which was to carry the war into enemy territory. Marching through eastern Northumbria and Lothian, the Normans crossed the Forth and penetrated the valley of the Tay, while a fleet which had shadowed them anchored in the estuary. Malcolm did not offer battle to the first feudal host seen in Scotland; he did homage to William at Abernethy and soon afterwards the Ætheling sought refuge in Flanders. The Conqueror had met so little opposition that it is easy to forget the dangers which attended his most far-flung campaign.

While Scotland was being brought to heel, Fulk of Anjou obtained possession of Le Mans. William hurried south and was again in Normandy at the beginning of 1073, preparing to defend his southern frontiers. A lightning campaign in Fulk's absence reduced the whole of Maine by the end of March and the first Continental challenge to the Anglo-Norman state had been overcome. William now turned the Conquest to his own advantage in France by transporting English soldiers to Maine, where the *Anglo-Saxon Chronicle* records that they greatly wasted the country, ruining vineyards and burning towns. There were now so many enemies south of the Channel, however, that William was to spend the rest of his life there, save for brief visits to England in 1075, 1080 and 1085; the first and last of these were in response to a crisis, the middle one was cut short by a disaster in France.

The Crown of England raised William, in prestige and in material resources, far above the others vassals of the king of France. Philip's supreme ambition was therefore to break the Anglo-Norman state. While his most obvious allies were Flanders and Anjou, the remnants of English resistance could be useful for France as well as for Denmark and Scotland. Edgar the Ætheling was offered a maritime base at Montreuil-sur-Mer in 1074, so that the last Old English prince again became entangled with William's external enemies shortly before Waltheof, the last native earl, leant himself to sedition at home. William prudently treated with Edgar, whose extraordinary career brought him once more to his supplanter's court, and Philip was forced to await the outcome of the rebellion of 1075. Its failure was mitigated for the French king by the escape of Ralf de Gael from Norfolk to Brittany, where he again began to threaten William from the border castle of Dol.

The events that followed do not strictly belong to English history but their extreme gravity stresses William's good fortune in having been able to break the worst resistance in England before 1074, the year when his Continental rivals first leant their aid to what had become a forlorn cause. Archbishop Lanfranc's government had already crushed the rebels in England when William arrived at Christmas 1075, so that within six months the king was again in Normandy, collecting troops for the siege of Dol. In September 1076 he invested the castle, only to be driven off by a relief army under the king of France himself. This first setback for over twenty years was the prelude to a renewed Angevin assault on Maine, which William managed to withstand, and to French penetration of the Vexin in 1077. Makeshift truces ended a strenuous year, which had seen Philip's power advance to the River Epte.

William's Achilles heel, like that of many masterful rulers, was found in his own family. Robert, whom the barons of Normandy had solemnly recognized as their duke's heir, was now in his middle twenties, and no longer content with the distant prospect of real power. Robert 'Curthose', so called from his short stature, was a strong, amiable, dashing young man, popular, a prey to youthful flatterers and without a shred of his father's calculation. In 1077, after vainly requesting control of Normandy and Maine, Robert failed to capture Rouen by surprise and was forced to flee with several younger members of the nobility. He made his way to Flanders and then to Germany, before an emissary from King Philip offered the support of himself and William's other enemies, Brittany, Maine and Anjou. The rebels accordingly were installed in the strategic castle of Gerberoi, and in January 1079 they won an unexpected victory over William's besieging army. The Conqueror's life was only saved by an Englishman named Toki and his empire received a blow more serious than the defeat at Dol.

William made peace with his son in the following year or in the spring of 1080. There was no choice, since one defeat was likely to start a chain reaction. The news of Gerberoi set King Malcolm again on the warpath in 1079 and on 14 May 1080 the north again approached anarchy with the massacre of Bishop Walcher of Durham and his retinue. Walcher had tried with some success to conciliate the Northumbrians until his Norman advisers became involved in the murder of a descendant of the Old

English earls; the bishop had then offered to clear himself by oath and had ridden for this purpose to Gateshead, where a mob had forced him into a church, set fire to the building and butchered the entire party as it ventured out. Vengeance fell, this time on the far north, when Bishop Odo harried the land, and a new earl was appointed in the person of another Norman, Robert of Mowbray. In the autumn Robert of Normandy led another expedition into Scotland, imposing fresh terms on Malcolm and strengthening the north on his return with an eponymous foundation at Newcastle upon Tyne.

Difficulties multiplied as William approached old age. He visited England in the summer of 1080, no doubt hoping to march in person against Malcolm, when another Angevin-Breton attack brought him back to Maine. Battle was averted, perhaps after clerical mediation, and a further pact was made. In 1082 the king was again brought back to England, this time by the activities of Bishop Odo of Bayeux, the former mainstay of Norman rule and the man who had benefited more than any other Norman subject from the Conquest. William arrested his half-brother for some nameless offence, perhaps for trying to lure Norman knights to Italy in a bid for the papacy, and the bishop, despite powerful advocates, was haled back to pass the rest of the reign in a Norman prison. Robert fled once more after 18 July 1083, to become a focal point for every intrigue that the king of France could procure, and Queen Matilda died in November. Abandoned by his heir and bereft of a wife whom he loved, the fat and elderly Conqueror learned in 1085 that Cnut IV, son of Sweyn Estrithson, was preparing a new invasion of England.

William's measures to meet the final crisis of his reign proved the strength of his work in England. He crossed the Channel with a force reported to be the largest ever seen in the kingdom, paid largely out of the proceeds of a heavy geld, and continued to support the troops by quartering them on his English vassals. He then set himself to devise further ways of exploiting the country's resources. At Christmas he was at Gloucester, where it was decided to conduct the most comprehensive survey made in any medieval country. The *Domesday* inquest had many aspects, which are examined below, but the motive immediately uppermost in the Conqueror's mind was probably the desire to know what extra taxes could be raised in his present emergency.

The Danish threat also produced another celebrated act, when 'all the people occupying land who were of any account' gathered at Salisbury to swear allegiance to William at Lammas-tide, 1 August 1086. It would have been impossible for every knight, still less for every freeholder to attend, even if the vague description in the *Anglo-Saxon Chronicle* may be taken to imply this, but every tenant-in-chief and all their principal tenants were present. Theoretically further oaths should not have been necessary but William, with his bitter experience, doubtless felt that the more recent the oaths the more binding they would be. It was not an artful royal attempt to cut across the traditional feudal divisions by appealing directly to the lesser barons; it was a reinsurance at a time of crisis. Thus the two most impressive displays of William's power were brought about in his last supreme effort to defend the land which he had won.

The end of William's reign in England was an anti-climax. Cnut's murder in July 1086 dispelled the threat of a Danish invasion, but Edgar the Ætheling again grew so discontented that it was thought prudent to allow him to leave for Italy. The king himself crossed to Normandy for the last time towards the end of the year. Bad weather and a worse harvest were followed by a winter of pestilence, further storms and famine, while much of London was consumed by fire in 1087. The

Anglo-Saxon chronicler ascribed these calamities to the people's sinfulness, which had also secured them a harsh and covetous king.

In Normandy, the Conqueror prepared a new campaign to exploit a change of fortune in the Vexin, where the county of Meulan had passed by marriage to his ally Robert of Beaumont. When Philip's troops advanced from Mantes into the duchy, William retaliated early in August 1087 with characteristic speed and savagery. Mantes was taken and sacked with the thoroughness that had been visited upon York, after which the Conqueror made his entry through a pile of burning ruins. As he did so he was seized with a terrible internal pain, perhaps after being ruptured by a jolt from his horse, and he was forced to retire to Rouen. Finding his complaint worse, he decided to be borne to the priory of Saint-Gervais overlooking the city, where the magnates hurried to his deathbed.

The scene lasted for several days, according to an account written soon afterwards by a monk of Caen and a more highly-coloured twelfth-century description by Ordericus Vitalis, an inmate of Saint-Evroul. If edifying speeches, expressions of penitence and pious bequests were normally ascribed to dying rulers, William was doubtless sincere in doing all that was possible for the safety of his soul. The political arrangements were more controversial. The king inveighed against his eldest son, who was still in exile, and desired to exclude Bishop Odo from a general amnesty of prisoners, while the bystanders urged leniency towards both. Perhaps William felt that he had attempted a superhuman task in holding together an empire which was the fear and envy of all his neighbours. More probably it was against his better judgement that the dying Conqueror consented to Odo's release and to Robert's succession in Normandy, for which he foretold an unhappy future; England passed to the king's surviving son, William, and the considerable sum of £5,000 was left to his youngest boy, Henry.

The sons hurried to secure their inheritance while their father was still breathing. The nobles followed suit as soon as William expired early on 9 September 1087, leaving the cell and the corpse itself to be despoiled by servants. A magnificent funeral procession none the less entered Caen, where appropriately enough a part of the town caught fire, and Henry was present at the service in the abbey of Saint-Etienne. Further interruptions came from a man who claimed that he had been robbed of the burial plot, and Ordericus says that the mourners had to hurry because of the smell from the coffin into which the fat body had been forced. Thereafter the Conqueror lay in peace until the religious wars of the sixteenth century, when all his remains were scattered save for one thighbone, which survived until the French Revolution.

*

When William died the subjection of England was complete. This is clear from his treatment of Edgar the Ætheling, who had sought help from the king of Scots, the Danes and the king of France, only to return to live on the Conqueror's bounty. Edgar, who was easily swayed, is said by William of Malmesbury to have been lazy and childish; certainly he recalls his great grandfather, Æthelred, rather than his father, Edmund Ironside, or any of his earlier, more robust ancestors. Even so it is astonishing that he should have been able to return in safety and that *Domesday Book* should record that the heir to Alfred's venerated line held a bare eight hides in Hertfordshire in 1086. The Ætheling was to appear again from Italy to play a fitful part in the rivalry of his supplanter's sons and to experience more adventures, in Scotland and as a crusader, before dying in English obscurity under Henry I.

The Conqueror also felt able to include Earl Morcar in his amnesty, as well as King Harold's younger brother, Wulfnoth; although the new king quickly returned them to gaol, the challenge to his accession came not from these representatives of a vanished order but from mutinous barons, stirred up by Odo and others of his own kin. The English fyrd may well have saved William II's throne in 1088, after which Odo sought refuge in Normandy, and it rallied again to support his younger brother in 1101. This was not a sign of reconciliation to the invaders; men simply preferred strong government to disorder. The long story of native rebellion under the Conqueror shows that the Normans were execrated everywhere but by a people incapable of planned resistance, often poorly led and sometimes reacting locally to provocation without any leader at all. It is possible to deny that there was any national resistance on the grounds that William used English troops in the west country in 1068 and in Maine five years later, that he won the co-operation of a few individuals and that his life was saved by an Englishman at Gerberoi. No doubt the native magnates who successively deserted him did so out of personal pique or fear rather than from what would now be termed nationalist motives, but the enduring opposition throughout the country can only have sprung from hatred of the foreigners.

As more Normans arrived to harry the country, to supplement the existing garrisons and to build new castles, the English efforts grew ever more fruitless. None the less, they might at first have succeeded if foreign help, particularly from Denmark, had been more reliable; even in the 1070s, when native resistance had lost much of its strength, the English could still distract William from other tasks and were always a danger. Their tenacity frustrated the hopes of a man to whom the Godwines had already denied a peaceful succession,

TABLE V

The Anglo-Norman Kings

WILLIAM I (the Conqueror),
king of England 1066–87;
m. Matilda of Flanders

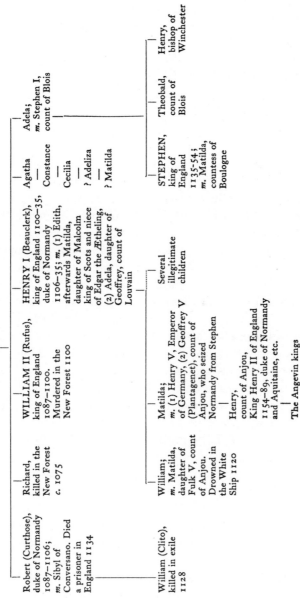

Robert (Curthose),
duke of Normandy
1087–1106;
m. Sibyl of
Conversano. Died
a prisoner in
England 1134

Richard,
killed in the
New Forest
c. 1075

WILLIAM II (Rufus),
king of England
1087–1100.
Murdered in the
New Forest 1100

HENRY I (Beauclerk),
king of England 1100–35,
duke of Normandy
1106–35; *m.* (1) Edith,
afterwards Matilda,
daughter of Malcolm
king of Scots and niece
of Edgar the Ætheling,
(2) Adela, daughter of
Geoffrey, count of
Louvain

Agatha

Adela;
m. Stephen I,
count of Blois

Constance
—
Cecilia
—
? Adeliza
—
? Matilda

William;
m. Matilda,
daughter of
Fulk V, count
of Anjou.
Drowned in
the White
Ship 1120

Several
illegitimate
children

Matilda;
m. (1) Henry V, Emperor
of Germany, (2) Geoffrey V
(Plantagenet), count of
Anjou, who seized
Normandy from Stephen

Henry,
count of Anjou,
King Henry II of England
1154–89, duke of Normandy
and Aquitaine, etc.

The Angevin kings

STEPHEN,
king of
England
1135–54;
m. Matilda,
countess of
Boulogne

Theobald,
count of
Blois

Henry,
bishop of
Winchester

William (Clito),
killed in exile
1128

proving that a single victory would not bring co-operation. This meant that the Conquest became much more thorough than had been envisaged. The setback, however, could be turned to William's advantage, since the Norman barons were forced to accept his authority in the struggle to maintain their foothold. It was the English who paid for thwarting their conquerors, as will appear in an assessment of the Norman impact on their land.

*

Although the Norman hold on England was assured by 1087, many of the effects of the Conquest became apparent only under William's successors. The first of these was a short, stocky and red-faced man of about thirty, nicknamed Rufus, memorable as perhaps the most evil, although not the most incompetent, king that England has ever endured. A wayward and blasphemous homosexual, William II was generally loathed when he met his death from an arrow in the New Forest on 2 August 1100, after thirteen years of extortionate rule. He was succeeded by his younger brother, who was probably also responsible for his murder. Henry I of England combined Rufus's greed with a much higher degree of statesmanship and governed with an iron hand until his death in 1135. He married Edith, daughter of Edgar the Ætheling's sister, Margaret Queen of Scots, thereby transmitting the blood of the West Saxon royal line to his descendants; unfortunately his only surviving legitimate child was a daughter, Matilda, so that Stephen of Blois, son of the Conqueror's daughter, Adela, was recognized as the next sovereign. Stephen was a kinder and simpler man than his predecessors, and the realm suffered accordingly; for much of his nineteen years' reign he had to contend with Matilda, who had married Geoffrey Plantagenet, count of Anjou, and on the king's death in 1154 Matilda's son succeeded as Henry II, the first of the Angevins. England thus had four Norman kings—the Conqueror, two of his sons and his grandson —whose reigns covered a span of eighty-eight years (Table V).

England and Normandy were not permanently separated after 1087. When William agreed to the break-up of his empire he was only conforming to custom, since his barons generally left their hereditary lands in the duchy to their eldest sons and their new lands in England to their second sons. This did not alter the fact that the division undid a large part of his life's work, to the benefit of Philip of France. Robert's hold on the duchy proved to be as feeble as his father had predicted, which encouraged William Rufus to launch an invasion in 1089–90 and again in 1094, with limited success; in 1096 the duke left on crusade after pawning Normandy to William, who thus died as ruler of both lands. Robert then returned to recover his inheritance and even to claim England, until he was defeated and captured by Henry at Tinchebrai in western Normandy on 28 September 1106, the fortieth anniversary of the landing at Pevensey. Tinchebrai proved second in importance only to Hastings among the battles of Anglo-Norman history, for Henry thereafter ruled a reunited Anglo-Norman Empire, while Robert lingered as a prisoner until his death in Cardiff castle at the age of eighty. Stephen soon gave up any attempt to hold Normandy against Matilda's Angevin husband, but Henry II's accession again brought kingdom and duchy under a single ruler, which they enjoyed until John lost Normandy to France in 1204. Henry was to secure still more French domains, from his father, Count Geoffrey, and from his wife, Eleanor of Aquitaine; the Conqueror's empire, which had stretched from Scotland to the hills of Maine, was succeeded by one which reached the Pyrenees.

These changes of fortune are important, for if Robert

Curthose had been able to hold his own against his younger brothers, Continental influence in England would have been much weaker. Under separate rulers the aristocracy could not for long have kept interests on both sides of the Channel, and in England the many native traditions which survived the Conquest for several decades might never have been extinguished. William the Conqueror ruled both lands for only twenty-one years, long enough to plant the Normans firmly on alien soil but not to prevent their descendants from becoming anglicized. It was Henry I and Henry II whose wars and diplomacy perpetuated the union for nearly a century, thereby ensuring that the rulers of England would remain French in speech and outlook until the later Middle Ages.

CHAPTER SIX

Feudal England

*W*ILLIAM'S reign saw the dispossession of an entire ruling class in favour of a foreign aristocracy. Land was confiscated at all levels, the first victims ranging from King Harold to the humblest peasant who had fought for him at Hastings, but it was the leading English families who suffered most heavily. The newcomers were granted estates in return for specific agreements to provide military service, whereas their predecessors had served the king merely by virtue of their rank or their general obligations as freemen. Wealth thus passed into new hands and military power assumed a different form.

*

A social revolution was inevitable. At Edward's death there had been four or five thousand Englishmen holding estates which the Normans were to rank as manors; the Northumbrians and Mercians had then been reduced in number at the battle of Fulford and the thegns of the south and east at Stamford Bridge and Hastings. William was bound to reward his followers at the expense of all who had fought for the Godwines, and continued resistance brought him yet more forfeited property. Later revolts in areas still unscathed completed the toll of victims. *Domesday Book*, which was inspired by many motives, is best considered as an administrative act; it is also a unique source of information on the lavish re-distribution of land. There were fourteen hundred-odd tenants-in-chief, who held estates directly of the king; about a hundred and seventy of these enjoyed an annual income of £100 or more and only two were Englishmen, both of whom had prospered at the expense of their countrymen. The full extent of the calamity is revealed, for a mere eight per cent of the land was left in native hands.

The thegns, who still existed everywhere as a class, lost their old standing. A knightly education and know-ledge of French became essential for social esteem and for advancement, so that many small men of thegnly rank drifted downwards into the mass of peasantry. The more adventurous and perhaps the most fortunate of the younger Englishmen emigrated; a few may have gone to Denmark or Ireland, others certainly fled with the Ætheling and Cospatric to Scotland, while yet more followed the Vikings by entering the service of the Byzantine emperors. An occasional Norman family is known to have acquired English lands by marriage and this practice may have been officially encouraged, since it would have buttressed William's claim to be the Old English heir. During the twelfth century, when bitter memories were fading and a new generation had been reared in Norman ways, Englishmen were to become more prominent and were even to be used as a counter-weight to the king's too powerful barons. In 1086, however, the bonds between Crown and barons were stronger than their differences, since both forces repres-ented an uneasy master race.

*

It was a delicate task for William to reward his followers in such a way that they would neither dispute one another's gains nor be emboldened to challenge the royal power. Continuity was stressed by bestowing on a baron all the lands of a pre-Conquest lord within a shire and by transmitting former obligations as well as rights. At the same time the total holding or honour of a magnate was scattered throughout several shires, so that a famous pattern of lordship was established which has been variously attributed to the king's deep cunning and to the piecemeal nature of the Conquest. Long distances certainly made it hard for a baron to consolidate his military power and later they were to hamper his exercise of seignorial justice in the face of royal competition. It remains unlikely that these advantages to the Crown were borne in mind during the settlement itself, which was based on the king's trust in individuals. Widely separated estates were held before Edward's death, so that William's originality has been exaggerated, and many under-tenants in the duchy were able to acquire English estates under the same lord; this transplanting of old loyalties must have helped to offset the dispersal of the magnates' new honours.

One result of granting scattered estates was that racial differences between the invaders quickly became blurred. A writ issued to 'Normans and Flemish and English' before 1069 does not distinguish the largest non-Norman element among William's followers, the Bretons, who had formed one of the three divisions of his army at Hastings. Brittany was not an advanced feudal state, for its ruler's authority was weak and knighthood was less a military qualification than a badge of rank. Members of this largely Celtic society jealously retained their place-names in England and might have been hard to assimilate into the Anglo-Norman kingdom if compact racial groups had been allowed to form. As it was, foreigners of all races mingled and quickly forgot all distinctions save the paramount one between themselves and the English.

The enormously powerful houses of Godwine and Leofric had no Norman successors. Beneath this vice-regal level the Conquest produced a small landowning class whose members individually were far wealthier than their thegnly predecessors. At the time of *Domesday* nearly half of the kingdom was enjoyed by William's tenants-in-chief, while the Church held about a quarter of the land and the king about one-fifth. The hundred and seventy-odd leading tenants-in-chief were themselves dominated by a favoured minority, for approximately half the land held by lay tenure had been granted to eleven men, headed by Bishop Odo of Bayeux and including the king's other half-brother, Count Robert of Mortain. All save two of these men, Count Eustace of Boulogne and Count Alan the Red from Brittany, were Normans, and all save two had played a leading part in the duchy before 1066. William's rule in England, as in Normandy, was to be based on close ties with proven associates.

The distribution of honours was linked with the needs of defence. William naturally entrusted the vulnerable parts of his kingdom to his most reliable advisers; Odo became earl of Kent on the morrow of the Conquest, Robert of Mortain was made earl of Cornwall some ten years later and the Breton Ralph de Gael was for a short time earl of Norfolk. In the Welsh marches the three great earldoms of Hereford, Shrewsbury and Chester arose from the estates granted to William fitz Osbern, Roger of Montgomery and Hugh of Avranches; fitz Osbern also received the Isle of Wight, while the six rapes of Sussex were all bestowed on great men, including Roger of Montgomery and Robert of Mortain. The enormous pre-Conquest earldom of Northumbria was left intact to a hapless succession of English and Norman viceroys, despite the fact that the southern part, Yorkshire, already existed as a separate county. Before William's death this ring of large and strategically placed lordships was reduced by the forfeitures of fitz Osbern's son, Ralph de Gael and Bishop Odo, who were joined by Robert of Mortain in the following reign. Although the mighty lords of the northern and western marches were to head many challenges to the Crown during the Middle Ages, every king had to permit some concentration of power in these exposed areas.

The Conqueror's grants of land are particularly important because of the military obligations which went with them. William adopted no rigid policy, based on the value of the lands; instead he struck a series of individual bargains with his tenants-in-chief, who agreed to furnish far more knights than were owed for estates of similar size in Normandy. These agreements were initiated around 1070 and were probably already furnishing mounted men for the Scots campaign two years later. The *servitium debitum* or service owed by each magnate ensured a force of about 4000 knights, to whom some 780 more were added by similar impositions upon the bishoprics and abbeys. All that the king had to do when preparing war was to send a terse writ of summons; the earliest known example is addressed to a native prelate who enjoyed wide powers as a regional governor, thanks to his unique place in the Conqueror's favour:

> William, king of the English, to Æthelwig, abbot of Evesham, greeting. I order you to summon all those who are subject to your administration and jurisdiction that they bring before me at Clarendon on the Octave of Pentecost all the knights they owe me duly equipped. You, also, on that day, shall come to me, and bring with you fully equipped those five knights which you owe me in respect of your abbacy. Witness Eudo the steward. At Winchester.

Comparisons between the knight-service owed in the

kingdom and in the duchy are based only on records of
the late twelfth century, but they show that in England
the burden laid on William's ecclesiastical tenants alone
approximated to that borne by the entire baronage of
Normandy. Few magnates in the duchy were encumbered
with the service of over ten knights whereas in England,
before the death of William's youngest son, eleven
laymen owed that of sixty knights or more and nine
ecclesiastical landlords owed that of forty or more.
Events between 1066 and 1087 show how urgently
this force was needed to hold the kingdom. Once military
tenure had been imposed by the king on his leading
subjects, England was on the way to becoming a feudal
state.

The second stage of the introduction of feudalism
followed naturally from the first. The tenants-in-chief,
burdened with knight-service, found it convenient in
England, as in Normandy, to lease portions of their own
land on similar conditions. Some eight thousand under-
tenants, including a few Englishmen, feature in *Domesday
Book*. This subinfeudation was a gradual process, since a
magnate was not bound to enfeof his followers and at
first he furnished his quota out of landless knights, paid
directly by him and maintained as members of his household. Large bands of 'household' knights, however,
proved to be an administrative burden and, with time on
their hands, they were a constant threat to law and order;
such men provoked many unnecessary clashes between
English and Normans, including the northern rebellion
of 1080. It was therefore in the king's interest to encour-
age subinfeudation, and William is known on occasion
to have interfered with baronial enfeoffments, which few
Continental rulers would have dared to do.

Baronial enfeoffments, like the king's imposition of
servitia debita, were not carried out in a regular fashion.
The enfeoffed knight had become a characteristic figure

by the time of *Domesday Book* but in the eastern shires, which lay under the threat of Scandinavian attacks throughout the reign, landless knights survived in greater numbers than elsewhere. The lord's rights to feudal incidents had not been regularized at the end of the century, the first knights' fees were not necessarily hereditary and the amounts of land granted to individual under-tenants varied enormously. A knight might be an obscure retainer or a substantial landowner who was the social equal of his lord and who could impose knight-service for his own lands. These prominent under-tenants were probably the men who flocked with the magnates to swear loyalty to William at Salisbury in 1086; they were the leading personages in the honour, the tenant-in-chief's natural advisers, his peers. In effect they formed a second baronial class, now termed honorial barons, which soon became indistinguishable from the first and from which many of England's noblest medieval houses were descended.

William did not grant lands only in return for knight-service, although this was originally the most honourable form of tenure. Land was plentiful and money was scarce, so that estates were bestowed for many special services. *Servientes regis* or king's sergeants appear in *Domesday Book* and their number increased for several decades. These tenants in sergeanty were usually members of the royal household and administration, or people connected with the king's sports; in Oxfordshire alone there was a dispenser by 1086 and later a naperer, who had to furnish a table-cloth worth 3*s.* every Michaelmas, as well as a herb gatherer, a larderer, ushers, falconers and foresters. Some sergeants had special military duties, including that of bearing the royal standard, and others were left with a once menial task which had become purely ceremonial and survived only at the coronation.

The sergeants' wealth and standing thus varied widely

and their functions ranged from the useful and onerous to the honorary and even to the ludicrous. In 1330 the Dorset manor of Kingston Russell was held by the service of counting the royal chessmen and putting them back in their box after use; earlier, Rolland of Hemingstone in Suffolk 'every year on Christmas Day at the court of the lord king had to make a leap, a whistle and a fart'. A benevolent sovereign was to commute Rolland's service after his land had fallen to an abbot, and many other picturesque sergeanties were likewise to disappear with the rise of a money economy.

The symbol of feudal power was the castle, whose very name of dungeon comes from the French *donjon* and ultimately from the Latin *dominium* or lordship. Here was the baron's home and here usually was the *caput* or centre of his honour; sometimes its dependent lordship was even known as a castelry. Above all the castle was a military safeguard, from which a baron could control the countryside and even defy the king himself. No rebellion was over so long as a single edifice held out, which it might do for months or even for years in the days before gunpowder; fire, which could reduce the early wooden structures, was of no avail against newer piles of masonry, and mining was slow and sometimes impractical, as well as dangerous.

In England, as in Normandy, private castles were not supposed to be built without licence; their numbers were rigidly limited by the Conqueror in his heyday, although they had proliferated in his youth and were to do so again under the weak rule of Duke Robert Curthose and King Stephen. If these strongholds held a threat to royal authority, they were indispensable in the Norman conquest of England. William's first act at Pevensey had been to build a castle and his triumphal progress was marked by at least thirty-six similar foundations, in and around London, in the south-west and later along the routes of his marches to and from the north. During his lifetime the castle did more than protect regal or baronial power, it ensured the triumph of a race (Map III).

Little is known of William's barons as individuals and no study has been made of them as a class. Their small numbers and individual riches would have made them more exclusive than Edward's thegns, even if there had been no racial differences to cut the new lords off from their tenantry. They introduced England to ordeal by battle and in due course to the tournament, a new and dangerous French pastime which at first resembled a battle without political motives. This martial enthusiasm does not mean that the Normans were more violent than their English predecessors, with whom they shared a love of hunting; Earl Godwine and his sons, Sweyn and Tostig, were as murderous as any baron. *Domesday Book* gives only the landowners who were established in 1086, with no details on when or how they had obtained their estates during the previous twenty years. Since those who appear in it most frequently, however, were either the men or the sons of men who had served William well in Normandy, it is at least clear that the chief beneficiaries from Hastings had not started as penniless adventurers; they were the men who had been best able to aid the duke in his greatest adventure.

The Normans contributed more to England's institutions than to her stock. If all the French-speaking settlers of Edward's reign are added to William's following, the foreigners would amount to tens rather than to hundreds of thousands, and continued arrivals during the next century still left them in a small minority, perhaps between 100,000 and 200,000 amidst a population of 1½ million. The fame of Hastings and the victors' virtual monopoly of wealth and position soon made Norman ancestry a source of pride, so that many voluminous lists of the invaders have been compiled from the twelfth century

CASTLES IN ENGLAND BUILT OR SANCTIONED BY WILLIAM THE CONQUEROR

MILES

0 20 40 60 80 100

N

NORTH

SEA

Newcastle on Tyne
Durham

York

Chester
Lincoln
Nottingham
Stafford
Shrewsbury
Rockingham
Norwich
Worcester
Huntingdon
Ely
Hereford
Warwick
Cambridge
Gloucester
Colchester
Oxford
London
Wallingford
Rochester
Windsor
Canterbury
Winchester
Dover
Old Sarum
Bramber Lewes
Hastings
Exeter
Arundel
Pevensey
Corfe

ENGLISH CHANNEL

onwards. In fact, while there are no more than three names today which belong to an Old English line, there are only some half-dozen families which can prove without a doubt that their ancestors came over with the Conqueror. This is not surprising, since the pedigrees of landowners alone have been preserved and the more prominent the family the more likely it was to end on the battlefield or the scaffold. On the other hand Norman blood is now spread throughout the English-speaking world, among the descendants of humble settlers or of barons whose heirs fell upon evil days. Names are an insufficient guide, since they change with fashion, and the men who could boast this traditionally enviable descent are unnumbered.

*

The entire apparatus of Norman baronial administration was transplanted to England. Each tenant-in-chief, although his lands lay in several shires, had a *caput* or principal seat, each had a household which resembled that of the king, and each had a court where his peers helped to deliver judgement. The honorial court was a general court for all the scattered tenants of a barons' honour, and it was there that knight-service was allocated on their lands; local regulations and disputes between lesser men, if they were tenants of the same manor, were dealt with at individual manorial courts, meeting under the lord's steward. The baron had clerks to draw up charters like those of the king, he was served by chamberlains, butlers and others whose style resembled that of royal officials, and he too received liege homage for his lands. The monarch enjoyed special powers and resources, which were to shape England's future; in the generation after the Conquest, the kingdom must have seemed like one vast honour, and the honours resembled miniature kingdoms.

The originality of these feudal arrangements in England

is a thorny problem. Nineteenth-century historians in general stressed the continuity of English history, minimizing the impact of the Normans; a reaction followed under the lead of J. H. Round, who concentrated on the subject of knight-service and demonstrated that this was an innovation which had no Anglo-Saxon precedents. The orthodox view today is that feudalism, in the form of military tenure, was indeed a Norman contribution to England's development, although more recently there has been a tendency once again to emphasize the similarities between pre- and post-Conquest society.

Clearly there were many features of the Old English kingdom which foreshadowed those of the Anglo-Norman state. Men were surrendering their freedom by commending themselves or their property to a lord, land could be held in return for services, and judicial immunities existed. None of these practices, however, was uniform and it is not certain that the lords could exercise justice in seignorial courts like those of the Norman barons. Thegns and housecarles were trained to arms and the old contrast between amateur Anglo-Saxon footmen and professional Norman cavalry was certainly exaggerated, yet similar customs do not make similar societies. The wholesale division of land into fiefs, granted after homage had been done and held in return for stipulated service, usually military service, was a Norman achievement.

No one disputes that this achievement, however it is rated, was primarily William's work. In Normandy he had found a developing feudal society, in England he forged one more complete and more to his own liking. The new king ruthlessly exploited the old authority of the English Crown, his own prestige as a conqueror and the danger in which the invaders still stood. The heavy quotas of knights, proof of the king's power, were not

matched by excessive baronial enfeoffments of under-
tenants; this again was in contrast to Normandy, where
barons built up private armies by rarely enfeoffing less
than three times the number of knights whose service
they owed to the duke. Moreover, William's success in
England strengthened him in the duchy, since the proud
families which recognized that they held their new
lands by royal grant could hardly deny that they were
similarly dependent in Normandy.

The force of four to five thousand knights which
feudal tenures ensured in England was not the king's
sole military resource. The old obligation to serve in the
fyrd and in the shire levies was recalled in 1181, when
Henry II specified the arms and armour which were to be
borne by every free man, as well as by those who held a
knight's fee. It has been seen that William himself was
soon making use of native troops, whose service was
assessed in hides and who were commanded, as before, by
local thegns. These continued English contributions did
not, as has sometimes been said, lessen the Norman
impact; they merely enabled William to have the best of
both worlds, since in Normandy he could call out the
whole army only to defend the duchy itself. Mercenaries
also diluted the feudal array, even in 1066, and were
retained by the Conqueror in varying numbers throughout his reign. The money-fief, whereby a man received
not land but an income in return for homage and the
promise of service, has been traced to William's time:
vassals of Henry I are also known to have paid scutage
or shield-money, compositions for military service by
cash payments which could then be used to hire mercenaries. The Anglo-Norman host, like that of every other
ruler, was never purely feudal and it grew steadily less
so under William's successors.

Feudalism in fact carried the seeds of its own decay.
Land was used to reward William's followers, since it was

more plentiful than money, and tenure in return for
military service was acceptable to warriors who had to
fight to keep their gains; the introduction of feudalism
thus met the king's pressing political and military needs.
Inevitably, as the danger receded and as men developed
local ties, those who owed service became less eager to
take the field in person; religious houses in particular
shrank from the burden of furnishing knights, while the
burgesses in the towns sought escape from individual
obligations. These defects in feudalism, always inherent
but increasingly obvious, do not detract from the Conqueror's achievement; he maintained the Norman grip
on England, strengthened his own authority and established the strongest military power possible in his day.

*

The legacy of feudalism lasted for centuries. Every
English king down to Charles I enjoyed the financial
perquisites of a feudal overlord, and private justice
survived for still longer. Honorial courts declined early in
the Middle Ages, with the difficulty of travelling to the
centre of a far-flung honour and with the replacement of
personal military service by cash payments; the courts of
the manor also attracted fewer tenants as the medieval
kings extended their own justice. On the other hand
unfree tenants and their descendants, the copyholders,
continued to use the manorial courts, which still provided
training grounds for rising lawyers under the Tudors and
Stuarts; it was during the eighteenth century that these
courts fell into disuse for all except the conveyancing of
copyholds, a form of tenure which was finally abolished
with effect from 1926.

Feudalism as the basis of England's defence had a
shorter and stormier history. During the early Middle
Ages every king struggled to make the cumbrous system
of military obligations work or to find satisfactory

alternatives. The problem grew more urgent after the French conquest of Normandy in 1204 deprived many families of an interest in Continental wars, as inflation eroded the value of the money payments which had become substitutes for service, and as the king in desperation sought ruthlessly to exploit those rights which were undisputed. Smaller quotas of knights had been assigned to the barons by the mid-thirteenth century and eventually mercenaries entirely replaced the feudal array. This long conflict over the Crown's military and financial rights produced many restatements of feudal custom, of which the most famous is Magna Carta.

CHAPTER SEVEN

The Conquest and English Society

*T*HE introduction of feudalism, effected for political and military reasons, entailed a social revolution. Within twenty years the downfall of the old aristocracy was complete, and for many smaller thegns the future proved equally grim. Their wealth and standing passed to foreigners, trained from childhood in mounted warfare, and laymen who were not knights enjoyed little respect. This confiscation of English estates was the immediate social result of the Conquest, and for their holders it was catastrophic. Landowners of any substance, however, were a minority; the Norman impact on the bulk of the population was slower and less obvious.

*

Anyone who happened to be in the path of a marauding army lost everything of value. Often entire families lost their lives as well, from hunger or pestilence if not from the sword. In the late seventh century, England had been swept by what was apparently the bubonic plague, a scourge which was to return in 1348 as the Black Death. During the intervening centuries most recorded epidemics sprang from starvation and were therefore linked with wars or bad crops. The Conquest took place at a comparatively fortunate time, since a generation separates the last and severest famine of Edward's reign, in 1049, from the heavy mortality of William's final years. The general outbreak of pestilence of 1086–7 was caused chiefly by the weather, which had ruined two successive harvests, and by murrain among the cattle; the king, however, may have contributed to this disaster by his high taxes, which discouraged cultivation, for many later chroniclers were to spy a connection between royal extortion, famine and pestilence. William can more confidently be blamed for the numberless deaths that followed his destruction of agriculture in the north.

Domesday Book, intended as a record of lordship and an assessment of the wealth of the land, not as a social survey, remains the richest source of information on rural life at the opening of the Middle Ages. Its compilers, when reckoning the value of estates at the Confessor's death and in 1086, used 'waste' to denote not untouched wilderness but former arable land. They show that William inflicted exceptional and unnecessary suffering over large areas, especially on his northern campaign of 1069–70. Abundant entries resemble the one for a small-holding at Chellaston in Derbyshire, which laconically records: 'There is land for half a plough. It is waste. There are four acres of meadow. In King Edward's time it was worth twelve shillings; now three shillings.' On the other hand Anglo-Saxon England had not been immune from devastation and some counties were more prosperous after twenty years of Norman rule than they had been in 1066; the Welsh marches had been impoverished by the raiders who had plagued Harold, and Northamptonshire had been laid waste by the Northumbrian rebels in 1065. Moreover, it was usual for enemy forces to live off the land, so that the peasant toll was countless in any war, and many of those who perished under William would have done so under any other conqueror.

The historic importance of the Norman Conquest lies in the fate of those who survived. Nine out of ten Englishmen lived on the land, to which they might be tied, and were burdened with services of varying heaviness. Although it is not always clear how accurately the lower grades of Anglo-Danish society are rendered by the Latin terms of the *Domesday* clerks, their survey reveals four main classes of peasant. First came the *liberi homines* or freemen, who owned their holdings and paid their own taxes; with them may be included for economic purposes the sokemen of the Danelaw, although these enjoyed a superior legal status in that they could be sued in court. Next came the *villani*, who enjoyed but did not own a full share in the village fields; their holdings varied enormously in size throughout the country but in general equalled those of their neighbours on the same manor and might comprise a quarter of a hide or thirty *Domesday* acres. Below the *villani* were the cottagers, the Old English *kotsetlan*, whom the clerks tried to separate into two classes by the name of borders and cottars; these men had their own smallholdings and might occasionally be prosperous, but they lacked a full share in the village lands and often had to supplement their income by casual labour or by finding special work, for instance as shepherds, blacksmiths or carpenters. At the bottom of the scale came the *servi*, whose lot is described below.

Domesday shows that rural society twenty years after the Conquest was much as it had been when the *Rectitudines* was compiled in the middle of the century. When William's clerks wrote of a 'manor' they may have meant merely a lord's house, and the word certainly did not yet signify the full medieval manor, where the peasantry of a consolidated estate was uniformly subject to the lord's jurisdiction and bound to labour services. Society was moving in that direction, as it had been moving for generations, but in *Domesday* the diversity of the past is more striking than the uniformity of the Middle Ages. In the Danelaw the manor, a tenurial unit, rarely coincided with the village, the older agrarian unit, and peasant freedom in 1086 was still far stronger there than in the English areas of the kingdom, save in Kent. Ninety-six per cent of the *Domesday* sokemen are found in Norfolk and Suffolk, while the *servi* are most common in the south-west. The holdings of the *villani* are still so varied that it is wise to retain the Latin term, which distinguishes them from the more uniform medieval villeins. *Domesday* also preserves the names of two minor classes: the radmen of the western Midlands, the *geneatas* of the *Rectitudines*, superior smallholders who performed riding services for their land, and the *coliberti*, recently freed peasants of Wessex and Mercia. These distinctions re-emphasize the fact that local pre-Conquest differences, including those between Englishman and Dane, persisted into the twelfth century.

Legal and economic variety survived because the Normans did not contribute to the peasant stock. The newcomers were a race of rulers, whose coming was not a popular migration. The Anglo-Saxon tribesmen and the rank and file of the Viking armies had settled down to till the soil, displacing many whom they found and inter-mingling with others. William's followers, fewer in number, dispossessed only the native ruling class and lived on the labour of the rest of the population. They brought with them no regular pattern of estate management to impose on a subject people and in general they had to accept the existing methods of working the lands which they took over. The basic routine of peasant life therefore continued unchanged.

Naturally there must have been many peasants for

whom life at once became harder. These cases cannot be numbered, since it is impossible to prove that the behaviour of any single Norman lord was worse than that of his English predecessor. One widespread Norman practice, favoured by the king and copied by many business-like barons, certainly led to oppression. Only a part of a baron's fief was needed for his own support and therefore kept as a home-farm, in demesne; the rest, which might amount to half of his lands, could be farmed out to men who provided an agreed profit and then recouped themselves as best they could. The lord thus enjoyed a guaranteed rent and the farmer had an incentive to extortion. Estates had been farmed in England before the Conquest but the habit spread so rapidly under William that the Anglo-Saxon chronicler seized his chance to bewail the resulting misery when describing the king's deathbed:

> The king and the chief men loved gain much and over-much— gold and silver—and did not care how sinfully it was obtained provided it came to them. The king sold his land on very hard terms—as hard as he could. Then came somebody else, and offered more than the other had given, and the king let it go to the man who had offered him more. Then came the third, and offered still more, and the king gave it into the hands of the man who had offered him most of all, and did not care how sinfully the reeves had got it from poor men, nor how many unlawful things they did.

It is this practice and what is known of the Norman character, rather than particular instances, which make it clear that some of the poorest in the land suffered from the change of masters.

If the daily round remained as before, there followed a gradual decline of freedom which in the long run may have affected popular living standards. The logical Normans preferred to relate a man's freedom to the services which he actually performed rather than to his ancestors' rights, and they could not be expected to appreciate the finer distinctions among the native peasantry. No clear breach was made with the past but the new lord's steward, unsympathetic to the English and determined to secure the maximum profit, tended to treat all peasants alike; since the baronial holdings were much larger than the average thegnly estates of Edward's day, the basis was laid for a uniform subjection. Ultimately the elaborate nomenclature of Anglo-Danish society lost its meaning, and degrees of freedom disappeared in an amorphous villeinage or serfdom. Prosperity does not always wither with freedom, and the material effects of this debasement are mainly a matter for guesswork. The only clear losers were those few peasants whose industry and good fortune, perhaps in serving a lord, might otherwise have lifted them above their fellows; an exceptionally favoured Anglo-Saxon churl could aspire to thegnhood, whereas the villein could never hope to become a knight.

Paradoxically the Conquest came to the rescue of England's most depressed class, the Anglo-Saxon *theows* or slaves. These men and women, whose condition was hereditary and who had no rights save that to the barest necessities of life, may have numbered over twenty-five thousand or nearly one-eleventh of the recorded population at the time of King Edward's death. Many thousands were still noted in *Domesday Book*, when the Latin term *servi* still denoted slaves, human chattels, rather than serfs, and they were particularly numerous in the south-western shires. None the less, their numbers had everywhere fallen since 1066 and within less than a hundred years slavery was to give way to a less absolute subjection, servitude. The *servi* of the thirteenth century were serfs, tied to the land and burdened with duties, but they were not denied all privileges and in practice had become indistinguishable from villeins.

This development removed a blemish which distinguished English from French society. It was encouraged by the prelates of the reformed Church and perhaps from equally high motives by William himself, who was anxious to suppress the English slave-trade. Humanity is so little associated with his race, however, that it is natural to seek additional and more practical reasons for the change. A slave had to be kept by his master whereas a peasant could support himself, so that it was easier and more profitable to rely on the forced labour of serfs. Moreover, Norman officialdom tended to view all peasants alike and the law came to treat them as one class, whatever economic differences might persist among them. The semi-emancipation of the slaves thus ran parallel to the depression of their hitherto more fortunate neighbours and formed part of that general levelling-out of the peasantry which took place during the hundred and fifty years after the Conquest.

*

The fate of the Old English aristocracy, peasants and slaves was shared by people of both sexes and all ages. None the less, while it is obvious that women were not a social class, their half of society was affected quite separately by the Conquest. The German tribesmen who had colonized Britannia seem to have treated their wives as partners, and the sexes retained a rough equality throughout Old English history. Many women are commemorated in a place-name and this sometimes denotes a woodland clearing, which suggests that they had a full share in the vital task of reducing the wilderness. Alfred's sister, Æthelflæd, had commanded victorious armies, Cnut had sent Ælfgifu of Northampton to govern Norway for her son, Harold Harefoot, and an abbess had always ruled men as well as women in a double monastery. There was no insistence that property should pass only through the male line and a rich lady could receive lands as well as bestow them where she liked in her will, even to the detriment of her own sons. Less is known about humbler women but Cnut's laws show that if goods stolen by a free farmer should be found under his wife's lock and key, she would be presumed to share his guilt; a woman, in fact, was expected to command access to her own store-room and boxes, and so to be mistress in the home.

Norman society, organized for mounted warfare, was more restrictive. Land was held in return for military services, which women could not perform, and an estate had to be kept intact. Male primogeniture therefore became the rule, while younger sons and daughters were thrown upon their fathers' generosity. A woman could still inherit land and in theory she could still alienate it, although she was not supposed to appear in court nor even to make a will without her husband's leave. St Paul's views on wifely submission, imported much earlier only to make slow headway, were more zealously propagated by the reformed Church. Women drew no comfort from the fact that men's consciences were sometimes uneasy, so that the law remained guiltily vague. A lady in practice merely passed from one guardian to another unless she was freed by widowhood, and even then the king might force an heiress into a new marriage or take money from her instead. The first glimmer of freedom did not come until 1215, when Magna Carta laid down that a widow could remain single if she promised not to remarry without her lord's consent.

The Conquest thus gave women in England an inferior status, placing ladies of property under legal disabilities which lasted until the abolition of feudal tenures at the Restoration. The intervening six hundred years, however, did not constitute an unrelieved dark age for feminism. William's own flinty nature was softened by devotion to his queen; Matilda of Flanders, who acted as regent of Normandy, was but the first of many royal

ladies whose station allowed them to wield authority
denied to other women. At the opposite end of the scale
the peasant's wife shared her husband's life much more
fully than she would have done had she been a noble lady,
and the Normans were not concerned to interfere with a
poor woman's rights. When a baron died his wife was
allowed only one-third of her husband's land by feudal
law; a villein's widow on the other hand could hold the
whole of his land so long as the customary services were
performed, and her place in the home was secure so long
as she lived unmarried. The feudal order was imposed on
the English from above and here, as in most respects, it
made the least impact on the largest sections of the
population.

*

The Norman innovation which bore most heavily on
the poor was the extension of forest land and the creation
of forest law. The Forest consisted of areas reserved for
the king, largely but not entirely wooded and not necessarily confined to the king's own property or royal demesne;
if a section of the Forest was enclosed, it might be called
a park. The purpose of the new measures was to protect
the vert, or young timber and undergrowth, and the
venison which it supported. The venison comprised the
red and fallow deer and the dwindling number of wild
boar, which royal foresters alone might take; at first it
also embraced the roe, which was excluded in the fourteenth century from the privileged 'beasts of the Forest',
because it kept the other deer away. Special licences
might be granted for the king's tenants to hunt lesser
game, occasionally including roebuck, inside or outside
the Forest, and the barons were allowed to create their
own deer parks. The king could also probably claim the
right of warren or hare-hunting over the whole of England,
although private warrens might be established by royal

grant, and he reserved for himself the wild honey of the woods, as well as the eyries of the 'fowl of the Forest'— hawks, falcons, eagles and herons. Wolves were always pests and the Angevin kings encouraged their extermination by payments which rose from a few pennies per head under Henry II to 5s. under John.

Hunting had been a passion of the Old English kings, from Alfred to Edward the Confessor. None of them had drawn up special regulations for the areas of their sport so as to put them outside (*foris*) the law of the land. The Norman kings, who also found their main solace in the chase, hunted over wider areas and followed the Franks in maintaining a hierarchy of officials to preserve what was described in 1184 as 'the peace of the king's venison'. No detailed statement of the Anglo-Norman forest law itself survives, but it is known that blinding and castration was at first a common fate for those who were convicted of destroying game; the Angevins, whose cruelty was softened by greed, preferred to rely on fines. Under Henry II itinerant justices held pleas of the Forest every three years, and in the following century the intervals increased to seven years, so that those who appeared in court had often already endured a long imprisonment.

For a century after the Conquest, save under the weak rule of Stephen, the royal forest grew in extent. The *Anglo-Saxon Chronicle* says that William indulged himself without heed to rich or poor, since he 'loved the stags as much as if he were their father'. The expansion which he started probably reached its limit under Henry II, when nearly a third of the kingdom formed a royal game-preserve, and only Norfolk, Suffolk and Kent are known to have been unaffected. The depopulation which this caused is hard to estimate; *Domesday Book* shows that some villages had again become waste, while some were laid under forest law and others survived as enclaves. The suffering in Hampshire was once exaggerated, perhaps because chroniclers loved to point a moral and found a golden opportunity to do so after the Conqueror's second son, Richard, and William Rufus met their deaths in the New Forest. Nevertheless, their father had expelled some two thousand people, when adding between 15,000 and 20,000 acres to the 75,000 sparsely populated acres which he had found there. William I's most notorious creation was not so large as the forest of Essex, which covered the entire county; it still deserves to be quoted as an example of Norman rapacity.

Those who were evicted were far outnumbered by those whose lives became more cramped and often fraught with danger. A cottager retained grazing rights, save during the month when the deer were fawning, and he was allowed to collect dead wood, but he could cut no living timber, and even an unauthorized hedge or ditch laid him open to a fine. Whole townships were held responsible for finding the slayer of a beast, on which an inquisition was always held, and the forest-dweller dared not keep a dog whose front claws were uncut, nor might he bear a bow and arrows. He was also bound to attend the forest court when summoned and to act as a beater when the king went hunting, an occasion which might involve the trampling of his own crops. While this harsh régime applied only to the king's preserves, it is unlikely that private landlords were gentler to men in their determination to protect the beasts.

The Forest, extended for royal sport and at such heavy cost to the poor, is important not only in social history. The Angevins drew a large income from the fines imposed under forest law or from granting permission to make clearings, while timber from the Forest was supplied for their buildings and ships, and venison fed their court as it journeyed ceaselessly over the land. Above all, exclusive royal hunting rights illustrate the power of the Anglo-Norman kings and of their Angevin successors;

across the Channel the weakness of Charlemagne's heirs
had allowed these privileges to be usurped by the nobility.

Inevitably the king's rights in the Forest later became
linked with his other rights as feudal overlord in the
contest between Crown and baronage. Henry II, by
insisting that churchmen should be subject to pleas of the
forest, multiplied the enemies of this arbitrary jurisdiction.
It was natural that the barons should seek to undo recent
afforestation and to empanel juries which were to inquire
into abuses of the forest law; accordingly they inserted
into Magna Carta two clauses which touched the populace
more nearly than did all the complaints over feudal
incidents. Two years later, in 1217, the forest clauses
formed the basis of a separate charter, which partly
amended earlier Norman brutality by protecting offenders
in life and limb. The oppression of forest law proved so
valuable to those who wished to curb the king that it
helped to shape England's constitutional development.

*

Less is known of eleventh-century urban ways than of
life in the countryside. The contrast was then less striking
than it is today, since the English towns of 1066 still
owned agricultural land and the inhabitants still included
peasants, as well as many townsmen who had not yet
given up working on their fields. None the less, on both
sides of the Channel there were people who were supported entirely by trade or industry and whose way of
life was quite different from that of the rural worker. In
the older English boroughs men already held their
messuages or plots by a special tenure, later known as
burgage tenure, whereby they paid a fixed rent for each
tenement of maybe 12d. a year and, unlike the *villani*,
were free to dispose of their property. A man was a bur-
gess only if he shared in the customary borough payments
as the holder of a messuage; lesser burgesses mentioned

in *Domesday* were probably non-residents who had purchased admission so as to carry on business in the town. Some burgesses possessed their own borough court, originally the hundred court, and had compounded for their rents and dues to the king by paying him a fixed annual sum. Many of these communities survived the Conquest unscathed, while others were laid waste by the invading armies; nowhere was growth permanently stunted. Urban development was already far advanced and the Normans were too astute to ignore a source of rising profits.

Domesday Book mentions neither London, the commercial capital, nor Winchester, the old West Saxon royal seat and the site of the treasury. Fortunately the prompt submission and continued obedience of these two cities makes it safe to assume that William's soldiers wrought very little damage there, except outside the capital itself around Westminster Abbey on Christmas Day 1066. Nature was far more destructive, for six hundred wooden houses collapsed in London during a gale in 1091 and at the beginning of Stephen's reign most of the city, including St Paul's, was destroyed by fire; the London of the early Middle Ages, with its many stone and tiled houses, arose after this catastrophe.

Several provincial centres of resistance did not escape so lightly. *Domesday* gives many examples of towns where the number of houses assessed for geld in 1086 was less than half the number which had been so twenty years earlier; in Oxford it had sunk from 721 to 243 although the king had nearly doubled the farm or fixed sum which was paid to his sheriff. York, the second city in the land, Chester and the other objects of William's wrath in 1069–70 fared no better than the surrounding countryside. The Normans' nation-wide measures to tighten their military grip entailed yet more suffering: in Gloucester 16 houses were destroyed to make way for the new castle, in Cambridge 27, in Lincoln 166. If each house contained a family of five, the total number of evictions ran into thousands.

Those who were expelled from the new forest land were sacrificed to the king's sport, those whose town dwellings disappeared were victims of military necessity. Empty tenements deprived the king of revenue and efforts to maintain the profits of King Edward's time, by forcing the remaining burgesses to pay larger sums, ended in still wider impoverishment. This was partly counterbalanced by the introduction of burgesses from the Continent; at Shrewsbury settlement was encouraged by exempting Frenchmen from the geld and at Norwich so many strangers were brought over under the ægis of the Breton earl, Ralph de Gael, that they were considered to form a new borough.

Municipal independence sprang from later prosperity, not from the Conquest itself. At the end of the eleventh century the boroughs still formed part of the shire organization, their officers being the king's men and their courts enjoying only petty jurisdiction. The towns' vital task of escaping from the sheriff and arranging to pay their own farm to the king was slow in fulfilment. Large sums were soon offered for royal charters which granted this privilege but it was only under Richard Cœur de Lion, the needy crusader, that spectacular strides were made. Meanwhile the formation of all the local traders into a single guild was furthering the cause of self-government; primarily an association to regulate commerce, with many charitable functions, the merchant guild drew strength from its own officials and from the fees which gave it an independent income. A later development was the rise of craft guilds, which limited the number of practitioners and enforced standards and prices, although a few industries, headed by the weavers, had taken this step by Henry I's time. The capital, with its folkmoot presided over by the sheriff, and its hustings court, under the aldermen, was naturally ahead of its rivals and was divided into wards for local administration by the early twelfth century. Even London, however, was riddled with the private 'sokes' or jurisdictions of great men, which the Conqueror confirmed in his charter, and the first mayor Henry fitz Ailwin is not known to have held office until 1191.

There is no need to deal separately with trade or manufacture. Since these activities together account for the very existence of most towns, their growth was both a cause and a consequence of urban development. The Conquest did not sever ties with Scandinavia, which continued to send gerfalcons and timber to England in return for corn; under Henry I, Danes might travel to any English fair and both Danes and Norwegians were allowed to spend a year in London, whereas other aliens stayed for only forty days. Merchants from Rouen still supplied wine and porpoises, but there was no flood of new luxuries, for which England had to wait until the Crusades. If the nature of imports was unchanged, the demands of the new aristocracy did not abate. The wine trade in particular must have flourished, for the duchy at that time could draw on its own vineyards to supplement imports from farther south; the Normans even attempted with limited success to cultivate vines in England. The concern of king and barons, the influx of foreign settlers and the more regular contacts with Europe are all likely to have inflated the volume of trade once the towns had recovered from the severities which attended the Conquest.

*

Moneylending, a concomitant of trade, flourished in Angevin times as an indirect result of the Conquest. Churchmen condemned this profession, while providing many good clients, and it was accordingly confined to the

Jews, a hunted race which was protected only by the whim of the ruler. Edward's kingdom had known no Jews, save perhaps the occasional visiting merchant, and the Jewish community established in London before the end of the eleventh century was a branch of the one at Rouen. The fiercely orthodox Normans had no love for Jews, many of whom were butchered at Rouen in 1096 by a band of departing crusaders, but such diligent and completely dependent men had their value for a business-like king. William of Malmesbury says that the Conqueror brought them over and the newcomers found room in London after the royal residence in the city had been abandoned. In part of an area called the king's soke and now known as Old Jewry, they formed the nucleus of a not entirely exclusive community.

The Jews were never free from popular hatred; under Rufus they were sometimes pursued like dogs by the London mob and under Stephen there was a massacre at Norwich. This did not prevent the spread of Jewish communities to several provincial towns, notably in the east of England, by 1159. In Norman times their activities are obscure and were relatively unimportant, and the prominence which they reached under Henry II lasted for a bare hundred years. Anti-Semitism hardened during the thirteenth century, as the Church marshalled her forces, and in 1218 the English Jews were ordered to wear a distinguishing mark, which suggests that inter-marriage had made them hard to recognize; in 1290 Edward I decreed their expulsion and they did not return to the realm until Cromwell's day. The arrival of this race under the Conqueror was thus only a prelude to the first sorry chapter of its stay in England.

*

The Norman Conquest brought widespread destruction of life and property. Estates were seized from native landowners, not because they were Englishmen but because they were rebels, and the new knightly class proceeded to raise higher the barriers which separated the people from its rulers. They bore hard on the wealthier peasants, ultimately eroding the legal status and so perhaps the economic prosperity of the peasantry as a whole. Thousands of wretches were evicted to create enormous game preserves, where savage laws burdened those who remained, and thousands more were uprooted in the towns. Everywhere appears the conquerors' determination never to relax their military grip and to wring the maximum profit, in cash or in kind, from their new land.

In fairness to the Normans it must again be stressed that they did not destroy an idyllic society in which sturdy churls and their emancipated womenfolk enjoyed the freedom of the country. The decline of the peasantry can be traced back for centuries, although the extension of lordship had been so piecemeal that there was no uniformity by 1066. The conquerors accelerated this trend, not by altering the Englishman's daily routine but by simplifying his rights and defining more clearly his duties, so as to create a more tidy and authoritarian society. In some respects the practical Normans turned out to be benefactors, by ending slavery and bringing new blood into the towns whose growth they fostered. Immediate misery must be weighed against long-term gains.

The unhappiness which followed the physical establishment of the Norman supremacy can be blamed on the selfishness of king and barons. It is hard to disentangle William's share in all this from that of his followers. For the deliberate destruction and the evictions the king himself was chiefly responsible, while the more gradual changes in town and country were wrought by his race. The administrative work of the same men, being more constructive, places the Normans and especially their leader in a more favourable light.

CHAPTER EIGHT

The Conquest and English Government

THE Normans, who brought no new new ideas on estate management to change the peasant's daily life, likewise left untouched the structure of Old English government. Their success as conquerors sprang from exploiting the achievement of other races, and there was no dogma to dictate that native institutions should be swept away. These were accepted, their powers simply being modified or expanded, in the light of the conquerors' own experience and in the interests of efficiency.

*

The backbone of the kingdom lay in the courts of the shire and the hundred. Here all manner of business was carried out—fiscal, judicial and police work. Some of these affairs arose locally, others at the behest of the king, and in either case the man chiefly concerned in their settlement was the sheriff, who was a royal agent. William the Conqueror, realizing the value of this system, exploited it for himself.

The Conquest, far from destroying the local courts, gave them fresh vigour by elevating the sheriff. Although these courts had no parallel in Normandy, the dukes were familiar with a similar agent in the *vicomte*, so that when Latin replaced English in official documents the sheriff was naturally described as a *vicecomes*. Even in Edward's day the sheriff had prospered because his grander colleagues, the earl and bishop, had spared less time for routine business; he flourished still more under William, since only a few strategic and smaller earldoms were allowed to survive and the bishops ceased to sit in the shire courts. The creation of separate church courts robbed the sheriff of influence in ecclesiastical pleas only to enhance his principal, secular role. The *vicomtes'* common duty of keeping the ruler's castles passed to many of the Anglo-Norman sheriffs, who combined it with the older function of commanding the shire levies. The collection of newly imposed feudal dues and the punishment of forest offences also magnified their authority, but above all they were raised up by the sheer energy of the new king. Royal writs bore a swelling flood of specific commands and often laid down rules for the recipient's own behaviour; sometimes he was directed to remit a case to the king's court, sometimes to assume its powers himself. Heavy as were the sheriff's military or fiscal duties, it is almost impossible to exaggerate his importance as the judicial head of the shire. Visits by royal judges to the provinces, which may have taken place under the Conqueror, became momentous only in the twelfth century. For the present men normally looked for justice to the local sheriff.

Often men looked in vain. Handsome profits came from the extension of the practice of farming the shire, a privilege for which sheriffs paid a special premium to the Crown. This procedure inspired private landlords to farm out portions of their own estates, and the oppression of baronial officials can hardly have been worse than the systematic plundering of some of the sheriffs themselves.

These men, whose judicial power made them dangerous enemies, were known to increase the farm without royal permission, extorting whatever they could; they and their agents have been accused of trespassing on the king's rights as well as seizing private and even ecclesiastical property. The most notorious sheriff, Picot of Cambridgeshire, imposed new carrying-services on the men of Cambridge, seized their common pasture, pulled down their homes to make way for three mills, and insisted that they should lend him their plough-teams nine times a year, instead of three times. More unhappily for his reputation, Picot also took lands from the abbey of St Æthelthryth at Ely and met protests by sneering that he knew nothing of the saint. 'Do you hear this, O Lord, and stay silent?' demanded one of the inmates as he rained abuse on Picot, comparing him to a ravenous lion, a filthy hog and many another beast whose belly was so insatiable that he would share nothing, even with God or the angels.

Some of the gains of Picot and his colleagues were so scandalous that they had to be disgorged. Others were certainly exaggerated, since no one loves a tax-collector and no monk could describe an injury to his house with dispassion. None the less, it is plain that in general the king prized loyalty and efficiency above humanity. Apart from the Crown itself, the shrievalty is England's oldest surviving secular office; never have its perquisites been so great as they were at the close of the eleventh century.

Another reason for the rise of the first Norman sheriffs was their personal standing with the king. The Conqueror's changing attitude to his English subjects is shown in their disappearance from local offices, which inevitably accompanied their deprivation as landowners. Although Kent, Berkshire and Middlesex were given Norman sheriffs at the start of the reign, out of eight of the Confessor's sheriffs who held office under Harold, six were retained for a time by William. The number was doubtless higher, for the names of many sheriffs are unknown, and it was not until 1071 that local administration passed entirely into foreign hands. The new men were barons, nearly all of them tenants-in-chief; most held office for life and some were succeeded by their sons. Since the kingdom's security depended on the loyalty of individuals, these vital appointments naturally went to those whom William could trust, as did the greatest estates. The higher the sheriff's prestige, the more effectively could he carry out the king's commands. Here, as in the imposition of feudalism, resistance to the Conquest strengthened the Crown. In the next generation, when the Normans felt safer, the power of the baronial sheriffs became a menace, which Henry I tried to meet by raising his own men 'from the dust'.

*

Norman adaptability is also shown in the survival of the Old English financial system. The king had lived on his own estates, on the customary dues paid by shires and boroughs, on the profits of justice and on his exclusive right to strike coins; recently, he had also come to rely upon regular levies of the geld. England and Normandy were both relatively precocious in their financial development and the traditional sources of revenue were similar to those which the duke already enjoyed at home, although the details of early Norman finance are more obscure. The introduction of feudal tenure added feudal incidents, hitherto unknown in England, to the king's resources, and William's strengthened authority after 1066 allowed him to exact these payments more regularly in Normandy.

Unhappily for the English, their conqueror's triumph made him so many enemies that his financial needs far outstripped those of King Edward. Royal estates were therefore farmed to the highest bidder and much heavier dues were demanded, even from places which had been pillaged by the invaders. The Normans ushered in a period of grinding taxation, designed to further Continental interests which were in no way connected with the security of Englishmen. This needs to be stressed, since it is common to enthuse over administrative genius without bothering to consider the uses to which it was put.

William naturally saw the value of the most advanced of all England's fiscal devices, the geld, which was assessed through the shire and the hundred upon the village. The Conqueror, who does not seem to have introduced this unique land-tax in Normandy, levied at least four gelds as king of England. Estates might secure special treatment and reductions were granted to several villages which had suffered from the march of his armies, but the profits remained enormous; in 1083 what appears to have been the usual payment of 2s. a hide was trebled to the crippling rate of 6s. The geld, falling only on land and weakened by exemptions, lost its value during the twelfth century and was last taken under its old name in 1162; by then attempts to cast a wider net by a levy on all movable wealth were presaging more modern taxation.

The chief agents in raising the royal revenue were the sheriffs, so that their prestige and William's hold over them were the key to his success. More specialized officials, to deal with debts and financial disputes, appear only under his younger son, Henry I. The treasure continued to be kept at Winchester, where in the Confessor's time it had already been the practice to test the purity of silver coins by blanching them in fire, as was later done in the Exchequer. The treasury itself, however, may still have been little more than a storehouse, containing the crown itself and other valuables, as well as loose money, and accounting was still done in the primitive fashion with split sticks, or tallies, on which the sums were recorded by notches.

William placed the central control of all his revenues under a Norman master-chamberlain, although the kingdom had its own officer after 1087 until it was reunited with the duchy following the battle of Tinchebrai. In England at an unknown date under the Conqueror or his sons the vital separation took place, when the treasure passed into the hands of two chamberlains known as chamberlains of the treasury; under Henry I they acquired a new head, the treasurer, who became one of the principal officers of state and an equal of the master-chamberlain. The latter continued in charge of the royal bedchamber but ceased to have anything to do with the treasury, which developed into a purely financial department. The Normans were such gifted financial administrators that they probably hastened this process. The Latin word *scaccarium* first occurs in 1110 and in the course of the century it gave its name to the Exchequer which evolved out of the treasury. *Scaccarium*, literally a chessboard, in this case described the chequered cloth which covered the table, on which counters were placed; calculation was done by the abacus, a frame with bells strung on wires, which had French or Lotharingian origins. It is likely that these practices of the Exchequer, and perhaps also its rolls of accounts, were imported by the Normans.

William thus retained and exploited the financial system which he found in England, adding the feudal dues to which he was accustomed in Normandy. His own power and that of his chief agents enforced prompt payment, and Norman efficiency in collection and record keeping laid the foundations of the medieval English financial system. For William himself an enviable revenue was assured, which allowed him to keep a magnificent court as well as to meet the unflagging assaults of his enemies. His total income as head of the Anglo-Norman state is unknown and any figures would be meaningless in modern terms, but by contemporary standards he was extremely wealthy. When the fruits of avarice, which the *Anglo-Saxon Chronicle* saw as his besetting sin, were inspected at Winchester by Rufus, 'it was impossible for anyone to describe how much was accumulated there in gold and silver and vessels and costly robes and jewels, and many other precious things that are hard to recount'. His nephew, Stephen of Blois, said that William's great bounty was nothing beside that of the emperor at Constantinople; he could not have made such a slighting comparison between the king of England and any other Christian ruler of his day.

The feudal incidents imported by the Normans brought profit to the Crown long after military service had become obsolete. A new court was set up under Henry VIII to exploit them more systematically than before and they expired only after the Civil Wars, together with the old idea that the king should 'live of his own'. In 1660 the Restoration was accompanied by an act which admitted that 'the Courts of Wards and Liveries and tenures by knight-service either of the king or others . . . and the consequents upon the same have been much more burthensome, grievous and prejudicial to the kingdom than they have been beneficial to the king'. Charles II then abandoned his position as feudal overlord, a hundred and thirty years before revolution forced the French monarchy to take the same step; tenures by knight-service disappeared and Parliament granted the king a hereditary revenue from the Excise in place of the feudal revenues which, in both senses, had been much abused.

*

The Norman kings issued no code of laws to rival the dooms of their Anglo-Saxon predecessors. Their chief innovations were forest law, which has already been described, and separate ecclesiastical courts, which will be examined in connection with the Church. The only other new regulation of any consequence was the *murdrum* or murder fine, imposed early in the reign for the protection of the conquering race; if any Frenchman who had arrived since 1066 were to be killed, his lord must pay forty-six marks and the hundred in which the man was slain must provide whatever the lord could not pay. This fine, which provides one more example of native hostility to the Normans, contrasts with the general policy of the new king. William's claim to be Edward's heir was strengthened by support for the pre-Conquest laws, which were still the laws of England at the time of *Domesday*.

A new legal procedure appeared in trial by battle, and William incongruously won a place among the opponents of capital punishment by substituting for the death penalty the more effective deterrent of mutilation. Trial by battle, which was common in other countries, was not intended to give foreigners an unfair advantage, since an Englishman accused by a Frenchman of murder or theft could still clear himself by compurgation, the identical testimony of a sufficient number of witnesses, or by a more familiar form of ordeal. The duel, which might have to be fought by witnesses as well as by principals, resembled the traditional ordeals in that it presupposed that God would give a sign; it had the same drawbacks, being open to corruption and leading to many decisions, usually acquittals, that were patently absurd. Moreover, the battle was not a method open to women, children or the aged, and it soon furnished a perilous living for professional champions. Its introduction therefore can hardly be called a step forward and in 1215 it was condemned by the pope, along with all other ordeals. Trial by battle and compurgation had become rare by the end of the Middle Ages, although neither was abolished until the early nineteenth century.

If William and his sons did not shine as legislators, they were forced to seek new ways of administering the law. Most cases could hardly be dealt with more conveniently than in the existing courts of the shire and the hundred. These were accordingly strengthened, by the new personal authority of the sheriff, and in one respect they were streamlined, by the withdrawal of ecclesiastical pleas. The wholesale change in ownership of land, however, gave rise to a series of disputes, often between magnates or affecting the Church, which called for a special assertion of royal power. The king's court itself was the obvious place for settling such questions, but William lacked the time and the necessary local knowledge. A number of great trials were therefore instituted by royal writ, presided over by a judge who was the king's deputy and attended by William's tenants-in-chief who came, as to the *curia regis*, out of feudal duty to their lord. Geoffrey, bishop of Coutances, was the man most commonly named to hear these pleas, which included a series over Picot's encroachments at Ely and a famous one in the 1070s at Pinnenden Heath in Kent, when Lanfranc secured judgement against Odo of Bayeux for occupying lands of the see of Canterbury. The interesting feature of these trials is that, although specially ordered by the king, they were held in full meetings of the shire courts where local men, including Englishmen, could pronounce on the customs of the country. Thus feudal obligations and native traditions were exploited to bring men of all races together so that they could assist the king in his primary task of dispensing justice.

These disputes over land were so common that there was not always time for the close examination of numerous witnesses. A quicker method of reaching the truth therefore arose in the delivery of a sworn verdict by a group of men appointed by the court. There is no

definite instance of this practice in pre-Conquest Normandy, although the principle of the collective verdict
was known to the Franks as well in the most thickly
colonized parts of the Danelaw. If the origins of the jury
are still in dispute, the credit for its widespread use in
England must go to the Conqueror. *Domesday Book*
itself was based on the verdicts of juries all over the
kingdom and the regular use of these bodies was William's
most lasting achievement in the history of English law.

*

England's strength lay in those institutions which
gave the king a unique means of asserting his will
throughout the country; these were appreciated and
preserved. Her weakness under Edward had been lack
of firm direction from the centre, caused not so much by
imperfect machinery as by the dominance of mighty
families over a feeble king. The Conquest corrected this
balance by destroying the three great earldoms, and the
flickering interest of Edward was replaced by the masterful energy of William. Constant watchfulness over the
loyalty of his magnates was essential for any medieval
king who was not to become a pawn, and much of the
new effectiveness of the government sprang from the
personal vigour of the rulers. Apart from the short-lived
Edmund Ironside, the eleventh-century heirs of Alfred
were listless and erratic; they could hardly have been
more different from the Normans and early Angevins.
Stephen alone, the most amiable of William's line,
allowed his grip to relax and, in doing so, taught men that
it was better to be governed harshly than not to be
governed at all.

All William's measures for collecting revenue and
maintaining order blended English with Norman traditions. There none the less followed certain changes in the
circle of royal servants out of which the great offices of

state were to arise. The Norman dukes modelled their household on that of the kings of France, who had a steward, a butler, a chamberlain, a constable and a chancellor. The first four were laymen, in charge respectively of the king's food, his drink, his bedchamber and his sport. Edward's court was presumably organized on similar lines, which are hidden by the vague Anglo-Danish title *staller* or placeman, borne by a variety of his attendants.

Time multiplied the duties of the chief Anglo-Norman household officers, whose history throws some light on the careful and practical nature of the new kings. The steward was responsible not only for the dining-hall but for the pantry, larder and kitchen, the butler not only for the wine-cellar but the chapel, the chamberlain for the laundry and the baths as well as for the beds, and the constable for the stables, kennels and mews. Apart from the escape of the treasury from the control of the chamberlains, the degree to which these posts were subdivided or became honorary is not of great constitutional importance. William stressed the personal character of his rule by retaining one principal holder of each of these offices for the whole of his empire after the Conquest, and no earl was allowed any of these dignities, save the trusted steward William fitz Osbern. The earliest detailed information on household organization comes from the *Constitutio Domus Regis*, drawn up on Henry I's death in 1135 for the guidance of his successor and covering every servant, from the steward to the scullions. The *Constitutio* gives each officer his allowance of food and drink, the highest enjoying clear wine and fresh simnel cakes, the humblest receiving ordinary loaves and apparently only beer. This scale was probably fixed under the Conqueror's business-like youngest son, Henry I.

The most highly paid personage in the *Constitutio*, with 5s. a day, was the fifth great officer of state, the chancellor.

This title, also known in France, had fleetingly appeared
in Normandy; the dukes, however, had possessed no
writing office to compare with that of the English kings,
who for their part had never given the chief of their
clerks a formal dignity. William's chaplain, Herfast,
mentioned as chancellor in 1069, thus became the first
chancellor of England, although the organized body of
clerks of which he was the head was undoubtedly of
native origin.

It was not until after 1070, under Herfast's successor
Osmund, that English gave way to Latin in the writs
and charters emanating from William's chancery. An
earlier change would no doubt have been impossible,
since the Conqueror needed the services of Edward's
clerks, even if a new official language had been envisaged
before the northern rebellion. At the same time William
started to widen the scope of the royal writs, until what
had once been a mere title-deed became a regular means
of conveying all manner of commands; this was a perfectly
logical step, furnishing yet another instance of his ability
to exploit the inventions of others. The chancellor was
also given custody of the Great Seal, which had been
used for authenticating Old English writs, and his
importance naturally increased as the scope of his office
was widened. He remained, however, a royal chaplain,
whose secretarial services ceased when they were rewarded
with a bishopric, and who had no special judicial duties;
the full glory of the medieval office is presaged only in
1133, when the current chancellor retained the Great
Seal on being elevated to the see of Durham.

The history of the Great Seal shows that Europe, as
well as England, stood to gain from the closer ties which
followed the Conquest. Single-faced wax seals were
known abroad, where they were placed directly on the
parchment, and Rome had for long used a pendant
leaden seal or *bulla*, which hung from a string and which

duly gave its name to papal documents. Edward the Confessor's seal, the first of the great royal series to survive, is unique in being a two-faced hanging seal of wax, attached to the writ itself by a thin strip of parchment. The king is shown on both sides seated in majesty (Plate Va), a posture adopted by the German Emperor Otto III and his successors, but since the imperial seals are single-faced it is doubtful whether they were copied by the English. Edward's seal was apparently a native invention, possibly derived from one used by Cnut as the head of a double monarchy. William, who may not have had a seal of his own before 1066, made use of Edward's device, although on the obverse he aptly substituted an equestrian figure for that of a seated king. The Old English method of sealing, used for letters patent throughout the Middle Ages, reached France during the reign of the Conqueror's younger rival, Philip I, and spread to Germany during the following century.

It was a matter of prudence for William, as for any other ruler, to take his greatest decisions with the advice of his magnates. The king wore his crown at Christmas, Easter and Whitsun, when he would be unusually well attended for the feasts of the Church, and the wide formal consultations which then took place kept him in contact with the baronage whose loyalty was vital. Some of the men whom he consulted on these occasions also belonged to his more intimate circle, because of their household appointments, their kinship or their personal value as friends and advisers. The larger assemblies constituted meetings of the great council, the smaller body may be termed the king's court, the *curia regis*, but neither was a formal body with defined functions; the great council might meet more than thrice a year and the status of many gatherings is indeterminate. The *curia* consisted simply of those advisers who usually followed the king; it assisted in everyday business and sat in judgement under William or his deputy on those cases which could not be dealt with elsewhere. There is little to distinguish the Anglo-Norman councillors from the Old English *witan*, save that William's crown-wearings were certainly regular, whereas those of Edward may not have been. The Confessor had been less alive to the possibilities of sounding opinion and of influencing it by splendid ceremonies; his need had not been so urgent.

It is commonly asked whether the germs of parliamentary government lay either in the institutions which the Normans found in England or in those which they introduced. The germs did not exist. The Normans were arrogant and oppressive, they created racial and social barriers, but they could not destroy what had not yet occurred to anyone. The notion of representative government presupposes a conflict of interest between ruler and ruled, which forces the people to control the government through certain laws and institutions. Nowadays such a conflict is assumed and the remedy is sought in legislation. Anglo-Saxon England knew of no such conflict, only of a benevolent, immemorial law which every official existed to enforce; the state's function was one of preservation. It did not matter whether the king acted alone, with tens or with hundreds of advisers, so long as his actions conformed to the law; the purpose of summoning many men was to decide the truth in a difficult case and reach a consensus as to what was or was not lawful. No one had a constitutional right to be the king's counsellor and no one could change the law by claiming to represent a majority or any special group; every man consulted among the *witan* was a representative of the race, whose well-being he must ensure by upholding the law. Democracy, the right of the majority to enforce its will, is a very different belief and one that is of later medieval growth, after the differing interests of Crown, baronage and commons had become plain. In Old English society men were not concerned with numbers nor with forms of government, they simply believed that every one had a duty to co-operate. The theory of partnership, like any other, was often submerged in practice, but it was general and persistent. William, who claimed to rule in the old tradition, had no wish to eradicate this deeply held belief; it survived the Conquest and it survives today.

*

William's skilful use of English institutions needs no further emphasis, yet the reign closed with a final display of his success. At Christmas 1085, with a Danish invasion again hanging over him, he wore his crown at Gloucester; there, after discussion in the great council, it was decided to conduct a nation-wide survey. The immediate purpose was to discover the taxable capacity of the kingdom, a second aim was to record how much land was owned by the king and by the individual barons on whose knight-service William depended, a third was to sort out problems of ownership and assess the effect of the Conquest by recording conditions not only in 1086 and when the land was given to its current lord but as they had been in Edward's day. William had specific reasons, fiscal, feudal and judicial, for ordering this inquiry, which at the time was commonly termed a *descriptio*, an assessment for taxation. The survey none the less served so many purposes that it cannot be neatly labelled; the Anglo-Saxon chronicler records that William himself was genuinely curious to learn more about the land which he had conquered, 'how it was occupied and with what sort of people'. The inquiry brought fresh terrors to his overburdened subjects and it is hard to imagine any other king who would have carried it through, but William remained alert and a man of iron until the end of his life.

Royal commissioners were appointed to gather information and the country was divided into seven circuits, only the few northernmost shires being ignored. Jurors from the hundreds were used to supply at least part of the details, and the reports of the first investigators were checked by the dispatch of second groups. The commissioners were to ascertain the name of each manor, of its holder on Edward's death and of its holder at the time of their visit, whether he was a tenant-in-chief or a subtenant; they were then to record the number of fiscal hides or carucates on which geld was normally assessed, the number of plough-teams, the number and degree of the inhabitants, and the amount of woodland, meadows, mills and fishponds. They were also asked to estimate the value of the manor, the sum for which it could have been leased in 1066, and to give its existing value, as well as to state the holding of each freeman and sokeman at these dates. A final instruction required their information to refer to three occasions—Edward's time, the date of William's bestowal of the manor on its new lord, and 1086—and that they should state whether they believed that the manor could be made to yield a higher profit.

The plan was too ambitious to be fully realized; it was not always possible to discover the value of a manor when it passed to its new lord, and many jurors may have shrunk from estimating how the yield could be increased. None the less, the returns dealt regularly with conditions in 1066 and 1086, and before the end of the latter year they had been shown to the king. The rolls were then stored in the treasury at Winchester but probably within a couple of years the material was already being rearranged in two volumes, which survive today and are known as *Domesday Book*. The second of these volumes, *Little Domesday*, is devoted to one of the commissioners' circuits, Norfolk, Suffolk and Essex, while the first volume, *Great Domesday*, covers the remaining shires. Among other texts is a survey known as the *Exon Domesday*, for Wiltshire, Dorset, Somerset, Devon and

Cornwall, all of which counties are included in the *Great Domesday*. *Exon Domesday* and *Little Domesday* are less orderly and more detailed than *Great Domesday*, which suggests that they are drafts; the first of these was later incorporated in the larger volume, the *Little Domesday* for some reason was left untouched. In all three volumes the details are set out geographically under the shires, but within each shire a feudal arrangement is followed whereby the lands of the king are followed by those of his tenants-in-chief; the amount of knight-service is not given, but this pattern records clearly where the strength of the barons lay (Plate VIII).

No book can be written on any aspect of Anglo-Norman history without constant reference to *Domesday*. It has been hailed as an administrative achievement without parallel in the Middle Ages, a voluminous literature has been devoted to the survey itself, and full translations of the entries for each shire are now being published as part of the *Victoria County History*. William's unique work was valued from the outset: under Rufus it was consulted, under Henry I it was quoted to settle disputes over land, and as the Middle Ages wore on the appeals to its authority multiplied. Later praises cannot rival the compliment paid by the men of the twelfth century, who gave the survey its name because the sentences based on it were final, like those of the last great day.

CHAPTER NINE

The Reformed Church

THE Church, of all England's medieval institutions, is the one which it is most dangerous to treat in isolation. Throughout the tribal migrations of the Dark Ages the Church had kept alive the common faith and common language of the Roman world, which she propagated so as to create new ties among the descendants of the barbarians in the west. If western Europe in the Middle Ages did not know the political unity which part of it had enjoyed under the Romans, neither did it know the sharp racial divisions of more recent centuries; states were not national but dynastic, theories and forms of government and society transcended their boundaries, and all men belonged to a single Church. When the Roman emperors' increasingly hellenized heirs were at last excommunicated in 1054, the resulting schism merely encouraged the churches of both east and west to stress their own claims: 'orthodox' was the description favoured at Constantinople, 'catholic' or 'universal' at Rome. There was never a doubt, before or after the Conquest, that English churchmen were members of a larger body, of which the pope was the head. No one tried, as did the Tudors, to forge a church with district observances and owning no outside allegiance. Although it is permissible to speak of the 'English Church', since the term *Ecclesia Anglicana* was used as early as the twelfth century, this implied none of the nationalism later associated with Anglicanism; during the Middle Ages the Church in England never became the Church of England.

This recognition of unity did not mean that the customs and organization of the Church were everywhere the same, still less that lay and ecclesiastical powers were always in agreement. The material and spiritual state of Christianity varied widely in the early eleventh century, largely because the papacy had sunk to one of its recurrent depths, in which the tiara became a trophy for the baronial house of Tusculum. In the year 1000 religion drew its main strength from the monasteries, and strenuous efforts to regulate clerical life, in particular to abolish simony or the sale of offices and to enforce continence, had started only as the work of individual princes and church-men; it was not until after the consecration of Leo IX in 1049 that the papacy became the spearhead of this reform movement. Since the quality of religious life depended so closely on the ruler, the English Church, like its counterpart in Normandy, naturally had peculiarities of its own.

If there was room for adjustment within the Church as a whole, Rome's espousal of reform brought a new danger from friction between Church and State. Leo and his successors made up for the wasted years by insisting that they alone should have the decisive word in enforcing ecclesiastical discipline. The pope was no longer content to be respected as head of the Church, to confirm appointments and to act as final arbiter; he developed an interest in details of ecclesiastical govern-ment, which had once been left in local hands. Recourse was had to the writings of the early Fathers, to the canons or commandments of church councils and to the decrees of previous popes in an attempt to justify these lofty claims, and the first of many new compilations of old laws appeared in 1050. Throughout the next century evidence was accumulated, much of it forged, until one universally accepted collection was published, the *Decretum* of Gratian; this was to remain until 1917 as the basis of the *Corpus Juris Canonici*, the canon law of the Roman Church.

Masterful rulers, even when they sympathized with the reforming spirit behind the pope's claims, naturally resented this stand and fought a long rearguard action, with some success. In Germany the Hohenstaufen emperors embarked on a contest with the papacy which, with many vicissitudes, was to last for two hundred years and to end in the ruin of their house. In England the challenge was at first less acute and under Edward the Confessor, who with his simple piety would not have recognized it as such, it was not felt at all. The Conqueror's reign, however, coincided with those of the reforming Pope Alexander II (1061–73) and his more zealous and domineering successor Hildebrand, the Tuscan monk who as Pope Gregory VII (1073–86) carried the trend to its logical conclusion by proclaiming himself God's sole mouthpiece on earth. It was perfectly reasonable for a king to resist these novel ideas while still declaring himself to be a good son of the Church, and the pope never achieved an authority that was uniform throughout western Christendom. Ideally, from the new Roman point of view, the only boundaries which mattered should be those of the Church's own provinces, but in practice the important frontiers remained those of the secular power. The popes, by corresponding with William and other individual rulers, always tacitly acknowledged these limits.

*

The Conquest was bound to effect the English Church, by tying the kingdom to Europe at the very moment

when the papacy, reinvigorated, was claiming unheard-of
powers and building up a body of law in support. The
effects were all the greater because the thoroughgoing
subjection of England involved a purge of the hierarchy
comparable to the fall of the aristocracy. They were
greater still because of the stature of the men chiefly
concerned. Hildebrand was one of the formative influences on the medieval world and all that need be noted
here are the fiery spirit and rock-like determination of the
pope who, at the height of his power, kept the Emperor,
Henry IV, waiting for three days in the snow at Canossa
and who died in exile without in any way abating his
claims. William for his part was an unusually devout
ruler who used his immense authority to improve ecclesiastical discipline in all his dominions. His age saw
nothing incongruous in lauding the piety of a red-handed
conqueror; an elaborate code, drawn up in Normandy
under a papal legate, imposed a year's penance for every
man slain at Hastings and enjoined that the severity
should vary with the status and motives of the killer, as
well as laying down further penances for woundings and
for other deaths before or after the battle. The *Anglo-
Saxon Chronicle* itself succinctly notes William's dual
character: 'He was gentle to the good men who loved
God, and stern beyond all measure to those people who
resisted his will.' The king, deeply concerned as he was
with all that touched the Church, had many preoccupa-
tions; if he laid down the general lines of ecclesiastical
policy the details were left to others, and it is impossible
to disentangle his part in specific decisions from that of
the archbishop whose views matched his own.

In April 1070 three papal legates held a council at
Winchester, during which Stigand was deprived of his
sees. Since one of the reasons for Rome's support of
William in 1066 had been a desire to rid Canterbury
of a man who had been excommunicated by five popes,

this final step was inevitable. William, like Harold, had taken care not to be crowned by Stigand, who had always been viewed askance by the English hierarchy. When the saintly Wulfstan of Worcester soon afterwards made to Lanfranc the due profession of obedience which he had withheld from Stigand, he recalled that he himself had been consecrated by Ealdred of York and that some of his fellow bishops had even resorted to Rome or to France. The tenure of the schismatic archbishop had been prolonged only by the king's other cares and by the delayed arrival of the legates; despite Stigand's part in the English resistance after Hastings he may have been sufficiently flexible for his deposition to be unnecessary on grounds of security, but the insular background and worldly character of this pluralist made it impossible for him to share in the reorganization which was envisaged. King and pope were at one in desiring his removal and also in their choice of a successor.

Long before the Conquest, Lanfranc had abandoned his hope of solitude at Bec, to win fame as a lawyer, a teacher and the antagonist of Berengar of Tours, whose denial of transubstantiation had been condemned as heresy. After opposing William's marriage Lanfranc had ended by pleading for the duke at Rome and in 1063 he was translated to the abbey of Saint-Etienne at Caen, one of the two foundations imposed on the ducal couple as a penance. Lanfranc's clear mind and practical nature fitted him for high office, particularly in William's service. While he and his sovereign saw the monastic life as the mainstay of Christianity, his early experiences had given him an outlook broader than that of men who had lived from childhood in the cloister; he respected the primacy of Rome but, having left Italy while the popes were still sunk in their abyss, he naturally preferred to identify the welfare of the Church with the strong rule of a devout king. Worldly-wise but not worldly, Lanfranc

XVII (a) Beak-head
ornament on the west
doorway of Bishops Teignton
Church, Devon, *c.* 1160
(the late *F. H. Crossley*)
(b) Detail from the south
doorway of Malmesbury
Abbey, Wilts, *c.* 1160
(*B. T. Batsford Ltd.*)

XVIII   Stone panel in Chichester Cathedral—Martha and Mary
greeting Christ, *c.* 1140 *(the Warburg Institute,*
photo by Otto Fein)

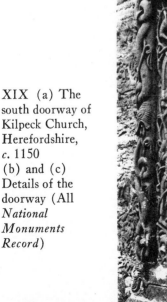

XIX (a) The
south doorway of
Kilpeck Church,
Herefordshire,
c. 1150
(b) and (c)
Details of the
doorway (All
*National
Monuments
Record*)

XX   The west front of Castle Acre Priory, Norfolk, mid-twelfth
century *(National Monuments Record)*

XXI   The Abbey gatehouse at Bury St. Edmunds, Suffolk, *c.* 1130 *(National Monuments Record)*

XXII   The chapter-house at Worcester Cathedral, first half of twelfth century *(A. F. Kersting)*

XXIII   The keep at Rochester Castle, Kent, first half of
twelfth century *(A. F. Kersting)*

XXIV (a) Somersaulting figure from the *Bury St. Edmunds Psalter,* second quarter eleventh century (Reg. Lat. 12 f. 90b, *Vatican Library* from *Late Saxon and Viking Art* by T. D. Kendrick, Methuen, 1949)

(b) Gymnastic initial from the *Arundel Psalter c.* 1060 (Arundel MS 60 f. 13, *British Museum*)

shunned public life: he would take no post at Rome, he moved to Caen only at the duke's bidding, and in 1067 he refused the see of Rouen. Only at the pope's insistence did this scholar, Italian by birth, Norman by adoption, cross the Channel to be consecrated archbishop of Canterbury on 29 August 1070, at the age of at least fifty-five.

Almost at once Lanfranc asked to be recalled. He pointed out to Alexander II, a former pupil, that when set over Caen, 'I found myself unequal to the task of governing a few monks. Therefore I cannot comprehend by what dispensation of the Almighty I have been promoted at your behest to undertake the supervision of an innumerable multitude.' Fortunately the pope was adamant and Lanfranc stayed to sustain the government of a kingdom, as well as to leave on the organization of the English Church an imprint rivalled by no later archbishop until Cranmer.

The essential first step was to assert the primacy of Canterbury. If the Church in England was to be brought into line with that on the Continent, Lanfranc's writ must run in the diocese of York. William too desired uniformity, with the added reason that an independent see in the disaffected north might be a political danger, but both men were at once defied by Thomas, the Norman monk who had been appointed to succeed the late Archbishop Ealdred shortly before Lanfranc's own arrival. Jealousy between the rival chapters enflamed the quarrel and it was not until April 1072 that a papal legate in council at Winchester gave judgement substantially in Lanfranc's favour. The papacy, naturally reluctant to see ecclesiastical boundaries coincide with those of a kingdom, never confirmed this decision and, although Lanfranc thereafter acted as primate, the dispute was not over. Lanfranc, following William by basing his claim on native tradition, had shown the legate and council some forged papal letters to support his case and the discovery of this in 1125 caused their decision to be reversed. It was once widely held that the archbishop himself concocted the fraud but all that is known of his character makes it virtually certain that he was deceived by his supporters and that he acted in good faith.

Stigand was not the only victim among the English bishops. His deposition from Canterbury and Winchester and that of his brother Æthelmær from Elmham, with the resignation of Leofwine of Lichfield at the same time, left vacant four of the fifteen English sees, to which a fifth was soon added with the removal of Æthelric of Selsey. Æthelmær and Æthelric, against whom the charges are obscure, may have been politically suspect, while Leofwine as a married man was bound to be among the first casualties of reform; a sixth see fell vacant with the outlawry in 1070 of Æthelwine of Durham, the only native bishop who went so far as to rise against the new king. In all six sees Englishmen were replaced by aliens. Timely deaths completed William's task, for in the nine remaining sees, of which York fell vacant on 11 September 1069, the deceased bishop was invariably followed by a man of French background. There was no need for greater urgency, since five of the remaining bishops who had been installed under Edward were foreigners and a sixth, Leofric of Exeter, had been educated on the Continent. Siward of Rochester and Wulfstan of Worcester alone survived from the old native episcopate and they too were to be succeeded by Normans; Siward died in 1075 and Wulfstan alone, who enjoyed William's singular respect, lived on into Rufus's reign.

The removal of bishops was primarily a political matter, determined by William and carried out by papal legates. New appointments were also William's concern and to this there was no opposition during his lifetime, although the papal objections to lay investiture, whereby the king gave the bishop his ring and staff and then received homage, were to lead to a crisis under his sons. Knight-service, already owed in Normandy, was imposed on the English sees in or after 1070, at the same time as quotas were assigned to the lay magnates, and it became more than ever important for bishops to be reliable men. William none the less took care to choose worthy nominees, who would reflect credit on the Church under his care; some were good, most were competent and none, save perhaps Herfast of Thetford, were of scandalous life. Osmund of Salisbury was later canonized, Gundulf of Rochester and the murdered Walcher of Durham would have been equally suitable for this honour, Robert Losinga of Hereford proved an eminent scholar and all of them deserve to be remembered as builders. As early as 1066 William had nominated one of his own chaplains to a Norman bishopric; this was an English practice which continued after the Conquest, so that every clerk who rose to become chancellor, as the head of the royal writing office was now known, in due course became a bishop. Lanfranc was no doubt consulted in all these appointments, but it is in the details of organization that his hand can more clearly be seen.

Individual bishops were presumably responsible for moving a number of cathedrals from remote villages to the cities where they remain today. Leofric had changed his see from Crediton to Exeter as early as 1050 but this trend, like many others which are visible before the Conquest, received its main impetus from the Normans. A church council meeting in London under Lanfranc in 1075 decreed that in future no cathedral should be founded in a rural setting, and the king approved the transfer of those at Lichfield, Selsey and Sherborne to Chester, Chichester and Old Salisbury. The first of these was moved again, to Coventry, in 1086, the year after the bishop of Wells made what proved to be an unpopular and hence a less complete move to Bath. Remigius abandoned Dorchester-on-Thames for Lincoln in 1072–3 and Herfast left Thetford for Elmham in 1078; in the following year the vast diocese of Lincoln was split, giving birth to Ely, and Herfast's successor finally settled at Norwich. The establishment of a seventeenth cathedral in 1133, at Carlisle, completed a pattern which was to be undisturbed until the Reformation.

The organization of many cathedrals was also changed. Whereas in Normandy they were served by clergy who lived in common and according to rule, with their own dignitaries, in England most of the great churches were attended by priests whose duties are now obscure and perhaps in some cases were never clearly defined. There are signs that the more energetic English bishops were trying to impose communal discipline on these bodies, but Norman eyes saw no virtue in the resulting variety and the old organizations were swept away by the founders of new chapters. Four cathedrals differed from the rest in England and had no parallel in Europe at that time, in that they were served by monks. These four—Canterbury, Winchester, Worcester and Sherborne—naturally attracted the king and his primate, who sought their finest recruits in the cloister, and three of them escaped the fate of most English anomalies. Sherborne ceased to be monastic but a threat to the monks at Winchester was averted by Lanfranc, who also protected those in his own city, while Worcester continued as before under its English bishop, Wulfstan. Before William's death Rochester and Durham had become monastic, and the transfer of many poorly endowed cathedrals to towns where there were already rich abbeys led to a further increase: Coventry, Bath, Ely, Norwich and finally Carlisle all became monastic cathedrals under Norman rule and remained so until the Reformation. The long-term results were unhappy: with the coming of the Cistercians in the twelfth century the black monks ceased to be the spiritual force that they were in Lanfranc's day, the business of administering large episcopal estates burdened too many of them with secular duties, and quarrels between bishops and their monastic chapters were to bedevil the history of many English cathedrals for the next four and a half centuries.

These unforseeable misfortunes were trivial in comparison with the benefits derived from Lanfranc's work. Diocesan administration, strengthened by the new location of cathedrals, was further reinforced by an order that all bishops should appoint archdeacons to supervise their clergy. Here too England was being steered firmly along a course which she might anyway have chosen, since such officials were known in the diocese of Canterbury under Edward, but once again it was only under the Normans that progress became rapid or consistent. At the same time Lanfranc advanced the parochial system by encouraging the existing trend whereby large 'minster' churches, attended by old-established communities, gave way to smaller churches under one priest, serving a single village. The parish priest himself was shielded by an edict against vagrancy or the wanderings of poor clerks, which required the bishop's permission for one to settle or seek ordination in any diocese but his own; monks too were forbidden to roam at will and were excluded from serving in the parish churches. Efforts were even made to protect the incumbent from his lay patron, who would claim the same personal services from a priest as from any other tenant; a priest's payments in money or in kind were only a substitute for labour and it was accordingly decreed that no benefice should be held by services heavier than those performed in King Edward's day.

Another of Lanfranc's tasks was to eradicate the vices of the clergy and to correct insular deviations from the doctrine of the Church. Here the regular summoning of church councils or synods under his presidency was of particular value, since it was only by continuous vigilance that such problems could be solved. William himself took a keen interest in ecclesiastical councils, which he attended whenever possible, and five had been held during his reign in Normandy before the Conquest. In England on the other hand the conciliar activity which had played a large part in the establishment of Christianity had long since lapsed; after the Danish invasions neither King Alfred and his many pious successors nor the energetic St Dunstan had attempted a revival. At least three and probably four more Norman councils were held between the Conquest and William's death, while the council held by the papal legates at Winchester in 1070 was the first of seven which met in England during his reign. These assemblies, which continued after Lanfranc's death, helped to win general acceptance for his work and allowed him to supervise its even progress throughout the kingdom.

Old English failings are often vouched for too emphatically. William of Malmesbury, acknowledging that high standards had once prevailed, believed that the love of learning and religion had decayed before the Conquest: 'The clergy, contented with a very slight measure of learning, could scarcely stammer out the words of the sacraments, and a person who understood grammar was an object of wonder and astonishment. The monks mocked the rule of their order with fine vestments and with the use of every kind of food.' Since England was superior to Normandy in literature and in most of the arts, as will be seen, this picture of degenerate materialism is clearly overpainted. Ignorance was no doubt widespread but it is impossible to assess the attainments of an average English priest and to compare them with those of his Norman counterpart. Moreover, William and Lanfranc tackled many abuses in England that had previously faced them in Normandy and were still rife on parts of the Continent. Simony was attacked simultaneously in councils at London and Rouen in the 1070s, and Lanfranc's assault on the married clergy echoed the much harsher general edicts of the papacy.

English standards in 1066 were certainly more haphazard than those of Normandy, where a zealous duke had temporarily suppressed abuses that were to recur throughout the Middle Ages. If simony is always hard to prove, vagrancy may have been unusually common in England, while Stigand was a blatant pluralist and Leofwine of Lichfield furnished an example of incontinence. In Tudor times Cardinal Wolsey still embodied the last two vices, although his pluralism was acceptable to pope and king and a prelate's incontinence was no longer advertised by marriage. Lanfranc was wise to insist on celibacy: the Old English laxity appears attractively honest, for it can hardly be said that Leofwine, with legitimate children, was worse than the Conqueror's own half-brother, Odo of Bayeux, the father of bastards, but clerical marriage involved the danger that offices would become the vested interests of a family. Although Leofwine is the only bishop known to have been married at the time of the Conquest, the practice must have been widespread at a humbler level, since at a council in 1076 Lanfranc strictly enforced celibacy on canons and the higher clergy as well as on all for the future, while prudently allowing established parish priests to keep their wives. Wulfstan, the last survivor of the old order, here surpassed his archbishop by facing all the priests of his diocese with a choice between their wives and their livings. This assault, vital to the Church's independence, proved to be slow work, for clerical marriage persisted into the following century.

The most momentous of all the Norman innovations in the Church, overshadowing the changes of personnel, the improvements in organization and the attacks on abuses, was the withdrawal of ecclesiastical pleas from the hundred courts. A royal writ, probably of April 1072, forbade bishops and archdeacons to submit any matter concerning the rule of souls to the judgement of the laity and ordered that 'anyone cited . . . shall not be tried according to the law of the hundred court, but he shall submit to God and his bishop in accordance with the canons and the episcopal laws', under pain of excommunication and constraint by the sheriff. Unlike many post-Conquest changes, this was in no way foreshadowed under the Confessor. The decision, a natural sequel to the establishment of archdeacons, reflected William's reforming zeal as well as his contempt for the lack of order which he found: 'I have ordained that the episcopal laws shall be amended, because before my time these were not properly administered in England according to the precepts of the holy canons.'

Unfortunately the holy canons were open to many interpretations. The Conqueror, a strong ruler in a kingdom where the new papal claims were not yet current, could afford to set up ecclesiastical courts without closely defining their powers, but his successors found that their authority was being undermined by a rival jurisdiction over which they had no control. Disagreement over the right to punish criminous clerks was ostensibly the occasion of the quarrel between Henry II and Becket, although this issue was soon engulfed in the wider struggle between king and pope. In the later Middle Ages popular resentment of the Church's wealth was fanned by the exactions of the ecclesiastical courts, and grievances smouldered for many generations before they were finally unleashed by Henry VIII.

*

William and Lanfranc were not concerned with the secular clergy alone. In 1066 England contained some thirty-five monasteries, including the monastic cathedrals, all of them self-governing and Benedictine, grouped mainly in the Severn valley, Wessex and the Fens. Their total population was less than nine hundred but the revenues recorded in *Domesday* have been calculated at £11,066, almost one-sixth of that of the kingdom; the incomes of individual houses varied widely, from Glastonbury with £828 a year and Ely with £768 down to Horton in Somerset with only £12. There were also nine nunneries, of which Wilton and Shaftesbury were wealthy houses with some £250 a year each. Both monks and nuns were drawn mainly from the landowning class, and the former were often ruled by men with the highest connections: Earl Godwine's brother, Ælfwig, was abbot of the New Minster at Winchester, Earl Leofric of Mercia had one nephew and namesake who ruled Peterborough and another, the married Leofwine, who ruled Coventry before becoming bishop of Lichfield in 1054. The new king naturally treated these monasteries as store-houses of wealth and centres of political influence, which would have to be brought under his control; moreover, both he and Lanfranc, whose spiritual home was always the cloister, saw the monasteries as nurseries for future churchmen.

The replacement of English abbots by Normans resembled the changes among the bishops, although William's political motives are more obvious because of monastic support for the native resistance. A number of abbots had fought at Hastings, where Harold's uncle Ælfwig had died, and hostility to the conquerors persisted at St Augustine's, Canterbury, the New Minster, Winchester, and among the fenland houses; at Peterborough Leofric's successor Brand, who ruled from 1067 to 1069, was the uncle of Hereward the Wake. Six formal degradations are known to have been carried out, at least two abbots having fled the country and three being imprisoned, and as the remaining English abbots died they were succeeded by Normans. At the king's death only three out of the twenty houses of which anything is known still enjoyed native heads, so the replacement of the higher clergy was ultimately as complete as that of the nobility. William was less drastic with the bishops and abbots than with laymen only because he could rely on time to do his work for him.

The Conqueror, being no doctrinaire, was ready to use an Englishman who could be trusted. Here he was slightly more successful with the clergy than with the laity, thanks to the wisdom of two men. Æthelwig, abbot of Evesham from 1059 until his death in 1077, won the king's confidence and was given exceptional judicial authority over seven west Mercian shires. The abbot's hopes of becoming bishop of the nearby monastic cathedral of Worcester had been dashed in 1062 by the appointment of the prior, Wulfstan, with the blessing of the papal legates and of the earls of Wessex and Mercia. Afterwards the rivals became friends and together they won fame as outstanding representatives of the Old English tradition, which died with them. Lacking the crusading spirit of the Norman reformers, both prelates were always ready by counsel and example to assist in affairs of Church and State. Wulfstan is remembered for his pastoral care, Æthelwig is renowned for wielding powers given to no other Englishman; both were devout and charitable men, who raised the number of their monks from a dozen to fifty at Worcester and to over thirty at Evesham. Their houses remained the last centres of native culture and furnished refuges for many of their fellow countrymen after the Norman ravagings in the north. Æthelwig and Wulfstan, unable to reverse the Conquest, helped in 1075 to put down a rebellion whose extension would only have led to wider misery, and Wulfstan was also instrumental in suppressing the baronial revolt of 1088 against Wlliiam Rufus.

Æthelwig's activities are proudly recited in a thirteenth-century chronicle of Evesham, whose author probably drew them from a contemporary account. Wulfstan is still better known, since shortly after his death in 1095 he was honoured with a full-scale biography by Coleman, an English monk at Worcester; this work, the last of the vernacular lives of famous bishops, is now preserved in a Latin translation by William of Malmesbury. Neither here nor in any other chronicle is Æthelwig or Wulfstan even mildly reproved for collaborating with William, although Wulfstan at any rate had been a close friend of King Harold. Both prelates saw what was best in Norman rule and it was recognized that they had worked to soften the blow. Tales of miraculous healings around Wulfstan's tomb led in 1203 to the canonization of the last of King Edward's bishops, whose life had done something to bridge the gulf between Englishman and Norman.

During William's reign twenty-four foreign superiors are known to have been imposed on English houses. The Norman monasteries rose to the challenge, for they supplied twenty-two of these heads and only three turned out to be failures. Geoffrey, a royal nominee drawn from Jumièges to rule the Confessor's wealthy foundation at Westminster, was dispatched home in disgrace by Lanfranc. Turold of Fécamp was sent first to Malmesbury and then, when the king aptly remarked that he was more of a soldier than a monk, to Peterborough, a hotbed of English resistance from which he was briefly excluded by Hereward but where he managed to maintain himself with notorious harshness for twenty-eight years. Thurstan, another martial figure, was appointed to England's richest house, Glastonbury, where his attempts to introduce new ceremonies and chants caused defiant monks to arm themselves with church furniture and take refuge before the altar, only to be shot down by Norman men-at-arms from the gallery; this scandal, involving at least two dead and twelve wounded, led to Thurstan's return to Caen for the rest of William's reign. The task of the new Norman abbots was more delicate than that of the non-monastic bishops, since they had to live among closed and hostile communities, and it is surprising that there were so few incidents of this kind.

Isolated outbreaks of violence do not do justice to the general resentment which smouldered in the monasteries. The monks of St Augustine's at Canterbury, after many years under the tactful Norman Abbot Scotland, rejected the successor named by Lanfranc and walked out from the presentation ceremony; the archbishop prevailed, but his death in 1089 was followed by riots in the city, in which St Augustine's was implicated, and the community had to be dispersed, twenty-three monks from the neighbouring monastery of Christ Church taking its place. This was an exceptional step, although a number of inmates were also removed from Glastonbury and Ely. Trouble sprang not so much from the high-handed behaviour of the Norman abbots, which has been exaggerated, as from a genuine lack of sympathy. Lanfranc himself, a firm but not a harsh man, hated the prospect of dealing with strangers in an alien tongue, and so did the saintly Anselm, a still more gifted Italian who succeeded him at Bec and eventually at Canterbury. Anselm wrote sympathetically to Lanfranc's nephew Paul, who had been appointed to rule St Albans; the barbarians would be unable to understand him but his labours would not be in vain, 'for what you cannot say to them, you can show by your life'.

Language problems and strange surroundings partly explain the distaste of many Normans for their new charges. Discipline and observances might also seem peculiar in England, although the Norman houses themselves were not subject to a single, clear-cut code which could be transplanted. While there is no proof of the widespread laxity condemned by William of Malmesbury, any deviations were certainly corrected by a new abbot; Thurstan was no doubt the most luckless of many who tried to bring the services more into line with the practices of their own Norman monasteries, which would have been more closely allied with those of Cluny. Lanfranc himself drew up a code of customs or *Consuetudines* for Christ Church, Canterbury, which he did not intend for general use but which were certainly adopted in other houses; selected from several Continental monasteries and modified so as not to offend the English, they differ remarkably little from the *Regularis Concordia* which had been published in England a century earlier. The one issue on which Lanfranc and other Normans caused deep offence was their suspicion of the numerous Anglo-Saxon saints whose cult and numbers had grown steadily over the centuries. At St Albans, Abbot Paul called his venerated predecessors uneducated simpletons, Saints Edmund and Æthelwold were dismissed as rustics by the abbot of Abingdon, and Lanfranc himself overrode his chapter by omitting many native saints from the calendar. The bitterness with which these attacks on cherished figures was met sprang from racial as well as religious feeling.

The Conquest did not herald a wave of important foundations in England, since the Normans' loyalty was already given to houses in their own land. William himself vainly asked St Hugh, abbot of Cluny, to send him twelve monks who could help in the work of reform, and accordingly turned to Marmoutier on the Loire in order to colonize the house which was to commemorate his victory, Battle Abbey. Apart from Battle the sole major foundation of his reign was Lewes Priory, which William de Warenne finally established as a Cluniac house, after overcoming the misgivings of St Hugh.

Battle and Lewes, both of them well endowed and soon virtually independent of their mother houses, were followed later in the century by foundations at Selby, Shrewsbury, Chester, Spalding and Colchester and by the transfer of the pre-Conquest monastery of Cranborne to Tewkesbury. Bermondsey, founded by an English citizen of London in the 1080s, was the only other Cluniac priory to rival Lewes, although the number of lesser Cluniac houses had reached thirty-six within a century of the Conquest. Land was also given to other small establishments which the benefactors tied to larger houses, in the hope that future growth would lead to independence. A still more common practice was for barons to give land in England to houses in Normandy, which often sent over small bands of monks to administer their new estates. In this way at least two hundred lesser houses, known as cells, came into existence by the year 1200. Few of them were of any value to religion and those in foreign hands, known also as 'alien priories', served mainly to channel wealth out of the country, until they fell victim to the rising tide of national feeling during the Hundred Years' War.

The Normans, for all the havoc which they wrought, were not to blame for the desolate religious life of the north. The foremost seat of learning in northern Europe during the century after Bede, Northumbria had so suffered from the Scandinavian invasions that no monastery survived north of the Trent, although a college of clerks guarded the bones of St Cuthbert at Durham. Ruined sites and famous names could still exercise their power, even on a conqueror, and a Norman knight named Reinfrid was so moved at Whitby in the campaign of 1069–70 that he shortly afterwards retired to Æthelwig's monastery at Evesham. From there he later set out in the company of an English monk named Ælfwig and of Ealdwine, the prior of Winchcombe, to seek solitude in the north, where their monastic garb was an object of wonder. Encouraged by Bishop Walcher, they took over Bede's roofless church at Jarrow, where recruits from the south soon turned their search for tranquillity into the rebirth of northern monasticism. This movement, 'a somewhat neglected example of effective Norman and Anglo-Saxon co-operation', led to the recolonization of Wearmouth and Whitby from Jarrow and to the arrival of twenty-three monks at Durham itself in 1083. Houses were still relatively sparse, so that in the following century the north offered a natural home to the austere followers of St Bernard of Clairvaux; these white monks or Cistercians, named after the abbey of Cîteaux in Burgundy and representing an entirely new influence, were to make the first of their celebrated foundations at Fountains in 1132.

The effect of the Conquest on the nunneries was less dramatic, since no abbess had to be deposed. It was also less important, for monks far outnumbered nuns in the days before the latter became famous as teachers and nurses. Nunneries being a natural refuge for high-born ladies in distress, the relatives of dispossessed Englishmen suddenly if inadvertently raised the number of inmates; Harold's daughter, Gunhild, became a nun at Wilton, where Queen Edith retired temporarily towards the end of her life, and the Ætheling's younger sister, Christina, entered the nunnery at Romsey in 1085. In spite of this influx only two or perhaps three foundations of any importance were made before 1100. The north remained bare until the mid-twelfth century, when an Englishman named Gilbert of Sempringham established several double houses; these were recognized as belonging to a new order, which spread to the Continent at the same time as the Cistercians were challenging the black monks in England.

Despite every native grievance, justified or otherwise, there is no doubt that English monasticism benefited enormously from the Conquest. The number of monks more than doubled before Lanfranc's death, rising much more dramatically than the number of monasteries, from one or two dozen inmates in a fairly large house to sixty or even to a hundred. Seizures of land by grasping barons, crimes which no chronicler would allow his readers to forget, had in most cases been met by new allotments before *Domesday* and were soon to be more than out-weighed by the gifts of benefactors; the king himself ordered a great deal of treasure to be seized in 1070 but it will never be known how much of this was true monastic wealth, since many valuables had been left for safe keeping by English laymen. No house was destroyed and ultimately many new ones arose, although the legacy would have been more fruitful if the foundations had been fewer and larger. The most valid criticism is that the imposition of knight-service turned abbots, like bishops, into feudal magnates and so helped to divorce them from their flocks. This disadvantage pales by comparison with the blessings which flowed from the stimulus to monasticism as a whole.

Monastic libraries before the Conquest, while housing a unique vernacular literature and innumerable works of art, were small and insular beside those built up under the Normans. Among the books brought by Lanfranc to Canterbury were the first volume of canon law, as well as a new text of the Vulgate, the Latin Bible, which resembled that in use on the Continent and was distributed to become the standard version of the English monks. Abbot Paul employed professional scribes at St Albans, to which he left twenty-eight tomes, Bishop Walcher's successor, William of Saint-Carilef, gave over fifty to the monastic cathedral of Durham, and the historian William of Malmesbury took great pride in the library founded by Godfrey, the third Norman to rule his house. The new abbots were builders in stone as well as collectors of books, and the first activity helped to preserve the fruits of the second by reducing the risk of fire.

In the mid-twelfth century the monasteries' monopoly of learning was to be undermined by the growing popularity of disputation, a practice which needed a freer atmosphere. Cathedral schools were to produce professional masters of philosophy and medicine, and bishops' households were to become centres of legal studies, leaving history and literature to adorn the more remote monastic world. In William the Conqueror's time the monks had no rivals, the Norman houses were enjoying a golden age, and Le Bec was the most famous school north of the Alps. Through the Conquest, England was laid open to the ferment of Latin Europe.

*

The most impressive side of William's ecclesiastical policy, although not where he achieved the most lasting results, was his treatment of the papacy. Rome had a special claim on English loyalty, since St Augustine's mission had been dispatched by Gregory the Great, and the kingdom's veneration had for long been expressed in an annual tribute in the form of a hearth-tax known as Peter's Pence. This payment, with the existence of monastic cathedrals, was the outstanding peculiarity of the pre-Conquest Church in England, paralleled only by payments from the Scandinavian countries and Poland. William himself had incurred a further obligation by submitting his case against Harold to the judgement of Rome, where he had been enthusiastically and perhaps decisively supported by Hildebrand. As the reformed papacy gained in prestige, it was inevitable that it should try to place its authority in England on a firmer footing.

The result was an apparently contradictory situation in which William, the Christian prince, accompanied his reforms by erecting barriers against papal influence. In fact the very recent conversion of the papacy allowed him to take his stand on tradition and to enjoy the support of his bishops. A meddlesome pope who was ignorant of local conditions could be irksome to a practical church-man like Lanfranc, as well as a menace to royal authority. King and archbishop recognized that the pope, as head of the Church, should confirm appointments, that he should be the final arbiter in important disputes such as the Norman claim in 1066, and that Peter's Pence ought to be paid; further than that they would not go. No record survives in which William clearly states the limits to his obedience, but in the following generation he was said to have insisted that royal approval was necessary for the recognition of a disputed pope, for the entry into England of papal letters, for a church council to initiate legislation and for the excommunication of any tenant-in-chief or royal official. The arrival of legates in 1070 did not dilute this resistance, for they came to effect the deposition of Stigand and his sympathizers, which was a necessary part of the king's own policy.

Relations were at their worst during the four years after the imperial humiliation at Canossa in January 1077, when Hildebrand was at the height of his power. His demand that English prelates should attend the court of Rome was unacceptable to William, who feared that the bishops might thereby become the pope's men and would return with papal letters, or at least with subversive ideas; he therefore ignored the demand and even allowed Lanfranc to be threatened with deposition rather than give way. An attempt to undermine the closely knit structure of the Norman Church by subjecting the see of Rouen to that of Lyons was resisted with equal success, after Hildebrand for a time had tried to with-hold recognition of William's nominee to Rouen. A third and still more direct line of attack came with a demand for fealty, apparently first put forward by

Alexander II but known chiefly from William's terse reply after the issue had again been raised by Hildebrand. The pope based his case partly on the new canon law and partly on Peter's Pence, which was tendentiously assumed to represent an age-old admission of vassalage, buttressing this by stating that William had promised homage for his kingdom to the Holy See in 1066. The king's undertaking to pay the arrears of Peter's Pence, accompanied by a flat denial that he or his predecessors had promised homage, left the pope with no choice but to abate his claims or risk an open breach. Hildebrand stayed silent.

The Conquest thus brought no extension of papal power in England, despite the growing prestige of Rome. William's triumph is shown by the fact that bishops continued without demur to receive their pastoral staff from the king, whereas the papal decree against lay investiture in 1074 precipitated a European crisis which brought the Holy Roman Emperor literally to the pope's feet. This decree did not even enter England until the end of the century, so sound was the barrier which William built. Political events in Italy came to his help, since in 1081 a revival of imperial power led to the siege of Rome and confronted Hildebrand with an anti-pope, Clement III; three years later the city was sacked by rescuing soldiers under Robert Guiscard, the Norman duke of Apulia, and Hildebrand had to leave for the last time, in the company of his execrated allies. Approaches were made to the Conqueror on behalf of the anti-pope and amidst this turmoil England went her own way without deference to either party.

William owed still more to his own political supremacy, stronger than that of the king of France or of the emperor in Germany; the pope had no chance to threaten him through a band of malcontents and there was no papalist party under Lanfranc. Above all the king was a true reformer, whose individual measures to reinvigorate religion accorded with the pope's own views. Hildebrand was not given to compromise and his acquiescence in the last resort sprang from a recognition of these good qualities. In 1081 the papal legates were told to restore the Norman bishops who had been suspended after William had kept them away from a council. Hildebrand explained his reasons and lucidly summed up the Conqueror's ecclesiastical policy:

> The king of England, though in certain respects he is not as scrupulous about religion as we could wish, nevertheless shows himself to be more acceptable than other kings in this: that he neither wastes nor sells the churches of God, that he causes peace and justice to prevail among his subjects, that when he was asked by certain enemies of the cross of Christ to enter into a plot against the Apostolic see he refused his consent and that he bound priests by oath to dismiss their wives and laymen to give up the tithes which they were withholding. Therefore it is not unfitting that his power should be dealt with more leniently and that out of respect for his upright conduct the shortcomings of his subjects and his favourites should be borne with indulgence.

This was a fair estimate, which William would doubtless have taken as a complete justification of his life's work. No other monarch in England has so successfully combined zeal for the Church with the defence of his own rights.

William's outlook was that of a reforming Continental ruler of his father's or grandfather's generation. It is certain that new ideas could not have been excluded indefinitely, and unlikely that the old royal prerogatives could have remained intact. Rufus, by his cynicism and unblushing spoliation, threw away the best defence of his father's stand; no one could see a reformer in the second Norman king, who deliberately kept Canterbury vacant for four years after Lanfranc's death in order to squander its revenues. At last Anselm, intellectually the most eminent of all the sons of Le Bec, was named archbishop in 1093; Rufus, dangerously ill, then promised restitution, only to return to his old ways as soon as his health was restored. Anselm proved a rigid opponent, who defied the king by refusing to receive the *pallium* from his hands and eventually went into exile. The struggle continued under Henry I until, after a second exile, Anselm agreed to a compromise in 1107. Henry promised to enforce the new Roman decree on investiture, a breach in the Conqueror's barrier which was never closed, although the king adroitly retained political control of his ecclesiastical tenants-in-chief by insisting on homage before consecration.

Henry I maintained his father's policy with some success. Under Stephen the weakness of the monarchy allowed the Church to extend her power, while the spread of canon law studies influenced a growing number of clergy in favour of the papacy. Henry II in effect hoped to turn back the clock by working with Becket as the Conqueror had worked with Lanfranc, and the results of his misjudgement are notorious. The importance of their quarrel lies in the fact that when Becket fled to France he made his own cause that of the pope, losing sight of the original dispute over the powers of ecclesiastical courts and insisting on the freedom of the English Church to obey the laws of the universal Church. After his murder the point was partly gained, for Henry II agreed to allow appeals to Rome and a new, extra-territorial jurisdiction was 'asserted in England, to be exercised with varying independence until the Reformation. In this way, while the Conqueror's work as a reformer endured, the conservative policy towards the papacy which he pursued with such skill ultimately proved of little avail.

CHAPTER TEN

The Submergence of English

*L*ANGUAGE is evolved as a means of communica-
tion by people among whom there are few barriers.
When men move apart or are otherwise cut off from one
another, their speech will diverge until it consists of different dialects; ultimately the speakers of these dialects may
no longer be able to understand one another, at which
point their dialects have become separate languages. Latin,
the common language of educated men in western Europe
under the unifying rule of imperial Rome, was adopted
by the barbarians who overran Gaul, Iberia and Italy,
but the rise of separate kingdoms produced a number of
regional dialects. Some of these have died out with the
amalgamation of small feudal states into the larger units
of modern times, others survive as the Romance languages,
of which the most widely spoken today are French,
Spanish, Portuguese and Italian. The Normans, who
abandoned Scandinavian speech for that of northern
France, thus spoke an early Romance tongue.

By way of contrast, the Germanic invaders of Britannia
retained their own speech although, like most newcomers,
they borrowed several words, in this case from the Romans

and the Celts. Despite the prolonged survival of petty kingdoms, the tribes which settled in England spoke very similar dialects and saw themselves as one distinct race. When political unity was at last achieved under the kings of Wessex, the West Saxon dialect became the standard official and literary language, which today is termed Old English. The Scandinavian invaders also spoke a Germanic language, Old Norse, which shared with Old English a common ancestor in some Proto-Germanic tongue of which no records survive. Englishmen and Scandinavians were still able to understand one another, and the Viking settlement was followed by an intermingling from which English emerged with a much larger vocabulary. When the Normans landed this blending was still in progress but it was already clear that English, which was spoken at court even under the Dane Cnut, would be the survivor.

The popular languages of Normandy and England in 1066 therefore had very little in common, although there was a remote relationship in that both belonged to the huge Indo-European family, as do all the national languages of Europe today save those of Finland and Hungary. On either side of the Channel Latin had been retained by the Church but in England this was not the sole language of administration nor, when learning revived after the Viking invasions, was it the usual language of the chroniclers. The triumph of the Normans brought a graver threat to the future of English than did the arrival of the far more numerous Scandinavians. The Vikings had spoken a kindred tongue whereas the Normans spoke French and, for the purposes of government, always used Latin. A gentle assimilation could not be expected. The question was whether the conquerors would abandon their own speech or whether that of the natives would be submerged. English was the most advanced vernacular language in Europe, far richer than the rudimentary French spoken in the duchy, but merit was of little avail. The issue was decided by political events: partly by the very thoroughness of the Conquest itself, mainly by the ties which kept England bound to the Continent for over a century after William's death.

*

The Conquest presaged the disappearance of English as an official language, over four hundred and fifty years after it is first known to have been written down in the laws of King Æthelberht of Kent. Royal charters had always been written in Latin and the only difference after 1066 was that their form and style began to resemble those favoured in France. Royal writs on the other hand, of which the earliest surviving example dates from the reign of Æthelred the Unready, appear from the start to have been written in the vernacular. These short letters to the local officers were not an invention to be discarded by a king of William's temperament, although it was logical that they should now be used for a wider range of subjects. For three years they remained unaltered and it was only after the great northern rebellion, which was followed by a general displacement of native officials, that English gave way to Latin.

This change was made inevitable by the Normans' continued ignorance of English, since every act of government still depended on the royal will. Although there is no evidence for the literacy of Alfred's successors, their use of sealed writs makes it probable that they could read English, even if they did not write it; charters do not make it equally likely that the kings knew Latin, since these documents were only formal records designed for display. If William and his advisers had mastered a new language the writs could have remained as they were, but the Conqueror was totally illiterate and the one dubious story that he tried to learn the speech of his new subjects admits that he failed. On the other hand the autograph crosses with which he authenticated documents make him the first English king who is known to have handled a pen.

William Rufus seems to have resembled his father and it was not until Henry I, who was probably brought up in England, that a king again understood the language of most of his subjects. Henry was exceptional in boasting an elementary knowledge of Latin, which earned him the nickname 'Beauclerk' two hundred years later, and William of Malmesbury improbably credits him with repeating the old saw *Rex illiteratus, asinus coronatus* (an illiterate king is a crowned ass), in the Conqueror's presence. Henry II and the sons who succeeded him were taught Latin and thereafter, although royal proficiency in any language is rarely proven, it is likely that every king could understand the documents with which he dealt. Writing, a more advanced stage than reading, is first attested only by a painstaking sample of Edward III's from 1330.

Even 1069 did not witness an abrupt change. A vernacular writ was issued at the end of the Conqueror's reign and men were still pleading in English in the shire courts under Henry I. Sometimes orders were given in both Latin and English, a device used by Henry I when confirming the privileges of London and by those who drew up a series of bilingual writs about the temporalities of the see of Canterbury, which extend into the reign of Henry II. Since French had no history as an official language, it was natural that Latin should be the immediate gainer from the eclipse of English. A language restricted almost entirely to the clergy, however, was inconvenient as the sole medium of an expanding administration. Eventually French crept into official documents, although there are very few instances of this during the first century after the Conquest; French also became the language of the law-courts and, in the thirteenth century, of early parliamentary procedure and of the first universities.

When English at last regained formal recognition it was at the expense of French, while Latin was retained for the most solemn documents as it had been before the Conquest. Although King Henry III issued a trilingual proclamation as early as 1258 the formal use of French, like the existence of alien priories, ended only with the Hundred Years' War: in 1362 the chancellor first read the speech from the throne at the opening of Parliament in English and a few weeks later English officially replaced French in the law-courts, although their records continued to be kept in Latin, as were those of all the medieval departments of state. Lawyers did not welcome the change and many continued to plead and write in 'law French', which became increasingly mangled and reached a pitch of absurdity in Dyer's famous report of 1631 that a prisoner, venting his rage on the judge, 'jecte un graund brickbat que narrowly mist'. This weird jargon, condemned by Oliver Cromwell, returned at the Restoration and was not finally abolished until 1731. The Conqueror's tongue survives now only in a few time-honoured formulae, which include the words signifying royal assent to a public Act of Parliament, *La Reyne le veult*, and to a personal Act, *Soit fait comme il est desiré*.

*

The eclipse of English as an official language was not a catastrophe, since old institutions and practices lived on. Far more serious was the withering of native poetry and prose. The English have always excelled in poetry; it forms the very basis of their literature, since the Germanic tribesmen already boasted a magnificent oral tradition when they colonized Britannia. A great deal of their poetry was never set down in writing and the records of much more have been lost, but it was of remoter ancestry and in general it remained more inspired than Anglo-Saxon prose. The oldest subjects were the mighty warriors of Teutonic history and legend, to which Christian themes were later added. Beowulf himself was a pagan hero long before his triumph over the monster Grendel was celebrated, with Christian reflections, in the poem which survives today.

Poets relied on alliteration, whereby a line was divided and at least one word in each half began with the same sound. Their verse, alliterative in form and heroic or moralizing in content, was sonorously recited in the halls of great men, to the accompaniment of a harp. So strong was the Old English taste for majestic alliteration that it appears even in formal phrases, unconnected with entertainment, including the formula denoting private justice, 'with sake and with soke, with toll and with team, and with infangenetheof'; here it was of practical value, since the king's writs were read aloud in the local courts and it was important that the occasion should be impressed on men's memories. Alliteration may still haunt the marriage service with the words 'for better for worse, for richer for poorer', and it coloured the wife's vow 'to be bonere and buxom in bed and at board', which was discarded at the Reformation in favour of a succinct promise 'to obey'.

The finest Old English poems, the religious works inspired by Caedmon, the anonymous *Dream of the Rood*, the epic *Beowulf*, are all of pre-Viking date, albeit preserved only in collections made during the late tenth-century monastic revival. On the other hand poems were meant for recitation and it was long before any were written down; most later Old English compositions may never have reached this stage, others may have been thrown away when the monasteries, where they would have been cherished, passed under alien rule, and still more works must have been destroyed at the Reformation. The survival only of early masterpieces is misleading, for a few minor examples show that native poetry was still flourishing on the eve of the Conquest.

The Normans therefore arrived when the English poetic tradition was probably still creative. Certainly they interrupted the enjoyment of native verse, by destroying the old aristocracy, and equally certainly they prevented many works from reaching posterity. The Conquest however could not stamp out the love of poetry itself, and one long-term result was beneficial. English poetry survived as popular entertainment throughout the age when it could no longer appeal to courtly tastes and, although alliteration was to revive in the west country in the fourteenth century, new devices appeared. The use of rhyme became more common, often mingled with alliteration in the same piece, and its triumph was assured by the time of Chaucer, who abandoned the ancient native conventions for the rhyming couplets of France.

*

Prose had developed more slowly, first in Latin and then in English. At the end of the seventh century and throughout the next hundred years England, in particular Northumbria, had been an oasis of learning; she had produced in Bede, a monk of Jarrow who probably never travelled beyond York, the foremost historian of the Dark Ages, and in Alcuin she had given Charlemagne a scholar to whom the emperor entrusted the direction of the revival which he sought to procure in Europe. The Vikings had destroyed this pre-eminence so effectively that no later writers of Latin ever approached the heights of Bede's *Historia Ecclesiastica*. The monastic revival of the tenth century, however, apart from inspiring historically valuable Latin biographies of the chief reformers, including St Dunstan himself, led to a flowering of native prose which once again made England unique in her time.

King Alfred had hoped for such an upsurge nearly a hundred years earlier. Remarking that knowledge of Latin had decayed whereas many could read English, this exceptional king had found time to master Latin and had himself translated a number of works for his subjects. No renaissance followed and it was natural for the monastic reformers to counteract persistent ignorance by further translations from Latin and by composing instructions for the rustic clergy in their native tongue. There resulted a body of religious writing which owed its greatest debt to Ælfric, abbot of Eynsham, for his *Catholic Homilies*, his *Lives of the Saints*, his *Pastoral Letters* and the *Heptateuch*, a translation of the first seven books of the Bible. At the same time Ælfric's friend Wulfstan, archbishop of York from 1002 to 1023, composed a number of more fiery tracts, of which by far the most famous was a terrible warning known after his own name as the *Sermo Lupi ad Anglos*, which blamed the sins of the English people for the renewal of the Viking scourge. Several religious works of less literary merit were also produced in this period, while secular writings survive most abundantly in a score of pseudo-medical treatises, concerned mainly with extravagant prescriptions known as leechdoms. If historical prose is placed in a class by itself, there remain Byrhtferth's *Manual* on astronomy and mathematics, a classical romance called *Apollonius of Tyre* and a book of marvels, *Wonders of the East*, to provide yet more evidence of the amazingly wide range of Old English taste.

This vernacular literature, which had no Continental parallel, did not satisfy its creators, for whom it was a temporary concession to the lamentable ignorance of Latin. Ælfric accordingly composed the first Latin grammar in any vernacular of medieval Europe, which he accompanied by a *Glossary* and by a text-book of homely dialogue, the *Colloquy*. His friend Æthelweard, an ealdorman of royal blood for whom the *Lives of the Saints* was written, set himself to translate the *Anglo-Saxon Chronicle* into Latin for the benefit of a kinswoman who was abbess of Essen in Germany. While Æthelweard's Latin was eccentric and in places meaningless, it is remarkable that England held a noble layman with literary interests who could undertake the work at all, in an age when no such figure existed on the other side of the Channel.

This output of English prose continued, in varying volume, for nearly two hundred years before the Conquest. The tradition which had been started by Alfred and had gained rapidly in strength at the end of the tenth century, a time of political calamity, survived the Danish kings and lived on under Edward the Confessor. The scarcity of extant works from the generation immediately before the Conquest is no evidence of dwindling energy. It is doubtful whether poetry stagnated and prose, with its more recent origins, is still less likely to have done so. Under the Confessor men may have been prone to copy the inspired works of an older generation, but too much has perished for this to be proved and the style of the few surviving examples shows no decline.

Latin works might win acclaim on the Continent whereas vernacular writings, however distinguished, could be enjoyed only at home. The Normans appreciated England's prose no more than her poetry, and the destructive effect of the Conquest can be belittled only by stating that the loss would have been still more disastrous if William had landed fifty years earlier. Prose, written for instruction rather than entertainment, suffered less immediately from the fall of the old nobility than did poetry; so strong was the appeal of the great homilists Ælfric and Wulfstan that their works were still being copied by their fellow countrymen a century after Hastings, and English prose even reached a new height in a treatise for nuns known as the *Ancren Riwle*. In the end, however, the fate of prose was more severe, since it was not sustained by the popular enthusiasm which ensured poetry a rude but vigorous life. French prose, being relatively backward in 1066, presented its challenge only a hundred years later, but Latin soon gained ground, especially in the chronicles. French works eventually predominated, as the French-speaking court grew more civilized, and English became confined almost entirely to religious tracts, catering for the humble and written in a variety of dialects.

*

One important branch of native prose was certainly still flourishing in 1066. Repeated reference has been made to the *Anglo-Saxon Chronicle*, which Æthelweard tried to translate and which is the chief source for Old English history. The extant narrative, going back to Roman times, was first composed in Alfred's reign, from Bede and a number of earlier annals which have now been lost. Copies were distributed among various monasteries, where further entries were sometimes made, of differing quality. The *Anglo-Saxon Chronicle* therefore consists today of several narratives, some of which fill gaps left by the others and some of which supply different accounts of the same event. While Latin continued to be the language of biographers, less important annals were almost invariably written in English, as was the *Chronicle* itself. The latter survives in seven manuscripts and one fragment, three of which concern events leading up to or following the Conquest. No other European country can boast so early a history, written over a period of two hundred and fifty years and in its native tongue.

The Conquest ultimately put an end to this tradition.

One of the three texts of the *Chronicle* concerning this period, written at Abingdon, does not go beyond 1066; a second manuscript, known only from a copy made in the twelfth century and found at Worcester, having probably been written either there or in the north, ends in 1079. A third version, compiled at St Augustine's, Canterbury, down to 1121, has also disappeared in its original form but survives in a copy made at Peterborough, where the narrative was continued until early 1155. A single version of the *Anglo-Saxon Chronicle* thus outlasted the Anglo-Norman kings, only to expire within one year and leave England with no vernacular history for over two centuries. The *Chronicle* had not outlived its usefulness, since the Peterborough version is a vivid source for the misery of Stephen's reign, and its long survival testifies to the strength of English tradition. None the less, its fate was sealed by the kingdom's continued ties with Normandy, which for long prevented the conquerors from becoming anglicized. There was no room for compositions in three different languages.

Norman French, the vernacular of the new aristocracy, could not fill the gap left by English in historical writing. No French account of the Conquest was written in prose, on either side of the Channel, although a Norman French poem appeared in the mid-twelfth century, entitled *L'estoire des Engles* and based chiefly on the details given in the *Anglo-Saxon Chronicle*. Histories in verse appeared in France and Germany at this time but these, by their nature, were less accurate than prose accounts. The famous *Roman de Rou*, an epic of the Norman dukes composed for Henry II, is valuable largely because of the lack of earlier narratives in French; it was in no way the heir to the *Anglo-Saxon Chronicle*.

The new language of the chroniclers, as of the king's clerks, was Latin. If the Normans possessed no history in their mother tongue at the time of Hastings, expanding education produced a series of Latin writers to record the glory of the Conqueror and his line. William of Jumièges, who ended his *Gesta Normannorum Ducum* or *Deeds of the Norman Dukes* about 1072, allowed the Conquest to divert his narrative from the events in the duchy which were his main concern; he is valuable less for his second-hand details of the war than for his expression of the typical Norman view, that Harold and his people were justly punished for their treachery. Shortly after this date an admiring biography, the *Gesta Guillelmi ducis Normannorum et regis Anglorum*, was written by William of Poitiers, an ex-soldier who became chaplain to the duke and archdeacon of Lisieux. Only part of this work has survived, an exultant record by an odious man who met a mysterious and perhaps an unpleasant end after the king's death. William of Poitiers is none the less a leading authority, for he knew the Conqueror well and visited England soon after Hastings, where he found material for what is by far the fullest, although not necessarily the most reliable, contemporary account of the battle. English history was thus being recorded in Latin by Normans during the Conqueror's lifetime.

William of Poitiers, essentially a Norman historian, has nothing good to say of the English. The next generation produced a true Anglo-Norman group whose most entertaining writer was Ordericus Vitalis, born in England about 1075 to a Norman counsellor of Roger of Montgomery, earl of Shrewsbury. Ordericus, called after the English priest at his baptism, was sent to his father's country to become a monk at Saint-Evroul, where his outlandish name was suppressed in favour of Vitalis. A self-proclaimed exile, he never forgot the land which he had left with tears at the age of ten, nor the Englishmen who had baptized and taught him. In middle life he paid at least two visits to England, which loom large in his cumbersome but distinguished *Historia Ecclesiastica*, a work not contemporary before the reign of Henry I but which was written from the vantage point of one who knew both kingdom and duchy. At the same time Eadmer, a monk at Canterbury, was writing a biography of Archbishop Anselm and also an undervalued account of ecclesiastical politics, the *Historia Novorum;* a number of purely factual entries of great historical value were being added by an anonymous monk known as 'Florence of Worcester' to a foreign general chronicle, while Simeon of Durham was describing the north under Norman rule.

Above all, the reign of Henry I is illuminated by William of Malmesbury, the most prolific and widely quoted of Anglo-Norman writers. Born in the south of England and perhaps dedicated to the Church, like Ordericus, by a father who had profited from the Conquest, William was sent as a child to Malmesbury Abbey, where he later became librarian. If a historian is one who sifts his evidence and seeks to explain events rather than simply to record them as an annalist, William of Malmesbury was perhaps the first true historian since Bede. He was not gifted enough to enjoy Bede's reputation but two of his works, the *Gesta Regum* or *Deeds of the Kings* and the *Historia Novella*, represented a new, critical type of history unknown to the Anglo-Saxon chroniclers.

The first wave of post-Conquest historical writing ends with the Anglo-Norman kings. William of Malmesbury's own narrative closes in 1143, that of his lesser contemporary, Henry of Huntingdon, in 1154 and those of the monks who continued 'Florence of Worcester' and Simeon of Durham in 1151 and 1153 respectively. It is not possible to discuss their merits in detail, nor those of their successors, but only to stress the debt which the Anglo-Norman historians owed to their Old English heritage. These men were born in England and showed as much sympathy as hostility towards the conquered race.

Their parentage in general is obscure, but Eadmer must have been an Englishman and it is possible that Ordericus, like William of Malmesbury, was of mixed blood. All of them took pains to learn of the kingdom's history and many of them relied on the *Anglo-Saxon Chronicle* for events before their own time. Even William of Malmesbury, with his famous attack on pre-Conquest decadence, avowedly took Bede for his model and saw himself as a successor to the greatest of English historians, who after all had written in Latin.

The second half of the fourteenth century saw the re-emergence of English in the chronicles and in other literary forms, as well as the beginning of its revival as an official language. The *Polychronicon* or universal history of Ranulph Higden, a monk of Chester, was translated from Latin into English about 1385, some fifty years after its original composition, and an increasing number of later histories were to be written in the vernacular. The *Polychronicon* itself provides the best evidence of this change. Higden noted that since the coming of the Normans schoolchildren had not been taught in their own language, that gentlemen learned French from their cradles and that a knowledge of French was the aim of any rustics who wished to advance themselves. He himself disapproved of what he called 'this corruption of the mother tongue' and would have welcomed the change noted by his translator, John of Trevisa. John traced the reawakening of English to the Black Death of 1348–9 and recorded that the revival had become so strong by 1385 that 'in all the grammar schools of England children are abandoning French, and are construing and learning in English', and that even the gentry was changing its ways. By the end of the century the king's own circle was listening to Chaucer's vernacular poetry, and the future of English as a national language was assured.

*

When English came into its own again it was no longer
the language of the *Anglo-Saxon Chronicle*. If communica-
tions are poor any language tends to develop into a
number of local dialects, although a standard form is
superimposed wherever the governing class speaks the
same tongue as the mass of the people. Before the
Conquest the supremacy of Alfred's line had made West
Saxon the standard language of literature and administration; this criterion disappeared with the native aristocracy,
and regional variations of English, now the language of
the uneducated masses, developed unchecked. Middle
English, as the depressed post-Conquest vernacular is
called, appears very different from Old English because
many Norman spelling conventions crept in, while
changes in grammar and punctuation also took place over
the centuries. Among the dialects which made the period
one of wide local variety was Scots, which emerged as a
consequence of the strengthened political division between the kingdom of Scotland and Northumbria. The
new standard literary English of the fifteenth century was
descended not from West Saxon but from the dialect of
the east Midlands, economically the most advanced area,
whose speech came to form the basis of that of the
citizens of London. Modern standard English is derived
chiefly from this east Midland dialect because the
West Saxon pre-eminence was destroyed by the Normans.

English owes to French a vocabulary replete with
synonyms. It is not strictly a Norman legacy since the
French spoken at William's court, already a northern
variant of Central French, evolved as a still more distinct
dialect in England; this is now known as Anglo-Norman
and was regarded as somewhat provincial in the thirteenth
century, when the English court preferred the purer
French of Paris. A few everyday words were borrowed
by the English soon after the Conquest and occasionally
a similar word was adopted some generations later;

'warden', for example, is of Anglo-Norman origin, while 'guardian' comes from Central French. In Anglo-Norman times, however, there was no need for the natives, who performed what were generally inferior tasks, to borrow lavishly from their masters, and French began to make a significant contribution only when English was again becoming the language of government and literature.

The origins of particular words must obviously be left to philologists and all that can be done here is to show that French loan words still emphasize the fact that the English were once a subject race. In many spheres the triumphant French word had been for so long the chief one in use that it naturally superseded the older English word, and in a few cases there was no English equivalent. Words connected with the central administration are largely of French origin—including 'government', 'crown', 'state', parliament', 'council' and 'nation'—and so, inevitably, are many legal, military, ecclesiastical and artistic words, as well as abstract nouns. Often the French word represents the aristocratic version of a humbler object, the Englishman dwelling in a 'house' and his master in a 'manor', the peasant tending 'oxen' in the field, the lord being interested in the same animals only as 'beef' at his table. Where two synonyms of different origins still exist, the one derived from French is usually considered to sound the more refined.

It is arguable whether English was truly enriched by most of these additions, which replaced perfectly good pre-Conquest words. Purists claim that the language has never regained its old inventiveness and that it could not have hoped to do so once it slipped into the habit of uncritically adopting so much foreign matter. At all events the English word-stock was broadened, if not by the Normans themselves, at least by the speech of their descendants. At the same time the language itself, basically Germanic in structure, remained so even in vocabulary; its most common words—the numerals, the names of one's kindred, the parts of the body—are of pre-Conquest origin. This would have been otherwise only if one people had exterminated the other.

The Normans, a conquering minority, arrived after most of the historic towns and administrative boundaries of England had already taken shape, so that they had little chance to alter or to add to the stock of English place-names. Occasionally a French name was directly transplanted, such as Richemont which reappeared in Yorkshire when Count Alan of Brittany founded his castle at Richmond, and a number of obviously alien names were perpetuated in monastic foundations called after their parent houses, including Gracedieu, Grosmont and Marmont. Ordinary French words might be used to describe a topographical feature, Egremont in Cumberland having been identified as *aigre mont* or sharp-pointed hill, and compounds of *beau* and *bel* are fairly common, including Beaulieu, Bewdley and Belsize. None the less, while older forms of spelling and pronunciation were widely influenced, the total number of truly French place-names in England today is very small.

Whereas place-names are now the objects of methodical research, personal names remain neglected. Among the Germanic peoples an individual bore a single name, in a Christian kingdom the one which he had received at the font, but kinship could be stressed by giving every child a name with the same initial letter or containing the same syllable. In the West Saxon royal family children of either sex were commonly given names beginning 'Æthel-' (noble), 'Ead-' (rich) and 'Ælf-' (elf); the second element in these names also came from a select group of words, including '-ræd' (counsel), '-weard' (guardian) and '-mund' (protection). The names of Old English kings therefore tend to look very similar, particularly as 'Æ' and 'ea' have now become simply 'a' or 'e' in those names which survive: Ælfræd, for instance, is now 'Alfred' and Eadweard' is 'Edward', while even those not in current use are simplified, so that 'Æthel-ræd' has become 'Ethelred'. These compounds were less usual among the Anglo-Saxon peasantry, who were given names like Bugge and Ragge which have never since been thought elegant enough to deserve revival. Additional variety was provided by the Scandinavian settlers, among whom 'Sweyn' and 'Harold' were common, although the latter had a rarer Old English equivalent in 'Hereweard'; Viking names, however, were chiefly confined to the Danelaw.

The broad similarity of well-known pre-Conquest names and the scarcity of those in use today obscures the fact that the Old English enjoyed a much wider choice than did the Normans. The invaders, who retained their own language, naturally clung to the names which dominate the history of their duchy. 'William', 'Robert', 'Richard', 'Hugh', 'Roger' and 'Geoffrey' were all common in eleventh-century Normandy, as they are in England today, although a few Norman importations have since grown rare, such as 'Fulk', 'Walter' and 'Raoul', the last of which had previously been known to the English as 'Radulf' or 'Ralf'. The Normans, as good sons of the Church, also favoured New Testament names, which had made little headway in England before their coming. Women's names, then as now, were more plentiful; those of French origin include 'Maud', widely favoured during the century after the Conquest in its Latin form 'Matilda', as well as 'Alice', 'Agnes', 'Catherine', 'Margaret', 'Joan', 'Mary', 'Elizabeth' and 'Anne'.

At first the Conquest vastly increased the stock of names found in England, by introducing an entirely new range; the ultimate effect was the reverse, since a few French names drove out a great many native ones. Old habits were more persistent than was once supposed and the pace of change varied between different classes and regions; men of substance set the fashion, London was more advanced than the provinces and Wessex was less conservative than the Danelaw. In spite of this unevenness, it is broadly true that for a hundred years after Hastings the nomenclature of the foreign aristocracy percolated downwards, through every rank of society. 'William' soon became the commonest masculine name in the kingdom, with 'Robert' as a runner-up, only to be overtaken by 'John' during the thirteenth century, while 'Thomas', a Biblical name like 'John', gained in popularity after Becket's murder. Saints' names were being increasingly used for women around the year 1200 although 'Mary', the most sacred of all, was slow to win the favour which it enjoyed by the end of the Middle Ages and which, after a brief setback at the Reformation, it has held ever since. Edward I, who succeeded in 1272, was the first monarch to bear an English name since the Conquest and his baptism, an act of royal policy, ironically preceded the virtual extinction of the last native names among his subjects. In the later Middle Ages eighty per cent of all Englishmen were christened 'John', 'William', 'Thomas', 'Richard', 'Robert' or 'Henry'; twenty per cent of these were 'John' and fifteen per cent 'William', so that refuge was naturally found in diminutives and nicknames.

The rise of surnames belongs to later history, since these were not general before the second half of the thirteenth century and many of them assumed no fixed form for another three or four hundred years. There are none the less signs that a few Old English personal names were becoming unduly common by 1066 and that already a peasant might have to be distinguished by his father's name. Surnames certainly owe a great deal to the Conquest, since they can also be traced to members of the feudal aristocracy who identified themselves by adding 'de' to the names of their castles or estates. This process had recently started when William invaded England, but French territorial surnames like 'Beaumont' or 'Montgomery' could be enjoyed by only a few families, nearly all of which had died out long before the end of the Middle Ages. As English regained its ascendancy 'de' gradually became 'of', so that most high-sounding surnames today that imply an ancestral heritage by including the French prefix are the bastards of nineteenth-century romanticism and snobbery.

The Normans' chief contribution to English surnames was more indirect but far more extensive. As feudal society developed it became increasingly urgent for royal and baronial officials to tell men apart, and the triumph of a very small number of French Christian names threatened to make this task harder than ever. Men were forced to find an extra means of identification, whereupon some described themselves after their calling while others were known by their colouring and many more by their locality. Thousands more practised variations on their Christian names, including the pre-Conquest habit of adding '-son', which in the days of the Godwines had served only to distinguish one generation but which later became hereditary. 'Johnson', 'Johnston', 'Jones', 'Jenkins', 'Jackson' and several less common surnames could all be derived from one Christian name or from its nicknames, and every popular Christian name was of Norman origin. In this way the names of the Conqueror's companions have never ceased to multiply.

*

The vicissitudes of English after the Conquest show how radically a people's culture can be changed by political events. It is too sweeping to claim that Old English literature died as the result of one battle but not that it fell victim to the revolution that followed. If William had proved to be a second Cnut, ruling his conquered kingdom mainly through native magnates, English would still have had powerful patrons and would probably have survived as an official and a literary language, despite the fact that it differed far more from Norman French than from Danish. Even personal names, which are dictated by fashion, could have remained unaltered under anglicized rulers. Native resistance and William's own ruthlessness, however, ensured the temporary submergence of English, and his successors' continued ties with the Continent threatened to make this permanent. Its revival in a different guise can be traced ultimately to another conquest, when the French overran Normandy in 1204, and more directly to the anti-French sentiment which was spasmodically provoked in succeeding generations until it received its final stimulus from the nationalism born of the Hundred Years' War. The fate as well as the form of what is now the most widely used language in the world was thus decided by the dynastic ambitions of medieval princes.

CHAPTER ELEVEN

The New Architecture

SINCE the past is most easily judged by its monuments, it is unfortunate for the Anglo-Saxons that
none of their large buildings have survived. The most
ambitious pre-Conquest architecture has suffered from
the energy of the Normans, who destroyed and rebuilt on
a grand scale, and many of the humbler churches, left
alone by the conquerors, were not made to last. Ordinary
dwellings of the eleventh century were mainly of wattle-
and-daub and the churches themselves were built in
stone only where this was readily available. The walls of a
solitary wooden church still stand at Greenstead in Essex,
where oak logs have been split and set upright in what is
called stave-work, but so little is known of construction
in wood that it is not even certain whether this was
typical. Other churches were probably half-timbered and
some perhaps of block-work, with walls of long horizontal
logs like the halls of Viking chiefs or the traditional log-
cabins of North America.

Fortunately good stone was produced in several
counties and it is these areas which possess most of the
two hundred-odd smaller churches that contribute to
present-day knowledge of Old English architecture. The
best stone was found in Yorkshire, Somerset and around

233

Peterborough, especially at Barnack in Northamptonshire, and plenty of less durable red sandstone lay in
Cheshire, Herefordshire and the Midlands. London drew
heavily on the hard but rough Kentish ragstone, which
could be shipped down the Medway from Maidstone,
while Edward the Confessor relied on soft Reigate
firestone for his new abbey at Westminster. There is no
sign that the Anglo-Saxons could make bricks or tiles,
although both they and the Normans extracted large,
flat bricks from the Roman ruins. On the other hand
mortar, usually one part of lime mixed with two to three
parts of sand, had been known from the earliest days,
and lead, in which England was comparatively rich
thanks to the mines of Derbyshire, had been used to
cover timber roofs since the age of Bede. Glazing had
also been reintroduced from the Continent in his lifetime, but for three and a half centuries the windows
of churches were always more likely to be filled with
fretted stone slabs, wooden boards or even strips of
material.

Old English construction was comparatively crude,
walls being built of rubble and varying in thickness from
two and a half to three feet. The use of ashlar or rectangular building blocks was rare and sometimes walls even
lacked quoins or large cut stones at the angles. A small
complete church at Bradford-on-Avon, however, shows
that men were capable of building with well-squared
stones, and when quoins were supplied they were often
set upright and flat alternatively, with striking decorative
effect, in what is known as long-and-short work (Plate IX).
Herring-bone work, where stones were split in shallow
layers and set diagonally in courses on rough walls, was
also used before the Conquest but this device became so
much more usual afterwards that it is generally credited to
the Norman masons who were first imported by the
Confessor. Surviving masonry suggests that Edward's

own subjects, although capable of fine workmanship, were in general not very enterprising.

When church building was resumed in England after Alfred had beaten back the Danes, it was natural for men to copy the Carolingian architecture of Europe. The centre of this widespread style was Germany, the heart of Charlemagne's empire, where it developed in the tenth century under his Ottonian successors. The Carolingian style resembled the succeeding Romanesque, at which the Normans were to excel, but it was far less ambitious and never tackled the problems which later builders were to overcome. Under the Ottonian emperors the early diversity of plan dwindled in favour of single-aisled or cruciform churches, with an east end which was either square or in a semicircular form known as an apse. Arches were always round and blank arcading was used to decorate the outside walls; if the roof was of stone it consisted of a barrel-vault, a continuous vault unbroken by cross-vaults and resembling a tunnel. Whereas the bell-towers of early Italian churches were separate structures, Carolingian towers formed part of the church; a single tower might surmount the crossing of a large building, or else one might be set over each transverse arm or transept. Another distinguishing feature was the importance of the west end, which was generally endowed with its own altar. The Carolingian church was therefore treated more as a unity than was its Romanesque successor, where the all-important east end was often in use long before work had begun on the nave, which became a mere processional way.

Since small churches are all that are left from Anglo-Saxon times it is impossible to make an exact comparison between native and foreign achievements. Documents show that the vanished major churches of England often had a transept at the east end, with a presbytery projecting beyond, but that these were not so spacious as the cathedrals and abbey-churches of the Continent. The typical surviving English church of this age consists simply of two rectangles, a larger one for the nave and a smaller one, almost square, for the chancel. Western sanctuaries on the Carolingian model, however, were popular and towers, unknown in England before the Vikings, were also introduced into many later plans. Further Carolingian influence may be seen in the round-headed double-splay windows, so called because they were set in recesses in the wall, as well as in the occasional use of small circular openings; archways were always semi-circular and narrower doorways had either round or triangular heads, to which again there are counterparts on the Continent. The blind arcading and thin slices of masonry or pilaster-strips which adorn many exteriors might also come from Europe, although it can be argued that pilaster-strips were once constructional, in that they bound the rubble, or that they represented the pattern produced by half-timbering turned into stone, in which case they were of native origin. The ornament supplied by these strips may be seen on the finest of all Anglo-Saxon towers at Earls Barton (Northamptonshire), built under Æthelred II (Plate IX).

English architecture from Alfred's day was thus a Carolingian offshoot; unlike sculpture, it owed nothing to Scandinavia and very little to pre-Viking Northumbria. It plodded along its unspectacular course until the eve of the Conquest, generations after the architectural primacy of Germany had yielded place to the Romanesque styles of northern Italy and France. None the less, a people which had borrowed heavily in the past was presumably capable of doing so again; Edward the Confessor pointed the way, by planning Westminster Abbey on Norman lines, and the latest achievements south of the Channel would doubtless have been recognized in England, even if there had been no Conquest. Moreover, a number of features distinguish the Old English style from its Carolingian parent: long-and-short work, the separation of windows with two or more lights by squat, bulging shafts known as balusters (Plate IX), their position high up in the wall, the preference for round, bulbous capitals rather than cubical ones, and the use of a porticus or side-chamber, which evolved into a large porch. The English also preferred the square end to the apse, thereby revealing that love of 'cool and rational cubes' which, as Dr Pevsner shows, has lasted for a thousand years. Moreover, they have left early traces of their celebrated empirical nature in the crooked planning of many churches, built free-hand and without a single true right-angle in a manner that would have caused horror on the Continent. Finally, before pre-Conquest building is condemned as entirely humdrum, it must be remembered that the best has perished.

*

The Normans live above all in their buildings, although unlike many races, they deserve to be remembered for much else. Their architecture was the most massive and the most consistent variety of the Romanesque style which evolved in Western Europe between the ninth and twelfth centuries. Round arches remained universal and the stone ceilings at first were still barrel-vaults, of which the Conqueror has left London an example in the chapel of the White Tower. The next problem was to introduce larger windows, without weakening walls which already bore an outward thrust from the arch at the top. The answer lay in groined vaults, achieved by the intersection of simple vaulting surfaces (Figure I). Most English buildings in the century after the Conquest were built on these lines and therefore were Romanesque, but this elegant term is too vague to do justice to their peculiar and, sometimes, superior points. By the middle of the eleventh century the Normans were branching out into a new, monumental Romanesque style, with buildings of heavier masonry and on a larger scale. Distinct features had appeared, which were to be developed in England.

A few basic features of Norman design and construction must be described. In the major churches, the interior walls were divided into three storeys: the main arcade, the tribune or *triforium* and the clerestory (Figure IIa). The main piers were uniform, frequently square with an attached shaft on each face, or alternated with slighter, often cylindrical, piers. Between the bays, a shaft ran up the face of each wall, either to buttress it or to

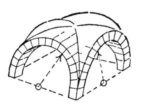 

Fig. I *Intersecting barrel-vault, or groined vault, viewed from above and below* (*Banister Fletcher*, A History of Architecture on the Comparative Method, *17th edition, Athlone Press*)

support a groined or ribbed vault, although a stone roof was rarely attempted at first. None knew better than the Normans, with their Viking blood, that buildings should be solidly constructed and safe from fire, so that the roofing of an entire church in masonry became a far-off goal.

Eventually, two main variants occurred in design and two more in construction. In Lower Normandy, around Caen, churches tended to follow the 'Benedictine' plan, with three apses at the east end, transepts with an eastern apse in each arm and an aisled nave (Figure IIIa). Around Rouen, but probably imported from central France,

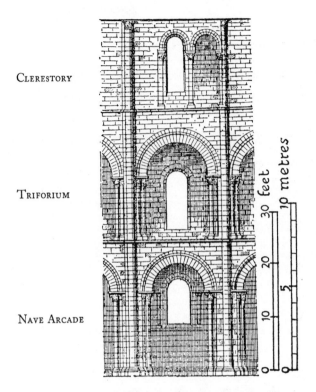

CLERESTORY

TRIFORIUM

NAVE ARCADE

30 feet

10 metres

20

5

10

0   0

Fig. IIa *Saint-Etienne, Caen: interior elevation of nave* (*T. S. R. Boase*, English Art, *1100–1216, Oxford History of English Art*)

Fig. IIb *'Thick' or 'hollow' wall at Saint-Etienne, Caen: plan at clerestory level* (*G. Webb*, Architecture in Britain, the Middle Ages, *Pelican History of Art*)

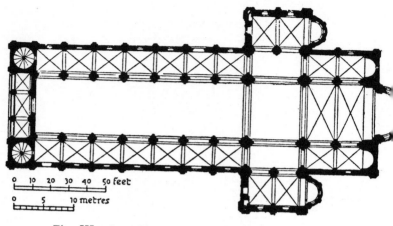

Fig. IIIa *Saint-Nicolas, Caen: the three-apse plan* (*A. W. Clapham*, English Romanesque Architecture after the Conquest, *Clarendon Press, by permission from* Congrés Archéologique de France, *vol. i*)

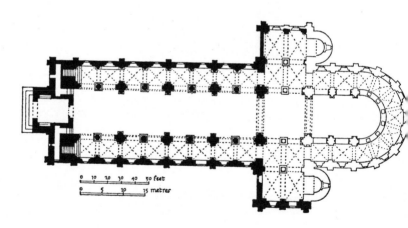

Fig. IIIb *Jumièges Abbey: the ambulatory plan* (*A. W. Clapham*, English Romanesque Architecture after the Conquest, *Clarendon Press, by permission from* Bulletin Monumentale, *vol. lxxxvii*)

appeared a fully developed ambulatory plan, with arcade, aisle and radiating chapels (Figure IIIb). Meanwhile, a new form of internal buttressing had arrived in the shape of a wall passage or gallery at the base of the clerestory, so that the original 'thin' wall became rivalled by what is confusingly known as the 'thick' or the 'hollow' wall (Figure IIb).

Among the famous churches in the duchy about the time of the Conquest, the three-apse plan is found in the parish church of Saint-Nicolas, Caen, and also in the abbey-churches of Saint-Etienne and La Trinité, sometimes known as l'Abbaye-aux-Hommes and L'Abbaye-aux-Dames, which were founded by William and Matilda to expiate their marriage; the curved, ambulatory plan was used in Rouen Cathedral, at Jumièges and Saint-Wandrille. Jumièges is the classic surviving example of the thin wall, while Saint-Etienne, Caen, and Cerisy have the hollow wall. Both sets of variants were to be used for a while in England.

More exciting is the development of the stone vault. The earliest great Norman church at Bernay, built between 1017 and 1045–50, has groined vaults over the aisles and a semi-domed apse, but no vaults over nave or transepts and only shafts up the inner faces of the choir piers to hint at higher aims. The builders' intentions at le Mont-Saint-Michel and Saint-Gervais, Falaise, are equally perplexing but a groined stone vault was at last achieved at Notre-Dame sur l'Eau, Domfront, about 1050–60, over the choirs of La Trinité, Caen, about 1062–6, and Saint-Nicolas, Caen, about 1083. These groined vaults, being rounded, were limited in height to roughly half the distance between the walls, although semi-circles could be distorted, as they had to be for diagonal arches (Figures IVa, IVb). None the less, it was possible to cover a main span. The Normans were now pre-eminent in northern France.

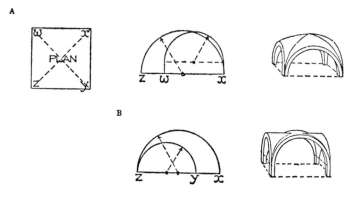

Fig. IV *The problem of regulating the height of ribs of different span over a square compartment*
a *The diagonal and transverse arms are purely semicircular, resulting in a rounded top*
b *The transverse ribs are stilted, so as to produce a level top* (*both from Banister Fletcher*, A History of Architecture on the Comparative Method, *17th edition, Athlone Press*)

*

In architecture, as in other fields, foreign influences reached England before the Conquest; in this particular sphere the source of inspiration need not be vaguely labelled 'Continental', for it undoubtedly lay in the duchy. The Bayeux Tapestry depicts the Confessor's abbey at Westminster as purely Norman in design, with an east end of three apses, following the plan which won most favour in the duchy and which William and Matilda chose at Caen. The abbey probably had a thin wall, unlike the Caen churches but like Jumièges, with a nave of thirteen bays and, again as at Jumièges, alternating piers. The originality of Westminster lay in its size, for the dimensions of the nave were greater than those of any known Norman church of that age. The remains of Rouen Cathedral, often cited as an example of the grandeur of Norman ideas, suggest that it was 305 feet long, while the foundations of Westminster Abbey give it an internal length of 322 feet. In England, Norman ambitions were already overflowing into new channels.

Since Edward the Confessor was half Norman in blood and more than half Norman in taste, other builders, such as Harold at Waltham or Leofric at Coventry, may not have followed their king. Employers, particularly prelates, sometimes helped to design their buildings, although this can rarely be proved, while planning, as well as constructing, might fall to the professional masons, who nearly all remain anonymous. In days when less depended upon knowledge than upon the masons' daring, there was probably less meddling by those who paid than there is now, but the patron's taste has always counted. Four of Edward's bishops in the west country were Lorrainers, if the foreign-educated Leofric of Exeter is included, and all survived the Conquest, which may explain Rhenish affinities in several western churches. William himself did not bring only Norman influences, for his army was drawn from many lands. None the less, Old English architecture could not absorb these new foreign styles as it had those of the Vikings or the Carolingian Empire. It succumbed completely before the century was out and native genius lived on only in a further development of the conquerors' skill, along lines whose persistence reveals a peculiar English taste. It is this emergence of insular preferences and the crowning of the Norman masons' aims in England that justifies the new school in the island being called Anglo-Norman.

Largeness was to be an Anglo-Norman characteristic. Already foreshadowed in Westminster Abbey, it is even more striking when the nave of Jumièges, completed in 1067, is compared with that of St Albans Abbey, mainly finished by 1093, for the first measures 145 feet by 65 feet and the second 275 feet by 77 feet. Massiveness was already notable in Normandy, where the key to stability was still sought in solidity rather than in the nicely

calculated interplay of stresses and abutments which was
to make medieval architecture so fascinating. This, too,
is more obvious in England, because of the amount of
rubble or rough material which had to be used.

If most houses were still made of wattle-and-daub, the
future lay with stone and mortar. At Lewes, William de
Warenne lost no time in substituting his Cluniac priory
for the wooden chapel of St Pancras and, although churches
of wood still existed in the thirteenth century, masonry
was employed much more widely after the Conquest. It
has been estimated, for a later date, that the carriage of
stone by land equalled the cost of the stone itself after
about twelve miles. Inevitably, local quarries continued
to be chosen wherever possible if there were no Roman
materials, such as the bricks used by Abbot Paul of Caen
at St Albans (Plate X). For the more ambitious churches
in East Anglia and the Home Counties, which called for
non-local materials, the Normans turned to their duchy.
The fine white stone of Caen was used from the Conquest
onwards in the south-east, although imports are not
clearly recorded until the rebuilding of Canterbury in
1175, and Caen became the staple freestone until partially
replaced by Barnack in the early twelfth century. Marble
fonts, tombstones and a few capitals are known from the
third quarter of the twelfth century but most were mass-
produced imports from Tournai, for the famous Purbeck
marble does not occur until the end of the period.

Norman building techniques were more varied than
those of the Anglo-Saxons. Herring-bone work became
much commoner, only to be abandoned as a primitive
device soon after 1100. Also under Henry I, more finely
cut ashlar was introduced, perhaps first at Sherborne
Castle in Dorset; this fine-jointed work helped to reduce
the amount of masonry which was needed. A good way of
dating stone is by the lines tooled on the external face of
the ashlar, for the lines of this period are all diagonal,

being succeeded by vertical ones about 1200. The rubble walls of the smaller churches became still more solid, being seldom less than 3 feet thick and, like the bricks of St Albans, plastered inside and out (Plate X). Mortar continued to play a vital part in the survival of stone buildings, while window glass remained a rarity until the thirteenth century. The Normans were quick to appreciate English experience in the use of lead and when the bishop of Coutances wished to repair his lightning-struck cathedral in 1091, he sent across the Channel for a plumber.

*

'You might see churches rise in every village, and, in the towns and cities, monasteries built after a style unknown before,' wrote William of Malmesbury in the early twelfth century. The thirty years after Hastings witnessed the most feverish building activity that this country has ever known. Traditional dates of construction are often misleading, since the east end would be consecrated while work began on the nave, but rebuilding started at nearly every cathedral and major abbey. Justice is now demanded for the Anglo-Saxons, whose cathedrals were probably far larger than once was imagined; none the less, when Henry I became king his senior bishop, Osbern of Exeter, was alone in having stayed satisfied with the edifice which he had found.

No apology is needed for concentrating on the Anglo-Norman cathedrals and great abbey-churches but only for being unable to cite more examples. There are survivals in nearly every English county and it is in them that progress in plan, construction and adornment is most obvious. At first, the newcomers deigned to found scarcely anything smaller, although their parish churches of the next century have escaped intact more often than grander buildings. Decoration in stone was unfamiliar to the conquerors, even as patterns on a surface, let alone in relief, but its later luxuriance leads naturally to a section on sculpture. The few domestic buildings that remain form another part of this chapter, together with military architecture, which developed much more slowly.

Anglo-Norman churches of the first generation cannot easily be divided into geographical schools. The three-apse plan was widely adopted and partly survives in important examples at Blyth Priory (Nottinghamshire), St Albans Abbey, Ely Cathedral, Christchurch Priory (Hampshire), Lincoln and, from the twelfth century, Peterborough: of these, Peterborough is the only major three-apse church with its original east end, while the nave of Blyth can claim to be the closest copy of a Norman-French church in England. The first church to be built after the Conquest, Battle Abbey, has disappeared, but excavations show that it followed the ambulatory plan, with radiating chapels. This may have been because Battle was colonized with monks not from Normandy but from Marmoutier in the Loire valley, although this plan also became widespread. The main ambulatory churches still existing in part are the cathedrals of Winchester, Worcester and Gloucester, Tewkesbury Abbey (Gloucestershire), Pershore Abbey (Worcestershire), and Norwich Cathedral: the last of these is the most complete of the great Anglo-Norman churches, with the original main apse, ambulatory and tower (Plate XI).

Externally, a central tower over the crossing was usual, although two western ones were often added. Accidents or a desire to finish more essential parts first have left few examples earlier than 1150, St Albans being the most striking exception. Sometimes the Carolingian rule of axial towers might be used, especially in the west; an enlargement of the late eleventh-century cathedral at Old Sarum, about 1125–30, included two

towers over the transepts and similar ones still stand at
Exeter, which has a Rhenish parallel at Murbach, in
Alsace. Another west-country variation was the horizontal
division of transepts and east end at Tewkesbury and
Pershore into four stages; this was quite foreign to
Anglo-Norman practice and has no known origin.

Rufus's spoliation led to a break in church building
during his last years, for the vacancies at his death
included Ely, St Albans, Bury St Edmunds, London and
Durham. Deep interest attaches to plans adopted in the
second Anglo-Norman phase, after 1100, as the three-
apse and ambulatory patterns both give way to square
east ends. Peterborough, St Bartholomew's, Smithfield,
and Leominster Priory (Herefordshire) persisted in the
old way, the last being founded as late as 1125, but
Southwell Cathedral (Nottinghamshire) and Romsey
nunnery church (Hampshire), begun about 1120, show
a reversion that soon became general. An Old English
love had been revived, to become a distinctive feature of
later architecture.

In spite of the example of Westminster, the thick or
hollow wall was to be the inspiration of Anglo-Norman
building. The object of introducing a gallery at the base
of the clerestory had been to thicken the wall above the
main arcades, so that there would be no need for internal
buttresses or attached shaftings (Figure IIb). Nevertheless, Romanesque differed from the Carolingian style in
preferring subdivisions, and half-round shafts were
usually retained, presumably because the vertical bays
were admired. Another feature of the hollow wall was to
be developed more logically and this was its low elevation,
proportionate to its length. The thin wall of Jumièges
had risen to 82 feet, but the later hollow one of Saint-
Etienne, Caen, had reached a mere 78 feet. In England,
this tendency was so exaggerated that the naves of Ely
and Peterborough were 86 feet and 81 feet high but

260 feet and 235 feet in length, while Winchester
boasted the longest nave in Europe, 318 feet from end to
end.

The Anglo-Saxons had favoured square or oblong
compartments and these appear in England more than in
Norman buildings elsewhere. Longitudinal emphasis,
like the triumph of the square east end, shows the early
reassertion of native prejudice. This English attitude to
architecture, angular rather than sculptural, has generally
persisted, reaching its height in the Perpendicular of the
later Middle Ages.

*

Meanwhile, the problem of stone vaulting was absorbing the attention of builders in the Norman Empire, in
France and in North Italy. In England, before the close
of the eleventh century, there are signs that it was hoped
to roof the main structure in stone at Gloucester, Norwich
and Chichester, but only a simple groined vault may have
been intended. The earliest high vault in groined form is
also the only one to survive, at Chepstow Priory (Monmouthshire) and dates from about 1120. The secret
of progress lay first in the ribbed vault, made up of a
framework of arched ribs, supporting thin stone panels
to cover the spaces between them, and later in the pointed
arch (Figure V).

The credit for the evolution of the Romanesque
ribbed vault has been claimed by Northern Lombard and
Anglo-Norman partisans. Although too much has been
lost for this ever to be anything save a subject for happy
dispute, the award is now usually given to a building not
merely in the north but at the remotest end of the Norman world. Since 995, the rocky fastness of Durham had
been a resting place for the bones of St Cuthbert; there, a
humble chapel had been replaced with a fine church of
wood and this, in turn, had been rebuilt in stone under

Cnut. Durham, lying in the path of invaders from Scotland, was made for storms and, as a natural rallying point for native hostility to William, it suffered more than ever in his reign. Hard times produced hard men and few more so than in the murdered Bishop Walcher's successors, William of Saint-Carilef, who died in 1096, and Rufus's evil genius, Ranulph Flambard. These political prelates sought many outlets for their ambitions and both of them found one in building.

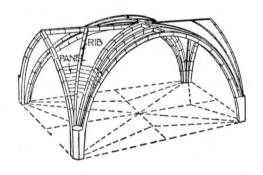

Fig. V *Details of a Gothic ribbed vault over an oblong compartment* (*Banister Fletcher*, A History of Architecture on the Comparative Method, *17th edition, Athlone Press*)

Work was started on Durham Cathedral in 1093, finished up to the nave by 1099 and completed by 1133, five years after Flambard's death, save for the upper storeys of the two western towers. The cathedral, not long by the excessive Anglo-Norman standards, is grand enough in scale to be placed in the front rank of Romanesque churches and was substantially finished in the very short space of forty years. A late Norman Galilee Chapel was added to the west end in the 1170s, the three original apses with the high vault of the choir were replaced in the thirteenth century by the Chapel of the Nine Altars and the central tower was rebuilt at the end of the Middle

Ages, but as a whole the early work remains remarkably complete (Plate XII).

Durham's internal structure is unique in England, with very pronounced alternating piers dividing the whole building into double bays, which are marked in the vault by cross-arches. The main arcades are over twice the height of the *triforium* gallery, while the clerestory in the choir consists of three arches, with one window in each bay. The major compound piers are elaborately shafted but no more impressive than the minor ones, massive cylinders, boldly incised with ribs and fluting (Plate XIII). Nowhere else can one be overwhelmed so easily by the strength of Norman architecture. Nowhere else is such confidence shown in the proportions or the placing of ornament. A remarkable over-all linear pattern was achieved, which was to be an obsession of later English architects. This may represent the first blending of two traditions for, if the bishops were Norman, the monks of Durham, with their illuminated manuscripts, formed an enclave where Anglo-Saxon taste lived on.

Above all, Durham is famous for being the first large building in north-west Europe to be roofed throughout with ribbed vaulting. The vanished high vault of the choir was probably ribbed, as the aisles still are, but this treatment at first may have been meant for the roof of the choir alone. The choir is 125 feet long by 32 feet 8 inches wide, both aisles being 15 feet 3 inches wide, while each transept measures 62 feet 9 inches by 33 feet 7 inches, excluding its aisle, and the nave 198 feet by 32 feet 4 inches, the nave aisles being 17 feet 6 inches wide. The decision to extend ribbed vaulting to the transepts and main nave was therefore a bold one and, even if the vault's planning has to be dated to 1115 or later, the builders' originality must still be admired. Durham has been said to assail the traditional primacy of France, as Constable and Turner anticipated Impressionism, and it stands not as a national but as a European landmark.

*

Meanwhile, Romanesque forms flourished, although embellished with increasingly elaborate carvings. These forms survived well into the second half of the twelfth century and may be seen in the nave which remains from Malmesbury Abbey (Wiltshire), apart from its pointed arch, in the cruciform rib-vaulted church of St Cross (Winchester), and the crypt of York Minster, all of which date from about 1160. Still later examples appear in the Galilee at Durham, Oxford Cathedral, the nave of Worksop Priory (Nottinghamshire) and the Lady Chapel at Glastonbury, the last of which was built between 1184 and 1186.

Many of these overlap with the early churches of the Cistercians, the austere white monks who, in architecture as in their way of life, reacted against the prevailing sumptuousness. Their founder, St Bernard of Clairvaux, condemned 'immoderate length, superfluous breadth, costly polishing and strange designs' but the buildings of his order, if stark, were not modest in dimensions. The Cistercians in England began by closely following Burgundian models, founding their houses in lonely valleys where the greenery today disguises the severity of the men who built there. In general, they adopted the pointed arch and so opened the way for Gothic. Pointed arches can vary widely in width while remaining the same height, so that there would soon be no need for the semicircular distortions into which the Anglo-Normans had been forced by a desire to keep the tops or 'crowns' of their vaults level (Figures VI, IVa, b). In Yorkshire, the ruined naves of Fountains and Rievaulx, begun in the 1130s, survive as the earliest Cistercian works, while Gothic influence is strong in their later abbeys at Furness

(Lancashire), Roche and Byland (Yorkshire), the last of which was begun about 1175.

Every style has a stage beyond which it cannot be carried without losing its identity. In construction, the Anglo-Norman school had reached that point at Durham. A better knowledge of thrusts and balances, with the finer cutting of stone, made it possible to abandon the solid masses of masonry on which earlier builders had relied; churches were slowly to assume a new aspect, as ribbed vaults and high pointed arches were exploited.

Fig. VI *Gothic solution to the problem of vaulting. The pointed arches can be made to any height, for any span, and still produce a level top* (*Banister Fletcher*, A History of Architecture on the Comparative Method, *17th edition, Athlone Press*)

Outside, buttresses and pinnacles would one day multiply to take the gathered stresses, while inside the ponderous, well-spaced arcades were to give way to a new emphasis on height and the great *triforium* galleries were to disappear, allowing the clerestory walls to become webs of stonework, filled with coloured glass. England's Gothic masterpieces owed much to the Île-de-France, whose influence in the last decades of the twelfth century is shown by the work at Canterbury of William of Sens and his successor, William the Englishman, after the fire of 1174. Taste varies but the century after the Conquest must always be a source of pride to the English, for those years of national humiliation were the only ones when a European style reached its perfection in the island.

✳

The English, eclipsed by the Normans as engineers, excelled in those arts which require sympathetic imagination and delicate treatment. Sculpture had vied with manuscript illumination in Bede's Northumbria, when it had been widely used for its own sake on individual monuments rather than as architectural decoration. Geometrical interlacements, curling foliage, birds, beasts and human figures had all been carved with great effect, notably on gigantic stone crosses of which the finest examples are now at Bewcastle and Ruthwell. The wars of Alfred's day proved less destructive to ornamental work in stone and metal than to the other arts, since the Vikings themselves were masters of several intricate styles. Northumbria therefore continued to be a centre of carving, where native forms blended with those of Scandinavia and Ireland, and it remains the source of most surviving pre-Conquest sculpture. This later northern work, however, is inferior to its predecessors, and the finest late Saxon carving comes from the south.

During the tenth century southern England boasted distinctive styles of decoration in metal-work and manuscript illumination. Unhappily there are not enough examples of sculpture to make clear the exact influence of one art upon another; the Winchester style of the manuscripts was derived from the Carolingians, who relied heavily on the acanthus as a motif, and this plant was certainly carved by the English in stone, both on panels and on the capitals of shafts and arches. As in earlier centuries, carving was used more for separate pieces than as an enrichment to buildings, although a post-Conquest development was anticipated by the occasional appearance of carving in an enclosed space over a door known as a tympanum. The towering crosses of Northumbria gave way to smaller ones, used as headstones for graves, while gabled or flat tomb-slabs were still more common. Churches were decorated with stucco-work as well as in stone, so that many isolated carvings which now exist were once part of a larger composition.

Late Saxon figure-sculpture survives only in a few works but some of these are so sophisticated that it was once thought that they could not date from before the Conquest. A rood at Romsey, with all the austerity and assurance of Byzantine art, at any rate is now accepted as English and as revealing the continued penetration of foreign influences, notably from Germany where the Byzantine tradition was strong (Plate XIV). If the Normans channelled their energies into problems of construction, the skill and emotions of the English stoneworkers found their fulfilment in carving.

The effect of the Conquest on sculpture was as decisive as on architecture, but for the worse. There was more to be destroyed and less to be gained. The newcomers had little taste for ornament and the eclipse of native patrons meant that sculpture was confined to rustic churches. It is therefore not surprising that the first generation of Anglo-Norman buildings, such as the cathedrals of Winchester, Gloucester and Worcester, are remarkable for their starkness. The change was radical: the Anglo-Saxons, with their free standing crosses and slabs, had practised sculpture on its own, but when it revived it was to serve as an addition to architecture.

The best of what little carving there was in the duchy had been mainly simple crocket foliage and a few crude figures on capitals, although Bernay boasts more sophistic-ated work of Burgundian inspiration. Arches were sometimes enriched with a diaper pattern of squares or diamonds, or with a billet ornament of short raised rectangles; these duly crossed the Channel. The simple imitation of the classical Corinthian capital known as the volute, a Norman favourite, was also introduced and can be seen in St John's Chapel at the Tower of London or in the chapel at Durham castle. A clear setback for the Normans has been seen in the English preference for the shallower cubical or cushion capital, which more easily linked a circular pillar to a square abacus. This suggests Rhenish influence, but the change is marked only after the Conquest and so must be due to the invaders, who used both designs in turn at Ely (Figures VIIa, b). Cushions could be curved further to become scalloped capitals; plain forms are found at first, in the crypts of Winchester, Worcester and Gloucester, the latest of which was begun in 1089, and eventually they were exported to Normandy. In the rare cases where the newcomers attempted figure sculpture, as in the pot-bellied devils on the capitals at Durham Castle chapel, the result lacked naturalism. Here, the richest series of early Anglo-Norman sculptures achieves startling decoration only by crude deformity (Plate XVa).

Abundant sculptured capitals show that a change was taking place in the early twelfth century. Elaborate figure subjects never became so common as in France but were attempted with some success in the choir at Hereford about 1115, on the tower arches at Southwell Cathedral about 1120 and the cloisters of Norwich, Reading and Hyde. At Canterbury, the plain cushion capitals of about 1100 were carved some twenty years later and have been detected as the centre of a southern school, which was later developed at Reading. An odd distinction in England is that, where such narrative subjects were chosen, they were rarely religious or moral ones; pictures of daily life, signs of the Zodiac, animals and, above all, mythical monsters were more popular (Plate XVb).

Capitals and the tympanum over the doorway were no longer the only subjects for sculpture. Outside, doors and windows might be framed with decoration, while projecting supports or corbels excelled in grotesque carving.

In the second decade of the century appeared the chevron, a zig-zag ornament for arches, found in the naves of Durham and Norwich but not in the earlier east ends

Fig. VIIa *Ely Cathedral: volute capitals*

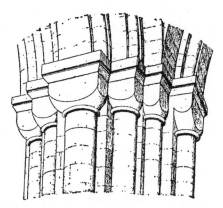

Fig. VIIb *Ely Cathedral: cushion capitals (both from T. S. R. Boase,* English Art, 1100–1216, *Oxford History of English Art)*

(Plate XIII). The chevron, the most typical Anglo-Norman enrichment, was soon followed by a variety of designs including the lozenge, formed by connecting two rows of chevrons, the disc ornament, especially in the eastern

counties, the embattled, chain, rosette and cable ornaments, all of which were being used by 1150. The
acanthus, the true Anglo-Norman foliage, appears
mainly on minor surfaces such as fonts or tympana.
Walls were sometimes given geometrical patterns, while
intersecting blind arcading, which had Islamic origins,
became a standard decoration. This was unusually
popular in England and probably first used inside
below the windows of the choir aisles at Durham; later,
it often covered outside surfaces, particularly those of
largely decorative parts, such as towers and west fronts
(Plate XX).

Among these decorations, the sinister beak-head
ornament has excited attention for its Scandinavian
appearance, consisting of heads with large eyes, gripping
the mouldings of an arch. This was particularly popular
in Oxfordshire and Yorkshire and, like the chevron, it was
later used in Normandy (Plate XVIIa). The first examples,
at Reading about 1130, have pre-Conquest precedents in
Deerhurst Church (Gloucestershire), but their immediate
source in the twelfth century can only be guessed. Indeed,
the whole question of lingering or revived pre-Conquest
traditions is confused, for it is rarely possible to date the
many village churches, where running foliage and
relatively superior figures hint at a parallel school of
native carving, unconnected with purely Continental
Romanesque. The flat, ribbon-like Scandinavian designs
had continued for a few years, as in a panel at Jevington
(Sussex), but they had almost disappeared by the early
twelfth century; only a capital at Norwich from as late as
1140 shows that this sinuous style may have lingered on
in East Anglian wood carving. Completely different
are two dramatic reliefs in the choir at Chichester, also
carved about 1140, which have no precursors, so that
their excellence is merely tantalizing (Plate XVIII).

Regional schools are not easily discernible, save in

Herefordshire during the 1140s. Here, confusingly exuberant carving in the little church at Kilpeck is now the best example of a group so unusual as to suggest a single pattern-book, based perhaps on copies made during a pilgrimage through France to Santiago de Compostella. Unlike the best work of the south, that of the Herefordshire school is found in modest churches, founded by laymen. For the first time since the Conquest, Continental influence is strong, although Celtic traces persist in lavish interlacements (Plates XIXa, b, c).

Europe now began to contribute more openly to Romanesque sculpture in England. Alterations to the late eleventh-century west front at Lincoln, carried out after a fire in 1141, show Italian influences, as well as French ones from Saint-Denis. Byzantine models were used, especially for a relief of the Virgin and Child at York Minster and a screen, of which two panels survive, at Durham. Western France was brought under the English Crown by Henry II and a prolific school of carving in Yorkshire, which reached its height in the church at Fishlake about 1170, was indebted to it. So were the main west doorway at Rochester Cathedral and Kent's most elaborate small church at Barfreston, where French motifs mingled with a profusion of local and often grotesquely humorous subjects. In choice and treatment of themes Malmesbury, the apogee of later Romanesque sculpture, which dates from 1160 to 1170, is linked with south-western France (Plate XVIIb). Foreign contacts were not always so fruitful. 'What profit is there in those ridiculous monsters?' demanded that baleful philistine, St Bernard, when faced with the riches of Benedictine and Cluniac sculpture. In northern England, the York-shire school eventually withered before the blasts of his disciples.

All this, however, is no part of the Norman legacy and it is enough to stress English survivals. Beak-heads and other native patterns still appeared at Lincoln and in the Yorkshire school, which applied its skilfully carved decorations somewhat wildly, while even at Malmesbury the form of the doorways, with their continuous orders, was English. Local vitality is obvious in the schools of fonts which flourished in the late twelfth century, especially in Norfolk, the Chilterns and Cornwall. The rectangular bowls of Norfolk, lovely chalice shaped ones from the Chilterns and the Cornish chalices with four shafts added, are all elaborate works (Plates XVIa, b). Here, as well as on larger surfaces, English craftsmen lovingly experimented with their own designs, which never succumbed before foreign ones but often were literally entwined with them.

The development of florid decoration has been deplored not only by those who relish the extreme simplicity of earlier years. At first, enrichment was mainly confined to the structural lines of the building, such as the chevrons on the arcades at Durham (although the patterns on the cylindrical piers break this rule) but it soon started to creep over the surface. Ely Cathedral and the nave at Gloucester show how the main forms were being broken up, while the mid-twelfth century west front at Castle Acre Priory (Norfolk), has every kind of motif spread across it and that of Malmesbury has become a screen, disguising the structure which lies behind (Plate XX). The effect now is not to awe with naked strength but to dazzle with fantastic decoration.

*

Domestic buildings from Norman days, while much scarcer than churches, are superior to most Continental remains and surprisingly plentiful. Those attached to monasteries are the finest, including a great covered staircase to the guests' accommodation provided by Lanfranc at Canterbury, the refectory of St Martin's

Priory, Dover, and an eleventh-century vaulted range from another at Westminster Abbey. These refectories could be very spacious: that at Byland measured 100 feet by 31 feet, those at Fountains, Rievaulx and Westminster were still bigger, while the one at Peterborough, remodelled in the thirteenth century, was 145 feet by 37 feet 8 inches. A number of monastic gatehouses still stand, the most complete being one of about 1130 at Bury St Edmunds (Plate XXI); dormitories, infirmaries and kitchens, on the other hand, are known only from plans. More important in its day was the chapter-house, where business was discussed. In dramatic contrast to the low vestibule, the vaults of a chapter-house might reach a span of 35 feet, as at Durham, Gloucester and Reading. For some unknown reason, Worcester produced a circular chapter-house, 56 feet in diameter, vaulted to a central column, which was the forerunner of a series of such polygonal buildings, peculiar to England (Plate XXII).

Apart from castles, occasional purely secular buildings show that the monks did not monopolize stone. The present fourteenth-century Westminster Hall incorporates the walls of Rufus's building $237\frac{1}{2}$ feet by $67\frac{1}{2}$ feet, and there remains a small courtyard house in Sherborne Castle, from about 1130, a chapel and doorway in Durham Castle, a hall at Wolvesley, near Winchester, and merchants' houses at Lincoln, Southampton and Bury St Edmunds.

This short list is not quite fair to the laity, since even the first castles were residences as well as military posts. It has been seen that those from which the invaders originally subjected the English were mounds, surmounted by hastily constructed fortifications of wood. Indeed, little else was possible, for freshly dug earth could not bear the collosal weight of Norman masonry. It is not surprising that there are only two great tower-

keeps or *donjons* in England which date from before
1100. The White Tower at London was begun in 1079,
on the site of a makeshift castle twelve years older and
possibly even of a pre-Conquest earthwork, while a
gigantic keep at Colchester was set up from Roman
materials. Both of these are distinguished by the large
space devoted to a chapel, while all the other floors are
divided into two unequal rooms.

From Henry I's time date Corfe Castle and Sherborne
(Dorset), Canterbury, Rochester (Plate XXIII) and perhaps Lancaster, but most of the grim Norman-style keeps
which stand today belong to the reign of Henry II. At
Dover, Castle Rising, Newcastle, Middleham, Richmond
(Yorkshire), Kenilworth and Carlisle there are tremendous
square towers, unmellowed by time, with flat buttresses
and once with a timber roof hidden behind the parapet.
Round or half-round towers, perhaps copied from
Byzantine models which impressed crusaders, were
introduced in the late twelfth century, starting with an
eighteen-sided castle at Orford (Suffolk), between 1165
and 1172, but these are no part of the Norman tradition.

Since castles were new to England, there is no problem about the blending of foreign with native traditions.
This is disappointing, for the names of military architects
have been preserved in accounts for years when other
builders are unknown. Strictly speaking, they were
designers of military engines who went on to plan the
defence works which housed or were to withstand them.
Ailnoth the engineer, so called from *ingeniator*, one who is
ingenious or contrives, is mentioned as a surveyor of the
king's buildings at Westminster and the Tower in 1157.
This is eighteen years before the appearance at Canterbury of William of Sens, England's first great cathedral
architect of whom much more is known than his name.
Ailnoth, who built, embellished and dismantled other
castles in the 1160s and 1170s, has an English sound.

Other engineers, including one who is called a *prudens architectus*, appear after 1170, in the service of kings and magnates.

*

The buildings of the late eleventh and twelfth centuries are now widely admired, not just because anyone can point to a rounded arch and pronounce it Norman. Today, sheer strength impresses and clean lines find favour, whereas a hundred years ago they repelled. The nineteenth century once more appreciated and copied the styles which earlier rationalists had contemptuously lumped together as 'Gothic'. Medieval architecture was then classified, too rigidly for modern purists but usefully for laymen; the fifteenth century, with its airy Perpendicular achievements, was generally shunned, but many loved the more robust 'perfection' of fourteenth-century Decorated, while the 'purity' of thirteenth-century Early English appealed still more widely. With the enthusiasm of antiquarians burning more fiercely as they looked back in time, it might be expected that the Normans would come into their own, but the revival passed them by. Ruskin denounced the 'suspensions in air, and other such tricks and vanities' of King's College Chapel, Cambridge, as 'a piece of architectural juggling', but he had no compliments for the century after the Conquest. Norman and Lombard Romanesque were alike dismissed as 'styles essentially infantine and barbarous, however Herculean their infancy or majestic their outlawry'.

At least these Norman works were spared the supreme contempt of the sterner Victorians. The elaborate delicacy of the later Middle Ages might be dismissed as 'effeminate' or 'decadent', parallels being drawn with the low public morality of that time, but such terms could no more be applied to the work of the Anglo-Normans than to the succeeding Gothic styles of Transitional and Early English. 'Massive', 'uncompromising', 'austere' have always described Norman architecture, just as these bleak adjectives are invariably visited upon its creators. It is always tempting to fill in a sketch of the Normans by deducing their character from their buildings, but not altogether wise.

The ruthless and inexorable military conquest of England did not march with a similar stately progress in the arts. Trial and error often brought disaster and only the triumphs remain as landmarks. It is true that Norman Romanesque was an unusually emphatic style, where no attempt was made to hide the bulkiness of piers, walls and arches. It was also a sombre style, in that aisles, transepts and other recesses were places of deep shadow. No lightness and little light are found, yet unrelieved gloom was never intended. The theories on proportion of Vitruvius, who wrote in the first century B.C., were known at least to a few scholars, but builders were not likely to be much influenced and there was none of the classical concentration on proportion and design. Chroniclers show that colour was the chief interest and that bright paint warmed even the earliest, plainest churches, while candlelight made metals glint and jewels sparkle in the deep recesses. Bold swathes of green, red and blue on walls and roofs, with gleams from the patches of mysterious darkness, once made the Norman church interiors far different from the grey caverns known today.

The severity of Norman *donjons* is an apt symbol of their rule but no conquerors should be judged by such monuments. Castles owed their aspect to the needs of warfare and when they became more elaborate they were to remain forbidding. Lack of sculpture on Anglo-Norman buildings is a better sign of natural harshness and no doubt the adventurous invaders found in problems of size and construction a more absorbing challenge than in the more intimate craft of carving. Yet, in less than a century, the full-blown Anglo-Norman style stands forth in all its lushness. Native craftsmanship occurs in examples of this development but many of the designs, although not the chevron, were imported from Normandy, where a similar movement was in full flood. If the invaders started as puritans, they soon threw off their restraints; indeed, since the final extremes of European Romanesque never crossed the Channel, there was probably an assertion of English reticence. The long nave and the square east end already reveal the angular prejudices of the English.

The Normans' most momentous achievement was the negative one of the mere fact of their conquest, which for ever turned England's face away from Scandinavia and towards Europe. The victors overlaid an undeveloped architecture and suffocated a tradition of brilliant sculpture. Since they both created and destroyed so much, final verdicts on their legacy in these fields must always be personal. The fate of Old English sculpture was a tragedy and, even in architecture, no one can honestly swear that the English and the Normans would never have built so well if one race had not mastered the other. Yet the sudden upsurge of building, the scale and, finally, the designs employed, suggest that the impact was decisive. The Normans brought new plans and methods, which were adopted throughout the land, and the habit of experimenting was born. Under them, the kingdom for a time gave a lead to Europe and, if the conquerors are given all the credit for this and every other disputable achievement, their work in England would still be distinctive. It was neither Saxon nor Norman, but something new.

CHAPTER TWELVE

The Minor Arts

*T*HE 'minor' arts treated in this chapter are not so called in an attempt to belittle their importance. The adjective applies to manuscript illumination and ivory-carving only in so far as these outstanding arts were known to a tiny fraction of the population and because most of the works were produced on a scale so small that they are harder to appreciate than the achievements of the mason. Metal-work, with which are included enamels and coins, was a minor art in a still more restricted sense because many of its products, although also on a small scale, were in widespread use; needlework can be dismissed briefly only because no more than two fine specimens survive, and pottery because it exists in a few fragments. Time and changing habits have left examples of the various arts in very unequal proportions; virtually nothing is known of Old English music or large-scale painting, and jewellery and pottery were better preserved in the earlier, pagan age, when it was the custom to lay ornaments and utensils in their owners' graves. Arts which are now poorly represented, if at all, were not necessarily neglected on the eve of the Conquest.

*

The masterpieces which have survived most abundantly from the later Old English period are manuscripts, illuminated in the monasteries. These are important because of their numbers and because they indicate a love of painting which must have produced many larger works on the walls of buildings. Above all, they are precious for their own excellence, in colouring and drawing. The colours, sometimes indescribably rich and diverse, sometimes delicate pastels that were peculiarly Anglo-Saxon, can be appreciated only in the originals or by means of the most expensive photography, and even the line drawings need close scrutiny to achieve their full impact. The effort is worth making, since it is a common-place that illuminated manuscripts reveal, more clearly even than sculpture, the artistic genius of Alfred's race.

Enjoyment is also hampered by the indifference to naturalism which was common to all early medieval artists. They worked in an age of faith and sought only to portray a figure or an event, normally a well-known subject from the Scriptures, and to illustrate a mood. Since everyone believed in the Crucifixion or the Resurrection, there was no point in seeking verisimilitude through accurate landscape or architectural details. If an object was not a necessary part of the story it was included either to compose a pattern or because it was a symbol which helped to identify the picture; scores of these symbols were in use, of which the best known include the haloes given to saints, the palms carried by martyrs, and the angel, the lion, the heifer and the eagle, which respectively denote the four Evangelists, Matthew, Mark, Luke and John. Such symbols were rarely drawn to scale and it may sometimes be suspected that artists in the Middle Ages did not know how to draw at all. Un-imaginative copying certainly perpetuated some odd mannerisms, an instance being the hunched shoulders of the Virgin in Plate XXIXa, but the brilliant marginal sketch in Plate XXIVa shows the daring and skill of which the best artists were capable. Although there is nothing life-like in the acanthus, borrowed from the Carolingians and used to denote all types of plant, it is known that men could perfectly well depict proper trees; the acanthus, a convenient symbol, was all that was felt to be necessary. If the natural representation of classical and Renaissance art can be forgotten, it will be seen how triumphantly the Old English masters and their medieval successors realized their primary aim, to stir the beholder's emotions.

*

Illumination in England for a century before the Conquest was dominated by the Winchester school, although the two monasteries of the West Saxon capital by no means monopolized this work. Its origins were varied and, like those of most styles, they have been disputed. Manuscript illumination had been highly developed during the golden age of Northumbria, reaching its zenith in the *Lindisfarne Gospels* about 710 and being carried on in Ireland to culminate in the *Book of Kells* some hundred years later. This so-called 'barbaric' style had been fantastically elaborate, excelling in geometric patterns and in the interlacement of strange creatures, but it had not survived the Viking invasions. Illumination, like literature, owed its revival in England to Alfred and its flowering to the reform movement in the monasteries.

English artists in the tenth century, presumably associating the old forms with northern heathendom, turned to Europe, where the classical tradition of representation maintained a debased existence. The primary source of the new style was therefore Carolingian and books henceforth were illustrated rather than merely decorated. Eventually the stolid Carolingian drawing was replaced by lighter work and the native feeling for pattern reasserted itself, either because long dormant tastes were reawakened or because the old Northumbrian or Hiberno-Saxon style, which itself had once penetrated the Continent, now re-entered the island from the south. At all events a style evolved which was unique to England, successfully solving 'the outstanding aesthetic problem of English pre-Conquest art, that of combining the glittering abstract patterns of insular "barbaric" illumination with the more substantial dignities and the gentler graces of the classical tradition in painting'.

The Winchester school may easily be recognized by its delight in curling foliage, which provided increasingly elaborate borders for formal, full-page miniatures, and by a uniquely sensitive outline drawing which is most noticeable in the flutterings of garments. The fully fledged style first appears exactly a century before the Conquest in the Foundation Charter of the New Minster at Winchester; the pious King Edgar, flanked by the Virgin and St Peter, who is denoted by his key, presents the charter to Christ, who is seated in an almond-shaped panel known as a mandorla. The Winchester border of acanthus has evolved and there are other distinctively English features in the white faces of all save the king and in a refusal to stress the trappings and position of royalty; Edgar's posture is not a stock one and the result, if contorted, testifies to the artist's vigour and originality (Plate XXV).

The most perfect example of the Winchester style is the Benedictional of St Æthelwold, dating from between 975 and 980, which was recently acquired by the British Museum from the Duke of Devonshire. The page illustrated is that showing the Ascension, one of twenty-eight large-scale illuminations, gloriously adorned and lavishly bedecked with gold. The border now has four enormous rosettes, a common later elaboration, and in no way confines the subject; Christ himself

appears to be moving, because of the new treatment of the mandorla, and the onlookers gaze up in
astonishment (Plate XXVI). Further elaboration of the
Winchester style is shown in the Pentecost from the
Sacramentary of Robert of Jumièges, a work of the second
quarter of the eleventh century which Edward the
Confessor's unpopular archbishop brought back to his
native duchy, where it remains at Rouen; this particular
page furnishes the most extreme example of a fantastic
border but other miniatures show the same frenzied
drawing, filling up every available space, which may
be deemed baroque or decadent according to taste
(Plate XXVII).

Sumptuous colours and ambitious composition often
distract attention from the sheer draughtsmanship of the
Winchester masters, which may better be seen in line
drawings. Some of these were intended for later illumination, others were lightly tinted and yet others deliberately
left in monochrome, or drawn in two or three colours of ink.
Many were mere sketches in the margins (Plate XXVIa),
but several were full-page illustrations and a few were
still more aspiring in that they formed a series of illustrations to a narrative, in which capacity they are more
successful than similar attempts in colour. The most
famous miniature drawings are those in an English version
of the ninth-century *Utrecht Psalter*, where the original
sketches have been faithfully copied in a more delicate
hand, although they are less well spaced, and in still
lovelier drawings illustrating the religious poems of
Caedmon. Slightly later, from early in Cnut's reign, is the
Liber Vitae of the New Minster at Winchester, whose
title page showing Cnut and Ælfgifu has been widely
reproduced and whose scene of the Last Judgement, in
which St Peter determinedly struggles with the Devil for
the soul of a pathetic little man, has been described as
'one of the most exquisite and most moving pieces of

English line drawing that has come down to us' (Plate XXVIII). The earliest known calendar pictures, one of which has been used in Chapter II to illustrate peasant life, are also drawn in line and date from the first half of the eleventh century.

The grace and sensitivity of Old English artists, tested in scores of masterpieces, was overtaken shortly before the Conquest by a bleak, alien influence. The difference is clear if the line drawing of the Crucifixion from a Psalter probably produced at Ramsey in Huntingdonshire between 974 and 986 is compared with a Crucifixion from the *Arundel Psalter* of *c.* 1060 (Plates XXIXa, XXXI); this second example is an illumination and has been chosen because it is more famous than a tinted line drawing, also in the *Arundel Psalter*, which reveals the same change. The dramatic yet subtle drawing of the earlier work has given way to harder, straighter lines, the painted version in the *Arundel Psalter* has a solid, muscular body on the Cross, betraying a new interest in the human form. Even the colours here are harsher, violent reds and blues eclipsing the greyish tints beloved by the English, and Ottonian or south German elements, themselves infused with Byzantine influence, pervade the work. The pre-Viking interlacements and curious animals had been perpetuated by English artists in a succession of initials, a few of which had been 'historiated' or inhabited; the *Arundel Psalter*, however, goes a step further by displaying the first of many 'gymnastic' initials, in which figures clamber about the framework of the letter (Plate XXIVb).

England, while boasting a unique and mature style of painting, therefore remained open to new influences. It is tempting to assume that Edward the Confessor imported foreign artists, since the king is known to have employed Norman masons, but this is only guesswork. Although Robert of Jumièges was sufficiently impressed with

XXV   King Edgar offering the Charter of the New Minster,
Winchester, to Christ, 966 (Cotton MS Vespesian A VIII f. 2b,
British Museum)

XXVI   The Ascension, from the Benedictional of St. Æthelwold, *c*. 975-80 (Add. MS 49598 f. 64b, *British Museum*)

XXVII   The Pentecost from the *Sacramentary of Robert of Jumièges, c.* 1008 *(Henry Bradshaw Society)*

XXVIII The Last Judgement from the *New Minster Liber Vitae, c.* 1016-20 (Stowe MS 944 f.7, *British Museum*)

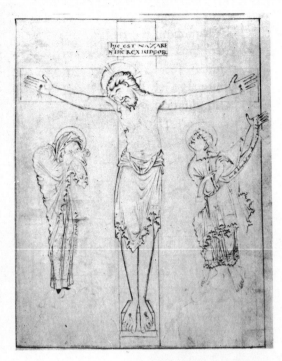

XXIX (a) The Crucifixion from the *Ramsey Psalter, c.* 980 (Harley MS 2904 f. 3b, *British Museum*) (b) The Crucifixion from the *Worcester Chronicle*, first half of twelfth century *(MS 157 f. 77b, by courtesy of the President and Fellows of Corpus Christi College, Oxford)*

XXX   The Ascension from the *St. Albans Psalter,* probably before 1123 *(the Warburg Institute)*

XXXI   The Crucifixion from the *Arundel Psalter, c.* 1060
(Arundel MS 60 f. 52b, *British Museum*)

XXXII (a) An ivory plaque
from Winchester showing two
angels swinging censers, c. 970
*(the Warburg Institute, photo
by Otto Fein)*
(b) An ivory plaque showing the
Adoration of the Magi, probably
late eleventh century *(Victoria
and Albert Museum, Crown
copyright)*

English illumination to take samples back with him to France, any new style which he may have introduced to England was not a truly Norman style. It can no longer be said that fine illuminations were unknown in pre-Conquest Normandy, since half a dozen illustrated manuscripts survive from le Mont-Saint-Michel; the artists, however, were indebted to schools outside the duchy and their work demands a great deal more research. English elements themselves had penetrated to northern France and Flanders, where the fluttering draperies and rosette borders of Winchester were adopted by artists of what has been termed the 'Channel' school, although harsher Ottonian influences are here more marked. Manuscripts circulated freely and Normandy was only one of several channels through which the rising Continental style might have reached the kingdom.

The Conquest was bound to affect painting in England, since it brought the monasteries under the rule of foreigners who were in closer touch with the latest Continental developments. On the other hand the newcomers had no rival style of their own, they were themselves acquainted with English elements which had previously crossed the Channel, and the importation of books from England into Normandy shows that this native achievement at least was admired. The result was what might have been expected. Book production was apparently halted for a time by the dislocation of monastic life, since no works can be ascribed to the fifteen years which followed Hastings, but when it was resumed the fluent drawing and favourite motives of the Anglo-Saxons lived on, side by side with the stiffer style and severe approach of the Romanesque artists. Norman attachment to native work is shown quite clearly in the Bayeux Tapestry and in the first body of post-Conquest manuscripts, produced at Durham for Bishop William of Saint-Carilef, who died in 1096, where frilly garments, elegant lines and 'barbaric' interlaced initials still appear. These works represent a transition from Anglo-Saxon to Romanesque, for their light primary colours and the repeated use of the gymnastic initial presaged a newer style.

Ultimately a tremendous change took place, as the intricate yet care-free Anglo-Saxon illuminations gave way to the more stylized compositions of the Romanesque world. The new art triumphed in the *St Albans Psalter*, often called the *Albani Psalter*, which was produced in England about 1120 and is now in the church of St Godehard at Hildesheim, in Germany. Heavily drawn and richly coloured, with solidly represented bodies, the Ascension depicted here is far removed from that in the Benedictional of St Æthelwold or from any products of the Winchester school, which by comparison appear to be all airiness and grace (Plate XXX). Appreciation of this change depends on personal taste, for Romanesque art has its own peculiar virtues; dignified and powerful, shunning all gaiety, it has been judged over-ambitious when practised on the small scale necessary in an illuminated book, yet many hold that even here it is the greatest of all medieval styles.

Byzantine influence, which before the Conquest had filtered into England via Germany, became very strong in the mid-twelfth century and may be seen in the Winchester Bible, produced by a series of artists who may have been attracted to the city by its gifted and sumptuous bishop Henry of Blois, the brother of King Stephen. The Crusades and the contact of the Normans in England with their fellow countrymen in Sicily undoubtedly furthered this trend, so that its sustained vigour may be traced to the Conquest. None the less, it is not surprising that Anglo-Saxon drawing lived on, since native prejudices had managed to reassert themselves in architecture, an art which suffered far more severely from the Conquest. A third drawing of the Crucifixion, which was added in the middle of the century to a chronicle begun at Worcester *c.* 1108, shows a return from the hard style of the *Arundel Psalter* to the movement of the Old English rendering made at Ramsey in the tenth century, and it was soon clear that the taste which created the *St Albans Psalter* was too alien to be accepted wholeheartedly. (Plate XXIXb). Even the *St Albans* Ascension includes the peculiar Anglo-Saxon motif of a disappearing Christ and, long before the Winchester Bible was completed, the old expressive lines and love of pattern had reappeared in the *St Swithun's Psalter*, a work which also has Byzantine features and may have been done for Henry of Blois himself. The softening influence of the Winchester artists can be traced through to the Gothic world of the thirteenth century, where it lived again in the brilliant outline drawings of Matthew Paris.

*

The arts of the eleventh century were more closely related to one another than are those of today, since the same designer and even the same craftsman might work in several fields. It is not known whether the Anglo-Saxons wove patterned fabrics, but skilled embroiderers were practising by the late seventh century and it is probable that there were many men like St Dunstan, an artist on parchment who is also credited with having designed pieces for needlewomen. Although stitchwork could hardly reproduce the flourishes of the Winchester school, the art of embroidering pieces of silk and linen was a delicate one, particularly when coloured silks were supplemented by gold and silver threads, made by winding thin sheets of metal around a silken core. It is hard to realize the high esteem enjoyed by this essentially medieval art, afflicted as it has been by the Reformation, the decline of ceremonial, the rise of painting and, most recently of all, by feminine emancipation. The work is also highly perishable, so that only one example survives of pre-Conquest embroidery in England.

When the tomb of St Cuthbert was opened in 1827 it was found to contain a maniple, a liturgical vestment in the form of a napkin-like strip which hung from the wrist, and seven fragments of a stole; the maniple, which is almost intact, is $2\frac{2}{3}$ inches wide and is today about 2 feet $8\frac{1}{4}$ inches long, while the stole is of the same width and now some 6 feet long. Both garments are of silk, embroidered in fine gold thread with the figures of saints and prophets between a border of acanthus scrolls and pairs of confronted animals. Although these beautiful and delicate textiles are of Byzantine inspiration, they undoubtedly come from England and may have been made at Winchester; inscriptions, stating that they were ordered by Queen Ælflæd for the bishop of Winchester, show that they were finished by 916 or soon afterwards. The St Cuthbert pieces, which must represent the very best work, prove that embroidery was a highly developed art a hundred and fifty years before the Conquest. Its later importance appears in *Domesday Book*, which records that in King Edward's time Alwid or Ælfgyth the Maid had held two hides in the Buckinghamshire hundred of Ashendon, 'which Godric the sheriff granted her as long as he was sheriff, on condition of her teaching his daughter embroidery work'. Godric himself fought at Hastings, beneath the magnificent banners of King Harold.

The next surviving textile is the Bayeux Tapestry, a work of art and also a historical source which is quoted as often as the *Anglo-Saxon Chronicle*. It differs from the earlier pieces in being not a vestment decorated in silk and precious metals but a roll of linen, now discoloured to a light brown, worked in worsted wools of eight colours. The roll, made up of at least six pieces which have been cunningly stitched together, is now 230 feet $10\frac{1}{4}$ inches long and $19\frac{3}{4}$ inches wide, and its final scene is largely a nineteenth-century restoration. The designer's theme is the tale of Harold and William, beginning when the earl takes leave of King Edward before riding to Bosham, as described in Chapter III, and concluding when the English are pursued from the field at Hastings; the end of the Tapestry is missing and the story once probably reached a different climax, perhaps the new king's coronation.

The Tapestry contains between seventy and eighty scenes. Their exact number can be variously estimated, since the narrative is continuous, but some guide is provided by the frequent introduction of a tree, a device commonly used in manuscripts as a kind of pictorial punctuation mark. Above and below the main scenes there are borders filled mainly with birds or animals but also with pictures of everyday life, of fable and of scandal, while the battle itself is accompanied by a frieze vividly portraying the horrors of war. The Tapestry has been estimated to contain 623 persons, nearly a third of whom are armed, as well as 202 horses and mules, 55 dogs, 505 other animals, 37 buildings, 41 ships and boats and 49 trees. This makes it a mine of information on a uniquely wide range of subjects—military, social, artistic and literary—and also the most vivid and the most detailed account of the Conquest. It was, however, designed simply as a strip-cartoon, for display in a church, where people could learn what happened to a man who broke his oath.

The Tapestry is so called because it was listed among the treasures of Bayeux Cathedral in 1476, when 'a very long and very narrow strip of linen' was hung around the nave on feast days. Early in the present century it was commonly held that the roll was embroidered some hundred years after the events which it depicts but today it is usually ascribed to a generation which could still remember Hastings. The prominence of Bishop Odo suggests that it was ordered by the Conqueror's half-brother, whose death in 1092 would in that case help to date the work. Sometimes it is claimed that William's own death five years earlier must have preceded the execution, since the duke is not given the dominant role which might be expected, but it is more probable that the mighty bishop commissioned it at the dedication of Bayeux Cathedral in 1077. The real credit for this ambitious work must go to the unknown designer, who may have belonged to the Canterbury school, and to the needlewomen, who are more likely to have been English than French. The use of certain letters and of English elements in the place-names is an indication, although not proof, of the Tapestry's origins, and the narrative scenes have their parallels in an illuminated copy of Abbot Ælfric's paraphrase of the Heptateuch of *c.* 1060.

Whatever the Tapestry's origins, it is clear from the chronicles that the Normans considered the excellence of England's embroiderers to rival that of her illuminators. William of Poitiers, whose gloating over the spoils of conquest assorts oddly with his contempt for the islanders, speaks of the wonder excited in Normandy by the new king's robes, and William of Malmesbury recalls a long line of famous needlewomen, which included the Confessor's queen and Edgar the Ætheling's sister Margaret. Matilda of Flanders employed English seamstresses and it is possible that Godric's Alwid was the widow 'Leviet' or Leofgyth who held land in Wiltshire at the time of *Domesday*, when it was noted that she 'made and still makes the gold fringe of the king and queen'. A number of English textiles surviving from the twelfth century are much cruder than the work which was lodged in St Cuthbert's tomb some two hundred years earlier, which suggests that embroidery was yet another art which suffered from the Conquest. None the less, native skills and preferences again proved to be firmly rooted, and the mid-thirteenth century was to witness the dawn of a golden age, when *Opus Anglicanum* was sought throughout Europe.

*

Another art which flourished in England at the time of the Conquest was that of bone and ivory-carving. It is convenient to describe all carved bone objects as 'ivories', since the tusks of the African or Indian elephant were the craftsman's most prized material, although only a small and erratic supply of ivory proper was available in the north. All manner of bones might be used for smaller objects, while walrus tusk or morse and whale's bone were employed in some of the largest and finest work. Morse and whale's bone rarely occur after the twelfth century but morse is the material which survives most plentifully from the great period of ivory-carving in England, which lasted for roughly a hundred years before and after the Conquest.

Ivories loom particularly large in Continental history, where the works produced for Charlemagne and his successors help to bridge the dark gulf between classical and medieval art. In England their story resembles that of manuscript illumination and embroidery, in that a flourishing art was probably cut short by the Viking invasions, only to revive in the tenth century. There is, however, some doubt on the extent of purely native achievements during this early period, since the material is easily portable and carvings were made both in the Latin and in the northern world. Although the art may have been re-established in England soon after Alfred's death, the first later examples are from the middle of the century, when illuminators were evolving the distinct style of the Winchester school. The dignity and also the woodenness of the Continent reappears in English ivories, as it does in the manuscripts, only to give way to more sensitive work which can be claimed as that of a national school. Many instances may be cited to show the affinities between native illuminators and ivory-carvers; here, the angels on King Edgar's charter should be compared with those on a triangular plaque found at Winchester and carved at very nearly the same time (Plates XXV, XXXIIa).

English ivory-carving thereafter often reached a high technical pitch and, even when the execution faltered, distinction was achieved by what has been called 'a subtle alchemy which infused a spirit of genuine emotional quality into much of the work produced in this country'. Boxes, knife-handles, pins, buckles, combs, chessmen and gaming pieces could all be made from ivory, while still finer work was produced for the Church in the form of crosses, heads of staves and of bishops' croziers, book-covers, caskets for holy relics and, most abundantly of all according to the inventories, liturgical combs. The patina which many of these pieces have today is often the accidental result of long burial but sometimes it was procured by staining, while jewels and gilding were also used to enrich the carvers' masterpieces. If the Norman chroniclers do not pay the specific tributes to England's ivory workers that they pay to her embroiderers, the conquerors had every reason to covet the works which they found.

The Normans cannot be accused of crippling the English tradition of ivory-carving, chiefly because it is difficult to date or even to establish the provenance of so many works. A change came over the art at about the time of the Conquest, for a crozier head of c. 1060, where figures from the Nativity and the Passion sprawl over the crook, is an entirely new composition. A plaque of the Adoration of the Magi, where figures have hard flesh and stiff draperies, also reveals a startling change, since the form is Romanesque and the work reveals all the power of that style. This plaque is now cautiously described by the

Victoria and Albert Museum as of 'English or north French' production, dating from 1120–30; it could be of much earlier date and if, as seems likely, it was made in England, the harsh alien influences apparent in the *Arundel Psalter* were also making themselves felt in ivory-carving (Plate XXXIIb). The scarcity of Norman art treasures precludes any comparison of achievements in England and Normandy in 1066, but the new influences probably came through rather than from the duchy. They may have preceded the Conquest, although they were undoubtedly strengthened by it, and the carvers continued for a hundred years to work in both styles, as did the illuminators. Ivories, unlike manuscripts, became scarce after the twelfth century, perhaps because the material was not available, perhaps because stone sculpture absorbed the craftsmen's skill; this decline, however, was one of quantity, not of quality, and it took place too late for it to be blamed on the Conquest.

*

'If the English women were renowned for the art which had wrought . . . the Fighting Man on the banner of Harold, the men were no less renowned for the art which wrought the cups of gold and silver, and the many other articles which adorned the tables of the great.' William of Poitiers, recalling how the Conqueror displayed his spoils, 'whose number and beauty surpass all imagination', has left posterity a certificate in place of the works of art taken by his compatriots to Normandy and now lost for ever. Gold and silver vessels have been the first objects to be plundered, by the Vikings, the Normans and the destroyers of the monasteries, as well as to be melted down in time of war or as fashions changed. It is therefore not surprising that very little survives from the later Old English period, when ornaments and utensils were no longer buried with their owners.

The Anglo-Saxons' skill in fashioning gold and silver, of which the second was by far the more common metal, had for long attracted the connoisseurs of Rome. Even the peasant was acquainted in England with silver coins, which had a far more widespread currency than in Normandy or any other state in France. This treasure, a sign of the kingdom's prosperity and a lure to both Vikings and Normans, cannot all have come from the silver and lead mines of Cumberland, Wales, Derbyshire and the Mendips. One promising theory is that extra supplies were imported from Germany, where there were rich sources in the Harz Mountains, and that they may have been exchanged for wool.

Metal-work, yet another art which was shaped by foreign influences, supplies further proof that England was by no means the remote, neglected island once pictured by the fiercer apologists of the Conquest. The Vikings contributed much to the designs on weapons and secular jewellery, and Germany and Byzantium to the ecclesiastical vessels which survive in greater abundance, although still in relatively small quantities. Often, as in the case of ivories, it is impossible to say where an object was made, since works were not only copied but might travel for hundreds of miles. Enamelling, the fusing of vitreous glazes on to a ground of metal, was an art brought to a high pitch at Constantinople in the tenth century, and Byzantine works often reached England, where they were attached to a native backing. None the less, in metal-work as in other fields, the English developed their own style and were themselves capable of the finest techniques.

The most beautiful example of pre-Conquest metal-work, the gold and enamel Alfred jewel, was made about 900. This exceptionally early date proves that at least one art was flourishing under Alfred himself and is a sign that the Viking invasions may not have been so destructive as the lack of other fine objects otherwise suggests. An old-fashioned and distinctively English style of ornament, with scrolls and interlacements in thin lines, persisted into the last third of the tenth century, when the monastic revival increased the demand for ecclesiastical vessels and when the influence of manuscripts became apparent. The most awe-inspiring of these pieces must have been the huge seven-branched candlesticks, placed before the altars of the larger churches at Eastertime, none of which has outlasted the Reformation; surviving ecclesiastical work includes a portable altar of red porphyry framed in silver and a number of censers, which differ from their Continental counterparts in being square rather than round, as well as a small bronze-relief of the Virgin and Child, the only figure work to exist. Among more mundane specimens there are a number of door hinges, strap-ends and finger rings, and a solitary jug which was probably a cruet. It is also clear from the chronicles that the rich had candlesticks and table vessels of metal, often silver gilt, and that metal was used for mounting objects of wood or horn, but all of this domestic ware has perished.

There are not enough dateable examples for the progress of metal-work to be assessed under Edward and again under William or his sons. The craft served so many humble uses that its daily practice throughout the kingdom can hardly have changed after 1066, but on its highest plane, where gold- and silversmiths worked for the Church or the court, it must have been affected by the Conquest. In the Old English monasteries, on which all the arts were centred, even the abbots had not scorned to try their skill at metal-work, an occupation for which they could find a precedent in the activities of the many-sided St Dunstan. To the Normans, on the other hand, manual labour had no appeal; monks continued at first to illuminate the manuscripts which they alone knew how to write, but heavier work was increasingly delegated to specialized laymen, many of them foreigners. The unique early twelfth-century Gloucester candlestick, which commemorates native taste, may not also be a monument to English workmanship. If the old expertise was not lost this development may have been beneficial, since it encouraged inventiveness. The goldsmiths themselves, while not contributing to England's future expansion so decisively as the wool-merchants, became so prosperous that within a century of the Conquest their number included Henry fitz Ailwin, the first lord mayor of London.

Coins could be discussed under many headings, since they throw light upon the authority and, in earlier centuries, upon the very existence of kings, as well as upon the spread of commerce and the rise of towns. They are more often collected for their historical associations than as works of art, even when in good condition, since most were struck from dies that were crudely cut and poorly designed. None the less, fine and original coins were produced, which may be traced to the dexterity and feeling which brought England to the forefront in many arts.

In the turmoil after the withdrawal of the Roman legionaries it is probable that coins ceased to circulate until *c.* 600, when Æthelberht of Kent struck a number of gold *thrymsas*, copied from those current in northern France. These gave way some fifty years later to a coinage of tiny silver *sceats*, which were replaced at the end of the eight century when the first silver pennies were struck at Canterbury. Offa of Mercia, who had won the overlordship of southern England, is associated with the first of these coins, although it seems that he merely took over the mint which was already issuing coins for the archbishop and the king of Kent. The silver penny, larger but thinner than a modern sixpence, survived the Vikings and the Normans, to become the staple English

coin for nearly five hundred years; Alfred and some of
his successors issued halfpennies, but from the reign of
Edgar to that of Edward I only pennies were struck and
lesser sums had to be obtained by breaking the coin into
two or four pieces. The royal portrait was placed on the
obverse of Offa's pennies and thereafter it appeared
sporadically until Edgar's time, since when it has rarely
been absent; one exception was a penny of Æthelred II
which portrayed the Lamb of God and a dove, probably to
celebrate the year 1000. A number of variations in
lettering and symbols are known, both with the king's
head on the obverse and with the name of the moneyer and
perhaps of the mint on the reverse, where the design
tended to centre on a cross.

These coins were made from a die which was cast by
the king's engraver and then distributed to the various
mints, where the moneyers had to abandon the old die and
pay for the new one. Every mint was accompanied by
an exchange, whose warden bought the bullion and
afterwards checked the weight, standard and design of
the coins which the moneyer had struck. Mints, which
were permitted only to towns of *burh* status, had multiplied with the extension of the political power of the
West Saxon house from a single one, in Canterbury, at
Alfred's accession to at least seventy-three under Edward
the Confessor. The sale of dies to the moneyers at an
average of 20s. a time was a source of considerable
profit to the Crown, which accounts for the variety of
coins issued by each monarch. Edward the Confessor
issued eleven types, appearing on the five earlier ones
without his traditional beard, and even Harold Godwineson in a reign of nine months succeeded in altering his
penny by omitting the sceptre.

There were few changes in the design of coins during
the eleventh century and these few took place before the
Conquest, as did so many innovations. Edward the

Confessor was the first monarch to be portrayed full face, to attempt the full-length figure of a king enthroned, and to inscribe his pennies with the word *Pax;* on the coins issued after Hastings, only the king's name was strange (Plates Vb, c). Dies were still frequently changed, so that thirteen types of penny were struck by the Conqueror and William Rufus, although the coins of father and son are not easily distinguishable since royal numerals were not added for another two hundred years. The number of mints decreased only slightly, if at all, for while no coins survive from sixteen of those operating under the Confessor, the products of twelve new mints appeared and the foreign moneyers known before the Conquest continued until the end of the century to be a small minority.

Under Henry I more aliens were brought in, which may explain why most coins of the twelfth century are of much cruder design and execution. Mechanization also helped to ruin art, for it was found to be quicker to use punches for the letters and even for the royal 'portrait' rather than to engrave a new coin-type with proper tools. Forgery was always a problem and in Henry's reign a mass of light-weight or impure coins was circulated by moneyers who hoped that clumsy workmanship would conceal their crimes. Complaints mounted 'because the man who had a pound could not get a pennyworth at a market', until at Christmas 1124 the moneyers of England were summoned to Winchester, where the *Anglo-Saxon Chronicle* records with approval and some exaggeration that every man was deprived of his right hand and castrated. This vengeance, which did little to improve design, at least put a temporary stop to systematic debasement.

Although the silver penny remained the only coin, larger units were needed for accounting. The pound, an Anglo-Saxon term for the weight of silver from which two hundred and forty pennies could be minted, was divided after the Conquest into twenty shillings of twelve pennies each; these units were equated by the Anglo-Norman clerks with the old Roman coins *libra*, *solidus* and *denarius*, which had their French equivalents in *livre*, *sou* and *denier* and survive in the modern English abbreviations *l.*, *s.*, *d. Domesday Book* shows that men also reckoned in marks, representing 13*s.* 4*d.* or two-thirds of a pound, and in gold marks, representing £6.

England in 1066 was noted for the fine quality of her silver coinage, which was already some three hundred years old. William, by leaving it virtually untouched, paid tribute to its high standard. His conservatism may also have sprung from political calculation, since the nation-wide handling of familiar coins must have helped to impress upon Englishmen the legitimacy of his rule. The next important step was taken when Henry II abandoned the practice of regularly changing the die, so that a single type of penny became current for several decades, including the entire reigns of his sons Richard I and John, who are not comemmorated as individuals on any coin. This was followed by Henry III's abortive attempt to introduce a gold penny worth twenty silver ones, by the appearance of half-pennies and farthings under Edward I and by the final establishment of a gold florin in 1344 under Edward III. These were revolutionary changes but none can be ascribed to the Normans.

*

Any survey of the arts, however sketchy, is worth while if it serves as a reminder that England can claim to have been the most civilized country in Western Europe at the time of the Conquest. It is fortunate for the Normans that stone buildings are so striking and so durable, since architecture seems to have been the only art in which they had anything to teach their victims. A study of the arts modifies the simple, old-fashioned conception of Englishmen and Normans, to the advantage of both peoples. The conquerors' later zest for elaborate carving and the remembrance that their massive early buildings were once highly decorated should dispel the idea that the Normans were a peculiarly sombre race. The English output of smaller masterpieces, unrivalled in conception and execution but appreciated only in the present century, must destroy the notions of Carlyle and other Victorians that the kingdom was peopled by sluggish degenerates. There remains the suspicion that the Anglo-Saxon craftsman, like the man of letters, had lost his inspiration while retaining his technical skill; this is certainly untrue of manuscript illumination and probably of every other art, which foreign influences were reshaping before William landed. The Normans should not therefore be accused of abruptly sweeping away native traditions, since these were already undergoing change, nor on the other hand should they be acclaimed for turning England from a cultural backwater into a respected province of Latin Europe, since England had led the Continent for two golden centuries between the decline of Germany and the dominance of France. They can be blamed for a lesser disaster, the disappearance of innumerable works of art, and they can be given the modest credit of having assisted the penetration of fashions for which they were not responsible.

CHAPTER THIRTEEN

Conclusion

*H*ISTORICAL research, although it aims at finding the truth, often raises more issues than it settles. There are few records of the Norman age and not one, whether the work of a royal clerk, a monastic chronicler or an anonymous craftsman, which is wholly devoid of mystery. Writs and charters prove to be forgeries and chronicles, on which later ages must chiefly rely, betray prejudice or turn out to have been founded on hearsay. Bald statements therefore have to give way to carefully qualified theories. The historian, faced with alternatives, dare not try to arouse interest as a simple narrator; he must either be a judge who sums up or a barrister who states a case, and run the risk that others will be confused or misled. The problem is acute with a subject as heroic as the Norman Conquest, which invites a confident description not justified by knowledge of the facts. Almost every detail of its course can be disputed, from the personal relations between the rivals to the size, equipment and disposition of their armies at Hastings.

When it is so hard even to tell the story of the Conquest without qualifying every sentence, an assessment of its long-term effects becomes still more daunting. The Old English kingdom was more of a national unity than was early medieval England, where society resembled the feudal world across the Channel, and hatred of the invaders was not confined to followers of the house of Godwine; the havoc of William's soldiery and the upheaval which attended his triumph bred such bitterness in all classes that a century after Hastings it was still said that Battle Abbey, dear to every Norman, was threatened by machinations of the English. Patriotic indignation is none the less out of place. All conquests are bloody and it is futile to rail at what has been an accomplished fact for nine hundred years. Moral judgements are only interesting if they embrace the full impact of the Normans upon England.

A new dynasty was founded and an Anglo-Danish ruling class was swept away by a French-speaking aristocracy. This alone makes 1066 more decisive than most dates which are cnosen to mark the limits of a historical period. None the less, the struggle for the Crown started under Edward the Confessor and was not decided until William had crushed the north, while many other changes began and ended in decades still further apart. The earlier that new influences once associated with William can be traced, the less momentous does the Conquest itself appear. The timing as well as the nature of these changes needs to be settled before the true importance of the Norman victory can be gauged.

The Norman achievement appears most impressive when it is remembered that Harold and his men were tough opponents, who destroyed the foremost Viking of their day. The duke, despite King Edward's favour, enjoyed none of the advantages which awaited an invader from the north and there was no foregone conclusion to the contest for the throne which loomed over the reign of the Confessor. Victory depended partly on luck, on the good fortune which favoured William in Normandy and in England and on the misfortune which befell

Harold. It also depended on the duke himself who, after curbing his subjects and checking his neighbours, assembled and maintained a force which he commanded with prudence and skill before, during and after Hastings. Even this would not have been enough without the Normans' mastery of mounted warfare and without the castle-building which allowed them to hold a hostile land in a grip of iron. The invasion would have had little chance if it had been launched during any other year, and in 1066 it is probable that no other man and no other race could have carried out the feats of William and his army.

The consequences were less spectacular than the performance. In every field—economic, military, legal, fiscal, ecclesiastical, literary, artistic—there are signs either that England was superior to her neighbours or that she was being influenced from the Continent before the Normans came. At certain activities—mounted warfare, the exploitation of military resources, reforms in the Church and perhaps architecture—Englishmen lagged behind Normans, but even here men were moving hesitantly along the road down which the conquerors were to stride. Feudalism itself, the most striking innovation, was foreshadowed by dependent tenures and private jurisdictions, and its establishment brought no revolution in the lives of the peasants, since rural economy was much the same on either side of the Channel. The administration of the kingdom, with its royal clerks and writs, its hierarchy of local courts and its national taxes, was unrivalled, so that the Norman kings were content to exploit English inventions; when William is rightly praised for his insight, moderation and adaptability, it is in reality the West Saxon line that is being honoured.

The importance of Hastings is diminished still further by the division of William's empire on his deathbed. A feudal baronage had by then been installed, on the ruins of the native landowning class, and there was no longer any hope that the new order would be overthrown. There remained, however, a strong possibility that the second generation of Norman settlers, cut off from their homeland, would adopt English ways; they were a small minority, under a royal house which posed as the successor to Alfred's line, and it was in their interests to win the hands of native heiresses. The prolonged life of vernacular prose and the coming reassertion of English taste even in architecture, the invaders' favourite field, show that England might have been governed by an increasingly anglicized aristocracy under William's sons. Rufus's penetration of Normandy and Henry I's triumph there, thanks to the weakness of Robert Curthose, followed by the extinction of the Conqueror's direct male heirs and the accession of a still mightier Continental dynasty, destroyed this prospect. The alien character of England's medieval rulers, while its origins lay in William's victory, was not determined solely in his lifetime.

There is much to deplore in the Conquest and its aftermath: the immediate misery, the lack of sympathy between king, barons and officials on the one hand and the mass of the people on the other, the subjection of women, the legal and to some extent the material debasement of the peasantry, and the cruelties of the forest law. After many centuries these injustices are no longer felt and at present, when pride in Old English civilization is being rekindled, the loss of numberless works of art is resented more keenly. The experiments of native craftsmen in every medium reveal a mature yet creative tradition which the invaders managed to obliterate, although magnificent Romanesque architecture provides some compensation. Even the most obvious legacy of the Normans today, the names and rich vocabulary of the English-speaking world, has to be balanced against the extinction of Old English poetry and prose.

Other results are dubious, unless administrative improvements are always deemed to be good in themselves: the elevation of the sheriff, the wider use of writs, the introduction of new feudal dues and the more severe levies of existing taxes. All these measures increased the efficiency of the government and, by strengthening public order, in the long run helped to bring greater prosperity; they also enabled William and his successors to exploit England's resources in pursuit of Continental ambitions. The firmer establishment and clearer definition of private justice increased the power of the lord at the expense of the peasant, and the separation of ecclesiastical pleas, although logical, can be disputed for ever between partisans of Church and monarchy. *Domesday Book*, a unique product of the newcomers' administrative genius, will always be treasured for the light which it sheds on the Conqueror's England; it should not be forgotten that this survey was attended by violence and that it was meant to reveal what further wealth could be extorted by the Crown, whose interests were not invariably those of the kingdom.

Among more welcome innovations the most valuable was William's use of the jury, a device which might never have taken root but for the land pleas held during his reign. The Normans, despite their reputation for harshness, must also be remembered for ending slavery, for encouraging the immigration of Jews and for fostering urban development. Although their motives here were doubtless material, the same cannot be said of efforts to improve the spiritual life of England, which reflect genuine piety in William and a number of lay benefactors, including Reinfrid, the knight who brought monasticism again to the north, as well as in the churchmen under Lanfranc and Anselm. It is unjust to deny the Normans the credit for these improvements by claiming that they might in time have taken place without a Conquest, since the same can be said about most of the darker results for which they have been blamed.

When the changes associated with the Normans are examined, they leave an overall impression that the Conquest was not so much good or bad as unnecessary. This would be a disappointing conclusion if it were the whole truth, but William has a more lasting claim to fame. Before his triumph there was always a danger that England would be drawn again into the northern world, not under the West Saxon line nor even under Harold Godwineson but by a new Viking conqueror. Afterwards there was little chance for a second Cnut, once military tenure had been established and when the kingdom was ruled from castles by a warrior aristocracy, trained in the most up-to-date techniques of mounted warfare. Few would deny the ultimate value of this protection, since western Europe was to enjoy the twelfth-century renaissance while Scandinavia was destined to stagnate for generations to come. The Normans did not drag England out of an insular twilight and attach her for the first time to the feudal Europe which was emerging. They accelerated her progress in the direction which she had already chosen and ensured that she would not be turned back.

Bibliography

The following list contains suggestions for further reading. It does not include every book or article which has been consulted, still less is it a complete bibliography of the period. Fuller guides are C. Gross, *The Sources and Literature of English History to 1485* (2nd ed. 1915) and W. Bonser, *An Anglo-Saxon and Celtic Bibliography, 450–1087*, 2 vols (Oxford, 1957); an invaluable modern list is in D. C. Douglas, *William the Conqueror* (1964).

Wherever possible, quotations from chroniclers and documents have been taken not from the separate editions listed below but from the extracts in *English Historical Documents*, II (1042–1189), ed. D. C. Douglas and G. W. Greenaway (1953).

ABBREVIATIONS

AHR	*American Historical Review* (Richmond, U.S.A.)
AN	*Annales de Normandie* (Caen)
BIHR	*Bulletin of the Institute of Historical Research*
BJRL	*Bulletin of the John Rylands Library* (Manchester)
ECR	*Economic History Review*
EHR	*English Historical Review*
MASC	*Mémoires de l'Académie Nationale des Sciences, Arts et Belles-Lettres de Caen* (Caen)
PBA	*Proceedings of the British Academy*
RS	*Rolls Series*
SAN	*Société des Antiquaires de Normandie* (Caen)
SHF	*Société de l'Histoire de France* (Paris)
SHN	*Société de l'Histoire de Normandie* (Rouen)
TRHS	*Transactions of the Royal Historical Society*

Place of publication London except where otherwise stated.

I. CHRONICLES, DOCUMENTS AND OTHER RECORDS

Anglo-Saxon Charters, ed. A. J. Robertson (Cambridge, 1939). See also *Facsimiles* and *Select Charters*

Anglo-Saxon Chronicle, ed. D. Whitelock, D. C. Douglas and S. I. Tucker (1961)

Anglo-Saxon Wills, ed. D. Whitelock (Cambridge, 1930)

Anglo-Saxon Writs, ed. F. E. Harmer (Manchester, 1952). See also *Facsimiles*

Bayeux Tapestry, ed. F. M. Stenton and others (2nd ed. 1965)

Chronicon Abbatiæ de Evesham, ed. W. D. Macray (*RS*, 1863)

Chronicon Monasterii de Abingdon, ed. J. Stevenson, 2 vols (*RS*, 1858)

Chronicon Monasterii de Bello (Battle Abbey), ed. J. S. Brewer (1846)

Chroniques anglo-normandes, ed. F. Michel, 3 vols (Rouen, 1836–40)

Correspondence of Pope Gregory VII, ed. E. Emerton (Columbia University, Records of Civilization, XIV, New York, 1932)

Domesday Book, ed. Record Commission, 4 vols. (1783–1816)

Dudo of Saint-Quentin, *De Moribus et Actis primorum Normanniae Ducum*, ed. J. Lair (*SAN*, 1865)

Durham, Simeon of, *Opera Omnia*, ed. T. Arnold, 2 vols (*RS*, 1882, 1885)

Eadmer, *Historia Novorum*, ed. M. Rule (*RS*, 1884)

— *Vita Anselmi*, ed. R. W. Southern (Edinburgh, 1962)

Encomium Emmae, ed. A. Campbell (1949)

English Historical Documents, II (1042–1189), ed. D. C. Douglas and G. W. Greenaway (1953)

Facsimiles of English Royal Writs to 1100 A.D., ed. T. A. M. Bishop and P. Chaplais (Oxford, 1957)

Facsimiles of Royal and Other Charters in the British Museum, I, ed. G. F. Warner and H. J. Ellis (1903)

Gaimar, Geoffrey, *L'estoire des Engles*, ed. T. D. Hardy and C. T. Martin, 2 vols (*RS*, 1888–9)

Huntingdon, Henry of, *Historia Anglorum*, ed. T. Arnold (*RS*, 1879)

Jumièges, William of, *Gesta Normannorum Ducum*, ed. J. Marx (*SHN*, Rouen, 1914)

Lanfranc, *Decreta Lanfranci* (Monastic Constitutions), ed. D. Knowles (1951)

— *Opera Omnia*, ed. J. A. Giles, 2 vols (Oxford, 1844)

Laws of the Kings of England from Edmund to Henry I, ed. A. J. Robertson (Cambridge, 1925)

Liber Eliensis, ed. E. O. Blake (1962)

Malmesbury, William of, *De Gestis Pontificum Anglorum*, ed. N. E. S. A. Hamilton (*RS*, 1870)

— *Gesta Regum Anglorum*, ed. W. Stubbs, 2 vols (*RS* 1887, 1889)

— *Vita Wulfstani*, ed. R. R. Darlington (Camden Society, xl, 1928)

— *Historia Novella*, ed. K. R. Potter (Edinburgh, 1955)

Ordericus Vitalis, *Historia Ecclesiastica*, ed. A. Le Prévost and L. Delisle, 5 vols (*SHF*, 1838–55)

Poitiers, William of, *Gesta Guillelmi Ducis Normannorum et Regis Anglorum*, ed. R. Foreville (Paris, 1952)

Recueil des Actes des Ducs de Normandie de 911 à 1066, ed. M. Fauroux (*SAN*, 1961)

Regesta Regum Anglo-Normannorum, I (1066–1100), ed. H. W. C. Davis and R. J. Whitwell (1913), II (1100–35), ed. C. J. Johnson and H. A. Cronne (Oxford, 1956)

Regularis Concordia (Monastic Agreement), ed. T. Symons (1953)

Scriptores rerum gestarum Willelmi Conquestoris, ed. J. A. Giles (1845)

Select Charters and Other Illustrations of English Constitutional History, ed. W. Stubbs (various editions)

Vita Ædwardi Regis qui apud Westmonasterium requiescit, ed. F. Barlow (Edinburgh, 1962)

Vita Haroldi, ed. W. de G. Birch (1885)

Wace, *Roman de Rou et des Ducs de Normandie*, ed. H. Andresen, 2 vols (Heilbronn, 1877)

Worcester, Florence of, *Chronicon ex Chronicis*, ed. B. Thorpe, 2 vols (1848–9)

II. MODERN AUTHORITIES AND WORKS OF REFERENCE

A. *Books*

Adam, R. J., *A Conquest of England* (1965)

Adams, G. B., *Councils and Courts in Anglo-Saxon England* (New Haven, U.S.A., 1962)

Armitage, E. S., *The Early Norman Castles of the British Isles* (1912)

Ballard, A., *The Domesday Inquest* (1906)

Barber, C. L., *The Story of Language* (1964)

Barlow, F., *The Feudal Kingdom of England* (1961)

— *The English Church*, 1000–66 (1963)

Baugh, A. C., *A History of the English Language* (1935)

— *A Literary History of England* (1950)

Blair, P. H., *An Introduction to Anglo-Saxon England* (Cambridge, 1959)

Boase, T. S. R., *English Art*, 1100–1216 (*Oxford History of English Art*, III, Oxford, 1953)

Bouard, M. de, *Guillaume le Conquérant* (Paris, 1958)

Briggs, M. S., *Architecture* (Home University Library of Modern Knowledge, 1947)

Brooke, G. C., *English Coins from the Seventh Century to the Present Day* (3rd ed. 1950)

Brooke, Z. N., *The English Church and the Papacy from the Conquest to the Reign of John* (Cambridge, 1931)

Burne, A. F., *The Battlefields of England* (1951)

Chambers, R. W., *On the Continuity of English Prose from Alfred to More* (1932)

Chrimes, S. B., *An Introduction to the Administration of Medieval England* (Oxford, 1959)

Christie, A. G. I., *English Medieval Embroidery* (Oxford, 1938)

Clapham, A. W., *English Romanesque Architecture before the Conquest* (Oxford, 1930)

— *English Romanesque Architecture after the Conquest* (Oxford, 1934)

— *Romanesque Architecture in England* (1950)

Complete Peerage of England, G.E.C., 13 vols (1910–59)

Conant, K. J., *Carolingian and Romanesque Architecture, 800–1200* (*Pelican History of Art*, XIII, 1959)

Corbett, W. J., 'The Development of the Duchy of Normandy, and the Norman Conquest of England', chap. xv of *Cambridge Medieval History*, V (Cambridge, 1926)

Coulton, G. G., *Social Life in Britain from the Conquest to the Reformation* (Cambridge, 1918)

Creighton, C., *A History of Epidemics in Britain from A.D. 664 to the Extinction of Plague*, 2 vols (Cambridge, 1891, 1894)

Darlington, R. R., *Anglo-Norman Historians* (Birkbeck College, Inaugural Lecture, 1947)

David, C. W., *Robert Curthose, Duke of Normandy* (Cambridge, U.S.A., 1920)

Dolley, M., *Anglo-Saxon Pennies* (British Museum, 1964)

Domesday Rebound (Public Record Office, 1954)

Douglas, D. C., *The Norman Conquest* (Historical Association leaflet LXXIII, 1928)

— *The Norman Conquest and British Historians* (Glasgow University Publications, LXVII, Glasgow, 1946)

— *English Scholars* (1951)

— *William the Conqueror* (1964)

Ekwall, E., *The Concise Oxford Dictionary of English Place-Names* (4th ed., Oxford, 1960)

Farrer, W., *Feudal Cambridgeshire* (Cambridge, 1920)

Finn, R. W., *The Domesday Inquest and the Making of Domesday Book* (1961)

— *An Introduction to Domesday Book* (1962)

Freeman, E. A., *The History of the Norman Conquest of England* 6 vols (Oxford, 1867–79)

— *The Reign of William Rufus*, 2 vols (Oxford, 1882)

Galbraith, V. H., *The Making of Domesday Book* (Oxford, 1961)

Haskins, C. H., *The Normans in European History* (New York, 1916)

— *Norman Institutions* (Cambridge, U.S.A., 1918)

Holdsworth, W., *A History of English Law*, rev. A. L. Goodhart and H. G. Hanbury, I (7th ed., 1956)

Hollister, C. W., *Anglo-Saxon Military Institutions* (Oxford, 1962)

Jolliffe, J. E. A., *The Constitutional History of Medieval England* (3rd ed. 1954)

Kelly, F. M., and Schwabe, R., *A Short History of Costume and Armour, 1066–1800* (1931)

Kendrick, T. D., *History of the Vikings* (1930)

— *Late Saxon and Viking Art* (1949)

Knowles, D., *The Monastic Order in England, 940–1216* (2nd ed., Cambridge, 1963)

Lemmon, C. H., *The Field of Hastings* (St Leonard's-on-Sea, 1957)

Lennard, R., *Rural England, 1086–1135* (Oxford, 1959)

Longhurst, M., *English Ivories* (1926)

Loyd, L. C., *The Origins of Some Anglo-Norman Families* (Harleian Society, CIII, Leeds, 1951)

Loyn, H. R., *Anglo-Saxon England and the Norman Conquest* (1962)

— *The Norman Conquest* (1965)

Macdonald, A. J., *Lanfranc: A Study of his Life and Writing* (Oxford, 1944)

Maclagan, E., *The Bayeux Tapestry* (King Penguin Books, 1943)

Maitland, F. W., *Domesday Book and Beyond* (Cambridge, 1897). See also Pollock

Matthew, D., *The Norman Monasteries and their English Possessions* (Oxford, 1962)

Mawer, A., 'The Vikings', chap. xiii of *Cambridge Medieval History*, III (Cambridge, 1922)

Medieval England, ed. A. L. Poole, 2 vols (Oxford, 1958)

Millar, E. G., *English Illuminated Manuscripts from the Tenth to the Thirteenth Century* (Paris and Brussels, 1926)

Morris, W. A., *The Medieval English Sheriff to 1300* (Manchester University Historical Series, Manchester, 1927)

Oakeshott, W. F., *The Sequence of English Medieval Art* (1950)

Oleson, T. J., *The Witenagemot in the Reign of Edward the Confessor* (Oxford, 1955)

Pacht, O., *The St Albans Psalter* (Studies of the Warburg Institute, XXV, 1960)

Petit-Dutaillis, C., *Studies and Notes Supplementary to Stubbs's Constitutional History*, 3 vols (Manchester, 1908–29)

Pevsner, N., *The Englishness of English Art* (Reith Lectures, 1955)

Philpot, J. H., *Master Wace: A Pioneer in Two Literatures* (1925)

Pine, L. G., *They Came with the Conqueror* (1954)

Pollock, F., and Maitland, F. W., *The History of English Law before the Time of Edward I*, 2 vols (2nd ed., Cambridge, 1898)

Poole, A. L., *Obligations of Society in the Twelfth and Thirteenth Centuries* (Ford Lectures, Oxford, 1944)

— *From Domesday Book to Magna Carta*, 1087–1216 (*Oxford History of England*, III, 2nd ed., Oxford, 1955). See also *Medieval England*

Poole, R. L., *The Exchequer in the Twelfth Century* (Oxford, 1912)

— *Studies in Chronology and History* (Oxford, 1934)

Powicke, F. M., *The Loss of Normandy* (2nd ed., Manchester, 1961)

Prentout, H., *Essai sur les Origines de Normandie* (*MASC*, 1911)

— *Etude critique sur Dudon de Saint-Quentin* (*MASC*, 1915)

— *Histoire de Guillaume le Conquérant* (*MASC*, 1936)

Reaney, P. H., *A Dictionary of British Surnames* (1958)

— *The Origin of English Place-Names* (1960)

Renwick, W. L., and Orton, H., *The Beginnings of English Literature* (2nd ed., 1952)

Rice, D. Talbot, *The Byzantine Element in Late Saxon Art* (Charlton Memorial Lecture, 1946)

— *English Art*, 871–1100 (*Oxford History of English Art*, II, Oxford, 1952)

Richardson, H. G., *The English Jewry under Angevin Kings* (1960)

Richardson, H. G., and Sayles, G. O., *The Governance of Medieval England from the Conquest to Magna Carta* (Edinburgh, 1963)

Rickert, M., *Painting in Britain in the Middle Ages* (Pelican *History of Art*, V, 1954)

Ritchie, R. L. G., *The Normans in England before Edward the Confessor* (Exeter, 1948)

Round, J. H., *Feudal England* (1895)

— *Peerage and Pedigree*, 2 vols (1910)

Salzman, L. F., *Building in England down to 1450* (Oxford, 1952)

Sayles, G. O., *The Medieval Foundations of England* (2nd ed., 1950). See also Richardson

Schram, P. E., *History of the English Coronation* (Oxford, 1937)

Smith, E. C., *The Story of Our Names* (New York, 1950)

— *Personal Names, a Bibliography* (New York, 1952)

Social Life in Early England, ed. G. Barraclough (1960)

Stenton, D. M., *The English Woman in History* (1957)

Stenton, F. M., *William the Conqueror and the Rule of the Normans* (1908)

— *The Free Peasantry of the Northern Danelaw* (Lund, 1926)

— *The First Century of English Feudalism* (Ford Lectures, Oxford, 1929)

— *Anglo-Saxon England* (*Oxford History of England*, II, 2nd ed., Oxford, 1946)

— *The Latin Charters of the Anglo-Saxon Period* (Oxford, 1955)

Stone, L., *Sculpture in Britain, the Middle Ages* (*Pelican History of Art*, IX, 1955)

Stubbs, W., *The Constitutional History of England* (various editions)

Tait, J., *The Medieval English Borough* (Manchester, 1936)

Taylor, H. M. and J., *Anglo-Saxon Architecture*, 2 vols (Cambridge, 1965)

Thompson, A. Hamilton, *Military Architecture in England during the Middle Ages* (1912)

Tout, T. F., *Chapters in the Administrative History of Medieval England*, I (1920) and VI (Index) (Manchester, 1933)

Valin, L., *Le Duc de Normandie et sa Cour* (Paris, 1909)

Victoria County History. (Volumes for various counties. In progress)

Vinogradoff, P., *English Society in the Eleventh Century* (Oxford, 1908)

Webb, G., *Architecture in Britain, The Middle Ages* (*Pelican History of Art*, XII, 1956)

Williamson, J. A., *The Evolution of England* (2nd ed., Oxford, 1944)

Wilson, D. M., *Anglo-Saxon Ornamental Metalwork in the British Museum* (Catalogue of Antiquities of the Late Saxon Period, I, 1964)

Wilson, R. M., *Early Middle English Literature* (1939)

Withycombe, E. G., *The Oxford Dictionary of English Christian Names* (Oxford, 1945)

Wormald, F., *English Drawings of the Tenth and Eleventh Centuries* (1952)

Zarnecki, G., *English Romanesque Sculpture*, 1066–1140 (1951)

— *Later English Romanesque Sculpture*, 1140–1210 (1953)

B. *Articles*

Brooke, Z. N., 'Pope Gregory VII's Demand for Fealty from William the Conqueror', *EHR*, XXVI (1911)

Brooks, F. W., 'The Battle of Stamford Bridge', *East Yorks Local History Series*, VI (1956)

Bouard, M. de, 'De la Neustrie carolingien à la Normandie féodale', *BIHR*, XXVII (1955)

Cronne, H. A., 'The Salisbury Oath', *History*, XIX (1934)

Darlington, R. R., 'Æthelwig, Abbot of Evesham', *EHR*, XLVIII (1933)

— 'Ecclesiastical Reform in the Late Old English Period', *EHR*, LI (1936)

— 'The Last Phase of Anglo-Saxon History', *History*, XXII (1937)

— 'The Early History of the English Towns', *History*, XXIII (1938)

Douglas, D. C., 'The Norman Conquest and English Feudalism', *ECR*, IX (1939)

— 'Rollo of Normandy', *EHR*, LVII (1942)

— 'Companions of the Conqueror', *History*, XXVIII (1943)

— 'Ancestors of William fitz Osbern', *EHR*, LIX (1944)

— 'The Earliest Norman Counts', *EHR*, LXI (1946)

— 'The Rise of Normandy', *PBA*, XXXIII (Raleigh Lecture, 1947)

— 'Edward the Confessor, Duke William and the English Succession', *EHR*, LXVIII (1953)

Galbraith, V. H., 'The Literacy of English Medieval Kings', *PBA*, XXI (1935)

Glover, R., 'English Warfare in 1066', *EHR*, LXVII (1952)

Hollings, M., 'The Survival of the Five Hide Unit in the Western Midlands', *EHR*, LXIII (1948)

Hollister, C. W., 'The Norman Conquest and the Genesis of English Feudalism', *AHR*, LXVI (1961)

Jamison, E., 'The Sicilian Norman Kingdom in the Mind of Anglo-Norman Contemporaries', *PBA*, XXIV (1938)

Mason, J. F. A., 'The Companions of the Conqueror: An Additional Name', *EHR*, LXVI (1956)

Musset, L., 'A-t-il existé en Normandie au XIe siècle une aristocratie d'argent?', *AN* (1959)

Navel, H., 'Recherches sur les institutions féodales en Normandie', *SAN, Bulletin*, LI (1953)

Oleson, T. J., 'Edward the Confessor's Promise of the Throne to Duke William of Normandy', *EHR*, LXXII (1957)

Prentout, H., 'Etudes sur quelques points d'Histoire de Normandie', *MASC*, nouvelle série, V (1929)

— 'Etudes sur quelques points d'Histoire de Guillaume le Conquérant', *MASC*, nouvelle série, VI (1931)

Prestwich, J. O., 'War and Finance in the Anglo-Norman State', *TRHS*, 5, IV (1954)

Sawyer, P. H., 'The Wealth of England in the Eleventh Century', *TRHS*, 5, XV (1965)

Sisam, K., 'Ælfric's Catholic Homilies', *Review of English Studies*, VII-IX (1931–3)

Southern, R. W., 'The Canterbury Forgeries', *EHR*, LXXIII (1958)

Stenton, F. M., 'The Danes in England', *PBA*, XIII (1927)

— 'English Families and the Norman Conquest', *TRHS*, 4, XXVI (1944)

— 'The Scandinavian Colonies in England and Normandy', *TRHS*, 4, XXVII (1945)

Stephenson, C., 'Feudalism and Its Antecedents in England', *AHR*, XLVIII (1943)

White, G. H., 'The Household of the Norman Kings', *TRHS*, 4, XXX (1948)

— 'The Battle of Hastings and the Death of Harold', 'The Conqueror's Brothers and Sisters', appendices in *Complete Peerage*, XII part i (1953)

Wilkinson, B., 'Northumbrian Separatism in 1065 and 1066', *BJRL*, XXXII (1936)

— 'Freeman and the Crisis of 1051', *BJRL*, XXXIV (1938)

Wormald, F., 'The Survival of Anglo-Saxon Illumination after the Conquest', *PBA*, XXX (1944)

Yver, J., 'Les Châteaux forts en Normandie jusqu-au milieu du XIIᵉ siècle', *SAN*, *Bulletin*, LIII (1955)

Index

Inheritance, laws of (English and Norman): 158–9
Intermarriage: 117
Ireland: 8, 28, 39, 118, 119, 138
Italianate churches: 235
Italy: 16, 35, 67, 129
'Ivories': *see* Carving

Jarls (three): 45
Jarrow: 205, 218
Jews: 167 *bis*, 291
John, King of England: 135, 161
John, Abbot: 14
Jousts (tournaments): 145
Judith (wife of Tostig): 89
Jumièges: Monastery, 12, 14; church architecture at, 241–2, 243, 247
Jury system: 62, 177–8, 291
Jury, trial by: 22–3
Justice, administration of: 22–3, 27, 291; Latin and Teutonic, 51–3; 54–6. *See also* Courts of Justice

Kent: 42, 63, 80, 118, 155, 161; Earl of, 140 (*see also* Odo, Bishop)
Kingdoms, fate of: 48
Knight service (feudal) in England and Normandy: 141, 142 *bis*, 143, 147, 149; origins of (?), 148
Knights, feudal: 19–21, 53, 142–57; landless and 'household', 142, 143
kotsetlan (cottagers): 49, 154

La Trinité, Abbey of (Caen): 90, 99, 241
Land tenure, feudal: 19–21, 49, 50, 53, 61, 90; after the Conquest, 140, 141, 143, 149, 150; urban. 163
Lanfranc, Archbishop of Canterbury: 34, 126, 177, 208–11 *passim*; his early life, 190–1; his church reforms, 190–206 *passim*
Languages: Anglo-Norman, 226, 227; English, 212–32 (*see also* English language); French (central), 215, 225, 226, 227; Germanic, 212, 216, 227–8; 'jargon', 216; Latin, 33, 39, 180, 212–16, 218–23; Middle English, 226; modern standard English, 226; Norman-French, 212–16, 222; of English poetry and prose, 216–18; of royal assent, 216; Old English, 213, 217, 226; Old Norse, 213; Romance, 39, 212; Scandinavian, 212, 213, 232
Lathes (in Kent): 55
Latin: culture (debased), 3; language, 33, 39, 180, 212–16, 218–23; terminations in place names, 6
Law, Anglo-Saxon: benevolent and

immemorial, 182. *See also* Courts *and* Justice
Le Bec, hermitage and monastery: 34, 207, 211
Le Mans: 88, 125
Le Mont-Saint-Michel Monastery: 13, 14 *bis*, 91, 241, 271
Leo IX, Pope: 89, 187
Leofric, Abbot of Peterborough: 199
Leofric, Bishop of Exeter: 192, 193
Leofric, Earl of Mercia (and family): 45, 75, 77, 81, 82, 85, 86; his sons and heirs, 95, 117, 122, 140
Leofwine, Bishop of Lichfield and Abbot of Coventry: 192, 197, 199, 240
Leofwine Godwineson, Earl: 108
Lewes Priory: 203, 204, 244
Liber Vitae: 269–70
liberi homines: 154
Libraries, monastic: 206–7
Lillebonne, Council of (1080): 23
Lincolnshire: 39, 50, 122; Lindsey, 101
Lindisfarne Gospels: 267
Litigation: 52–3
Lives of the Saints (Ælfric): 219, 220
Local institutions in England: 57
London: 7, 64, 65–6, 101, 108, 164, 215; pre-eminence of, 65–6; extent and site of, 65; Bridge, 115; defies the Conqueror, 115; capitulates, 116; Tower of, *see* Tower; courts of, 165–6; foreigners allowed in, 166; Jews in, 167; Church Council at (1070), 197
'Lordship': 49; and judicial power, 52–3
Lothair (son of Louis IV): 11, 12
Louis IV, King of France: 11, 12
Lugdunensis Secunda (province of Gaul): 7
Luxuries: 166 (*see also* Arts, minor)

Mabel: of Bellême, 88; of Montgomery, 32
Macaulay, Thomas Babington: 68
Macbeth, King of Scots: 85, 93
Magna Carta (1215): 151, 163
Magnus, King of Norway: 71, 76 *bis*
Magnus II (son of Harald Hardrada): 87
Mainard, Abbot: 12, 13
Maine, County of (France): 88, 124–7 *passim*, 132
Malcolm, King of Scots: 93, 102, 118, 122, 124, 125, 127, 128 *bis*, 131
Manors: 49–50, 137; in *Domesday Book*, 154, 155
Manuscript illumination: 253 *bis*, 266–72, 281
Marble, Purbeck: 244
Marches (northern and western), Lords of: 141–2